Editor's Preface

The idea of editing this book came to me originally during the early days of the Drama Therapy Centre. Students from all disciplines both in the arts and caring professions, come together to develop and use creativity in therapeutic situations. For some it is the first time of working alongside people from other disciplines, and often there is a struggle for dialogue across specialization barriers. It became apparent that the students, whether psychiatrist or poet, were discovering not just some techniques, to take home, but that the creative techniques in themselves provided new forms of expression, communication and relationship within the group itself. It is important not only to foster creativity in one's clients but to develop one's own creativity and express it in different ways.

It is always very encouraging to see the psychologist suddenly discovering that he can use his body to express his feelings and ideas; or the drama teacher realizing that the blocks in her work were not due to artistic inadequacy but to personal problems that could be resolved through intensive therapy.

There is little available literature on creativity and therapy and I feel it important that existing practitioners should be encouraged to write about their experiences and philosophy not only on the use of creative skills, but also on the creative process in itself. The reader will thus find a collection of ideas based on extensive experience, and with tremendous variety.

This variety illustrates the creativity and autonomy of each individual author. This is no attempt to make a uniform statement about creativity in theory or practice, and it does not dwell on definitions. Rather, it is a bringing together of disciplines and artforms and I hope will challenge assumptions about the nature of creativity. Too often we see creativity merely as the end product of the art object, rather than the creative process which may or may not work towards an art object. Also, we may not necessarily be using the 'arts' — we may be working in a creative way.

This book moves with the times, and speaks to and with the multi-disciplinary team and skill sharing group. I hope it will provoke, stimulate and encourage; but most of all foster the creative potential in all of its readers. Many people in many ways have contributed to this book both in ideas and practice. However, I must mention Larry Butler, Carlos Chan, Carole McIntyre, Roy Shuttleworth and Tony Solomonides for many formative discussions. I must thank Julia Solomonides for her translation and George Solomonides (who took the photographs for Chapter 2) for advice on photographs. The photographs in Chapter 4 were taken by Cedric Barker and in Chapter 10 by David Kingston. A special thank-you must go to Jenny Hedley who gave very valuable time in detailed editorial work and manuscript preparation.

Lastly, I must thank my own children Andrew, Rosalind and Hal and foster son David for their long-term patience with my pre-occupation.

Sue Jennings

Creative Therapy

EDITED BY

SUE JENNINGS

PITMAN PUBLISHING

First published 1975

Sir Isaac Pitman and Sons Ltd
Pitman House, 39 Parker Street, London WC2B 5PB, UK

Pitman Medical Publishing Co Ltd
42 Camden Road, Tunbridge Wells, Kent TN1 2QD, UK

Focal Press Ltd
31 Fitzroy Square, London W1P 6BH, UK

Pitman Publishing Corporation
6 East 43 Street, New York, NY 10017, USA

Fearon Publishers Inc
6 Davis Drive, Belmont, California 94002, USA

Pitman Publishing Pty Ltd
Pitman House, 158 Bouverie Street, Carlton, Victoria 3053, Australia

Pitman Publishing
Copp Clark Publishing
517 Wellington Street West, Toronto M5V 1G1, Canada

Sir Isaac Pitman and Sons Ltd
Banda Street, PO Box 46038, Nairobi, Kenya

Pitman Publishing Co SA (Pty) Ltd
Craighall Mews, Jan Smuts Avenue, Craighall Park,
Johannesburg 2001, South Africa

ISBN: 0 273 00750 5

Text set in 11/12 pt. IBM Journal, printed by photolithography,
and bound in Great Britain at The Pitman Press, Bath

G18:15(13)

Contents

I

The creative process: self-expression and self-transcendence

ROSEMARY GORDON

Part I: Nature of the creative process

Introduction

The impulse to create is one of man's most basic impulses. The recognition of it as primary implies that it is irreducible and that it cannot be thought of as a substitute or a defence against some other drive, a thesis which Freud seemed at times to propose.

One of the reasons which first of all attracted me to Jung's theories is the seriousness with which he treated man's need to create and the importance which he attributed to that need. In his *Psychological Factors Determining Human Behaviour*, Jung classified creativity as one of the five main groups of instinctive forces in man. Indeed just because it is so basic and primary it can provoke conflicts as daunting as any of the other instincts. Moreover, its expression often demands courage, will and perseverance; the ability to tolerate doubt and pain and whatever the anxiety provoked when one dares to jettison the old and to risk instead, to make something new, something as yet unknown. Prometheus incurred the wrath of Zeus for just that and as a consequence he suffered the agony the god saw fit to impose — the daily devouring of his liver — that organ so generally associated with fortitude and bravery.

1

Definition

According to the *Oxford English Dictionary* to 'create' means
to 'bring into being, to cause to exist, to form, to produce'.
Creativity involves in fact a number of qualities such as
'productivity', 'inventiveness', 'originality', 'divergence', etc.,
but it is very important to recognize that it is none of these
or any of these alone. For the most important quality that
marks a product as 'creative' is that it expresses a man's need
and search for meaning and that it is imbued with value and
excellence. Consequently creative activity forms an integral
part of the process of personal growth, and is an expression
of that process. Thus it is not just novelty or doing or making
something 'different'; rather it has to do with whether what
one creates truly reflects one's own inner experience and
resources and whether it is genuine, regardless of whether
or not the product happens to resemble something previously
made or created.

Even these few introductory remarks point to the fact
that when we discuss 'creativity' we must distinguish clearly
between (a) the creative process, and (b) the product of the
creative process. There is a tendency to think of creativity
only in terms of the arts, or, even more specifically of the
fine arts. But such a use of the term limits it excessively and
unnecessarily, though one can see how this has come about.
For the artist, perhaps, more than anybody else, has been
interested and concerned with the actual process and the
actual experience of the process of creation and has
provided many introspective reports and insights. Also the
process of making art involves perhaps the largest register of
mental activities such as making, forming, inventing and
discovering, among many others. It is thus from artists that
we have learned most about the process of creation; this
paper will therefore deal mainly with them. But I should
like to stress that I recognize that creativeness does enter into
many other activities. For instance, the object created need
not be a tangible object; it could also be a philosophical idea,
a scientific hypothesis, an answer to a problem; it could be
an insight into oneself, or an empathetic understanding of
somebody else. Certainly relationships can carry the mark

of creativeness and so can the making of oneself. Professor Maslow has in fact listed a great number of characteristics shared by those who make works of art and those whose life style and personal development is open and creative.

Artists and mystics

The seriousness and commitment with which poets and artists speak about their work suggests to me that man's creative activity has much in common with religious and mystical experience. One of the essential features which artist and mystic seem to share is their passionate need to find meaning, not just facts. This seems to evolve from their desire to find some order and unity behind the discontinuities of the world of objects and stimuli, and to discover some sort of significance which helps them to transcend the immediacy and transitoriness of actual experience. Again, both artist and mystic share a greater than average capacity to experience wonder and awe; their availability to these experiences implies that they have sacrificed enough of their need for personal omnipotence so that they can risk awareness that there might indeed exist something mysterious and unknowable — be this located inside them or outside them — but which in any case eludes control or manipulation. Einstein has expressed just this with particular feeling and lucidity:

> 'The most beautiful emotion we can experience is the mystical. It is the sower of all true art and science. To know what is impenetrable to us really exists, manifesting itself with the highest wisdom and most radiant beauty, which our dull faculties can comprehend only in their most primitive forms — this knowledge, this feeling, is at the centre of true religiousness and art . . . '

Thus there seems to be a common pattern of personality traits and a common quality of experience which marks both artist and mystic.

However, undeniably, there are also qualities that differentiate them. For instance, the mystic's primary concern is to achieve the experience of fusion and union with 'The All', 'the Absolute', 'the Godhead'; that is, he strives and longs for what Freud has called 'the oceanic experience.' With him passivity preponderates and he tends to avoid matter, sensation, the sensuous, in other words — form. It is in this that he is most essentially different from the artist; for the artist lives, precariously poised, between the need for fusion states on the one hand and the excitement and the pain of separating, delimiting, differentiating and defining on the other. Harold Rugg, for instance, when speaking of Blake describes how the poet followed the intuitive path in times of partial withdrawal from the physical world, but then, instead of continuing that path to the point of final union with the Absolute he undertook to 'endure the ordeal of return'. He thus seemed to strive to bring together the sensory with the intuitive and the temporal with the eternal.

A young and gifted artist brought me a dream in which this 'ordeal of return' was expressed clearly and dramatically:

'You are with me — or it is my mother — we are on a long and dangerous voyage; we meet ruffians and robbers and pirates and we cross the sea. We are on our way to heaven. But I tell my companion that we must not cross the threshold of the gates of heaven. When we get there it is all as expected: my warning prevails and we resist the temptation to enter; we return. On our way back we pass the town where I had been as an art student and from the distance we see my art college. We stand and look at it.'

But when he comes to tell me of the latter part of the dream the patient breaks down and weeps bitterly.

Another artist, a successful painter and engraver, who has for many years been also interested in Indian philosophy and meditation, dreams the following dream:

'I am going to see a wise Indian, a sort of guru. I want to bring him a present. I have a lump of some brown, semi-soft stuff in my hand, but then I think that it is not the appropriate sort of thing to give him. So I leave it behind . . . It is rather like a lump of shit.'

And after cogitating about it longer, she suddenly remarks:

'Perhaps it is even more like a lump of clay or plasticine.'

Essential then to the activity of making and creating is what I have called the urge to make form, to 'incarnate', 'to make flesh'. Speaking of art-making from the point of view of a philosopher of aesthetics, Professor Louis Arnaud Reid has also called it 'creative aesthetic embodiment.' Professor Reid has explored this new concept in considerable depth: he has suggested that in such 'creative embodiment' the

> 'perceived sounds, shapes, rhythms etc. are not only instrumental to the grasp of aesthetic meaning; the experience of attentive perception to them is an essential part of the apprehension of meaning. Attention to perceived forms is both instrumental and intrinsic to the understanding of aesthetic meaning. Content and medium are indivisibly and uniquely united.'

Clearly these two concepts — 'incarnation' and 'embodiment' — overlap considerably. But in my use of the Latin form — 'incarnation' — there is somewhat greater implicit emphasis on the element of sacrifice which inexorably accompanies the acceptance of limits and limitations that impose themselves when the abstract, the idea, the ideal, the spirit is given form, body; for whatever is expressed in a work of art cannot be grasped *apart* from the sensuous forms that express it.

This integration of form and content that is 'embodiment' is truly an appropriate analogue, a sort of mirror reflection of our own essential psycho-physical existence. The urge to 'embody' or to 'incarnate' rests on the fact that we sense and that we dream and that we always live at the same time in a world of facts and a world of meanings. There is thus a constant striving to bring these two worlds together; and while on the one hand we always search for evermore adequate forms through which to express the ever-changing world of our experience, we also always need to imbue with meaning and significance the sensuous forms that we encounter.

Nature of the creative process

The creative process is the process *par excellence* in which
contradictory but mutually reciprocal qualities are mobilized:
activity and passivity; receptivity and productivity; consciousness and unconsciousness. The interaction and interdependence
of these contradictory processes emerges clearly if we consider
the stages of the creative process as these have been discovered
and identified by most artists and researchers. Nearly all of
them seem to agree that there are four of them—though these
four stages may vary in relative importance or relative duration
from one person to another or even from one particular
creative act to another particular creative act in the same
person. What is more, the process may be a continuing one, so
that the last stage in one work or one part of a work can lead
to the first stage in the next phase of a work or of an altogether
new work.

The four stages of the creative process have been identified
as follows: first comes the stage of preparation, which is the
time when a person immerses himself in a problem and feels
himself drawn into a period of conscious concern and struggle
To enter this stage and keep faith by it a person needs to be
humble but persistent; nor would it help him to guard against
any increase in knowledge or information.

The second stage, the stage of incubation, has been named
by Whitehead, the philosopher, as the state of 'muddled
suspense'. It is the stage when, one might say, a person 'sleeps
on his problem', either literally or metaphorically. He lets go
of it, he withdraws his attention from it, he takes his mind
off it. Instead he feels baffled and confused. He cannot
see a solution and, as it were, admits his ignorance, his
defeat.

Then, if he is lucky, the third stage may 'happen' to him.
There is a sudden flash of light, an inspiration, a happy idea
occurs to him. This third stage, the stage of illumination,
tends to be unexpected, sudden and often marked by a
feeling of certitude. It happens when the mind is in a state
which Harold Rugg has described as 'relaxed concentration'
and one experiences a sort of 'creative emptiness'; it is
therefore often accompanied by a feeling of having been

passive, a mere bystander in what has occurred. Max Ernst, the painter, for instance has described this when he writes:

> 'I had only to reproduce obediently what made itself visible within me.'

And even so rational and logical a person as the mathematician Gauss, wrote as follows:

> 'Finally, two days ago, I succeeded, not on account of my painful efforts, but by the grace of God. Like a sudden flash of lightning the riddle happened to be solved.'

In this phase exuberance and ecstasy are often experienced.

But the fourth stage is a sort of 'coming-down-to-earth' stage. It is the stage of verification; a period of critical testing, when the ideas received in the period of inspiration are tested, organized and given relevant and appropriate form and expression.

When one examines these four stages and thinks about their implications it becomes clear that creativity depends on a person being able both to use and to surrender his ego functions. Inevitably ego functions must predominate in the first stage when knowledge and skill are needed and when a problem poses itself and challenges to battle. Again, the ego functions must re-assert their predominance in the fourth stage when the 'inspiration' requires critical evaluation and testing and needs work to be done with it and on it. But, during the second and the third stages the capacity to surrender ego functions and ego control is essential. For these two stages rely on what Ehrenzweig has named the process of 'de-differentiation' or 'unconscious scanning'. He has suggested in his *Hidden Order of Art* that this is a process vital to all creative work. It depends on a person's capacity to relinquish the normal compulsion to differentiate sharply; instead he can allow himself to scatter his attention and to let boundaries dissolve until 'everything seems to fuse into a single oceanic image.' He has also called this the 'creative suspension of frontiers'. The value he sees in it for the work of creation rests on his belief that the unconscious itself yields spontaneous form elements and possesses a hidden order which comes from levels deeper than the area which psychoanalysts have

until recently designated as originating primary process
activity; these primary processes have been regarded by them
as producing only raw material consisting of chaotic and
wild sexual and aggressive phantasies; these must then be
tamed and shaped by the 'secondary process' before they
can become aesthetic and communicable. I must add here
that already in 1956 Marion Milner had forecast that the
facts of art and of aesthetic would sooner or later call
for a revision of the whole concept of the nature and
function of the primary process. Such a revision is in fact
now under way.

Ehrenzweig's hypothesis of the existence of such a
'hidden order' in the deep unconscious has developed on the
basis of quite a lot of research, such as Desmond Morris's
collection of ape paintings, Kellog's collection and analysis
of infant scribbles, Charles Fisher's experiments with Rubin's
double profile — this produced evidence that unconscious
vision does not differentiate between figure and ground.
Ehrenzweig also draws attention to musicians who are quite
familiar with what is called 'horizontal' hearing, which is
in fact polyphonic and occurs when attention is not focussed
on a single musical theme or instrument.

The potential effectiveness of the two middle stages in the
creative process depends then on the capacity to suspend ego
control, to risk 'not-knowing' and 'not-controlling' and to
make oneself available to a possible experience of 'sacred
awe'. It is this that the poet Keats has called, 'negative
capability' and which he has described as the capacity to be
'in uncertainties, mysteries, doubts, without any irritable
reaching after fact and reason.' The process of creation then
demands that a person be available to freely moving oscillations between control and surrender, and between periods
of conscious work and periods of passive acceptance.

How and when to use the product of a creative process
has been most succintly and amusingly expressed by
Kekule, the discoverer of the benzine ring, when he admon-
ished his colleagues:

'Let us learn to dream, gentlemen — then perhaps we
shall find the truth. But let us beware of publishing

our dreams before they have been put to the proof
by waking understanding.' (*A Hundred Years of
Chemistry* by A. Findlay.)

Or there is Paul Klee's more poetic description of how the
artist may experience the creative process:

> 'From the root the sap rises up into the artist, flows through
> him, flows to his eye. He is the trunk of the tree. Over-
> whelmed and activated by the force of the current, he
> conveys his vision into his work . . . he does nothing other
> than gather and pass on what rises from the depths. He
> neither serves nor commands, he transmits. His position
> is humble. And the beauty at the crown is not his own;
> it has merely passed through him.'

The interaction and interdependence of consciousness
and unconsciousness, of control and surrender, of activity
and receptivity seems to have been recognized, understood
and conceptualized by psychoanalysts like Marion Milner and
Hannah Segal, in their description of the creative process as:

> 'A genital bisexual activity, necessitating a good identifica-
> tion with the father who gives and the mother who receives
> and bears the child.'

This conceptualization of the creative process is also echoed
in Eric Neumann's thesis that every artist is an essentially
bisexual type of person. This has more recently been supported
by MacKinnon's studies in which she found that in a sample
of architects the more creative ones scored higher on femininity
than did the less successful and less creative ones.

Nor is the analogy between giving birth to a baby and
creative activity the invention or discovery of modern psychologists. The poet, Rilke, for instance, among many others,
has talked about it in just these terms when he described the
making of a poem as:

> 'Like a birth which is drawn urgently out of the biological
> and spiritual depths of the poet.'

Also mystics, ecstatics and contemplatives — whose affinity
with artists I have already discussed earlier on — often describe
their experiences as a union between the sexual halves of their
own individual natures; thus they reveal to us another link
between the religious and the creative process.

In as much as the analytic process is also a creative venture,
so analyst and analysand are also likely to experience these
oscillations between activity and passivity, between certainty
and doubt. They too are likely to pass through periods of
'incubation', marked by the feeling of 'muddled suspense',
a 'dead point', or what Stephen Spender has also called the
experience of the 'dim cloud'. If they are lucky they may
then both be available to 'inspiration' which in that particular
work-context would have to do with the discovery of a new
insight or a novel experience. Certainly in my own work as
an analyst I am quite familiar with the experience of feeling
baffled, out of my depth, confused and unable to make sense
of something, be it a dream or a particular situation that
has developed in the transference between the patient and
myself. I have learned to value these moments of bewilder-
ment, to accept them and not to battle against them. Naturally,
these moments can be very painful and they may well dismay
the patient and call out his anger, his despair, his frustration.
But I know now that this is how it must be for me. Often
these periods of bafflement herald a new understanding.
Furthermore, in my acceptance of this 'not-knowing', in my
shedding of the mantle of omniscience and omnipotence —
whether I verbalize it and so make it explicit or not — I know
that I may ultimately help the patient to find release from
his own compulsion to cling to the known and the controllable.
And my acceptance of 'not-knowing' may mediate for him the
awareness that he too may dare to grow and to create, which
means taking the risk to make something, even if one is not
in possession of perfect knowledge or perfect skill or perfect
control; and so a 'good-enoughness' may come to seem good
enough.

I believe that there has in recent years been an interaction
and a reciprocal relationship between the studies of creativity
and art on the one hand and the theoretical and clinical
developments in the field of analysis and psychotherapy on

the other. The pioneers like Freud and Jung first drew attention to some of the unconscious roots in art; indeed they helped to decipher some of the symbolic codes embedded there. In their turn, students of the factors operative in the creative process seem now to have affected and modified analytic thought and ethos. One can, for instance, detect that some analysts have come to value anew their patients' experiences of silence or of alone-ness — (not to be confused with loneliness) — and have re-explored the effectiveness during certain stages in the analysis of such analytic procedures as non-intervention and '*un*-interpreting', as Masud Khan has called it. In this context I am thinking in particular — apart from Jung — of the more recent work of analysts like Balint, Milner, Little and Winnicott, as well as Khan. It seems to me unlikely that it can be an accident that these are all analysts who have been particularly interested in and concerned with art, with play and with creativity and that the ideas they have developed about analytic practice seem to parallel and to reflect the qualities and processes that are characteristic and intrinsic to the less controlling and less active and conscious phases of the creative process.

Freud himself had of course already expressed considerable intuitive awareness of the value of such an attitude for the analytic work, as is well shown in his paper 'Recommendations for Physicians on the Psychoanalytic Method of Treatment'. In this paper he enjoins upon analysts:

> 'a calm quiet attentiveness of evenly-hovering attention' in which 'all conscious exertion is to be witheld from the capacity for attention.'

And in this same paper he cites, with obvious approval, an old French surgeon who had taken as his motto the words, 'Je le pansai, Dieu le guérit', to which he added that the analyst might content himself with a similar understanding of his role.

What psychological forces or conflicts might then hinder the functioning of the creative process? A few of them stand out immediately:

Clearly delusions of omnipotence or omniscience and an excessive narcissism — (these would interfere with the capacity to test and to evaluate one's work and one's inspiration) — the refusal to recognize one's dependence on the knowledge and information previously acquired by other people at other times or in other places, an attitude of haste and impatience, a general lack of persistence and commitment and devotion — (the sort of butterfly mind that makes a dilettante) — all these could interfere with the work to be done in stages one and four.

Other qualities can make stages two and three difficult to attain or to use: thus the need to be always in control and carefully aware of all that goes on — (this is likely to abort any creative work much like the impatient cook who cannot let the cake rise peacefully inside the oven but needs to peep at it and so makes it collapse.) Such a need may in fact have its origin in a number of different unconscious fears and phantasies. There may, for instance, be a generalized fear of 'undifferentiation' and terror of the unknown due, as Anna Freud has suggested, to an experienced disbelief that the psyche contains spontaneous ordering forces and that these are truly intrinsic to it. Or there may be a dread of the possible disappointment that the object created may turn out not to be as 'good', as 'fabulous' as the excitement experienced at the moment of inspiration. Again there may be distrust in the 'good-enoughness' of one's own inner world and the suspicion that it contains forces so dangerous and destructive that, if externalized, they will wreak disaster or else provoke revenge. Or the obstacle may present itself in an exaggerated dependence on other people's judgement which brings in its wake great apprehension lest the work that one has drawn out of the very depth of one's self might in fact evoke ridicule and dismissal rather than admiration and praise.

The first group, we might therefore say, consists of those persons who are overwhelmed and caught-up in non-ego processes, which they may in fact idealize, while the second group is marked by excessive distrust of the non-ego forces. Ultimately creativity in both groups of people is seriously hampered by their inability to have and to tolerate the ebb and flow, the rhythm and oscillation between conscious and unconscious, that is between ego and non-ego.

Part II: Psychological processes involved

Having discussed creativity as an attempt to embody the ever-changing experience of facts and meanings, it seems to me important that we should now examine those psychological functions which enter significantly into this process and in fact make it possible.

Perception

Clearly perception is one of the primary psychological functions to consider here. Our senses are, after all, our doors, our gateways which open to us the external world, provide us with knowledge of it and help us relate to it. Of course, this world, external to us, is infinitely more rich than we can discover through our own sensuous equipment, though we have enlarged our awareness of it through the various scientific instruments like the microscope and the telescope which act, so to speak, as extensions of our own senses. But even without straying beyond the limitations of our sensuous equipment, many respond to our world with delight, fascination, curiosity, admiration and awe.

Inevitably the very will-to-form which, as I have suggested, is basic in creative individuals, depends of necessity on a person's sensory equipment and on his concern with the sensuous world that surrounds him and within which he exists and has his being.

It seems likely that the artist is quite particularly able to open himself up to this world, to see it, hear it, smell it, touch it, and that he probably does this with more naivety and innocence than the average grown-up person; in other words he is probably more able to approach an object again and again as if he had met it for the first time; moreover he feels driven to fashion whatever form most truly expresses his particular experience of it.

A great deal of research has shown that we never see the world just as it is, but that what we 'see' is the result of a combination of the actual qualities possessed by an object plus all the information, expectation, needs, hopes and wishes of the percipient.

In a most stimulating paper, 'The Childhood of the Artist', the American psychoanalyst, Phyllis Greenacre has described some of the characteristics which, she believes, are particularly strong already early on in childhood in those persons who later on reveal themselves to be endowed with special creative talents. The characteristics that she dwells on are primarily concerned with perceptual processes; it seems therefore appropriate to describe and discuss them at this point.

Having studied the biographies and autobiographies of artists, and drawing also on her clinical experience with patients in analysis, Greenacre suggests that there are four main qualities which gifted children seem to possess in great measure. They are:

(1) a greater than average sensitivity to sensory stimuli and stimulation;

(2) an unusual capacity for awareness of similarities and connexions between various stimuli;

(3) a predisposition to an empathy of wider range and deeper vibration than is usual;

(4) an efficient and well co-ordinated sensori-motor equipment which facilitates the projection, the embodiment of the expressive experiences.

The first quality — great sensitivity to stimuli — together with the second — awareness of the similarities and connexions between the various stimuli — is likely to make for more than usually intensive and extensive sensory experience. One of the consequences for the baby may be that by heightening the awareness of the sensory qualities of the primary objects, such as the breast, faeces, mother, etc., he discovers earlier and more easily sensory similarities with other objects; and so the gifted child in comparison with the average child may discover and enjoy sooner possible substitutes for the primary objects.

There is a marvellous example of such early and sensuous vitality in Kazantzakis's autobiography, in which he describes his first memories. The richness of the sensuality of these

impressions is truly prodigious, and I feel I must quote
them here:

> 'Still unable to stand I crept on all fours to the threshold
> and fearfully, longingly, extended my head into the
> open air of the court-yard. Now I not only looked, I
> actually saw the world for the very first time. And what
> an astonishing sight that was. There was a buzzing from
> the thousands of invisible bees, an intoxicating aroma,
> a warm sun as thick as honey. The air flashed as though
> with swords . . . '

> 'Next I remember a woman, Annika, a neighbour of ours
> . . . That evening I was playing in the yard. I must have
> been about three years old. The little garden smelled of
> summer. The women leaned over, placed me in her lap,
> hugged me. I, closing my eyes, fell against her exposed
> bosom and smelled her body; the warm dense perfume,
> the acid scent of milk and sweat. The newly-married body
> was steaming. I inhaled the vapour in an erotic torpor
> hanging from her high bosom . . . '

> 'On another day a man with a thorny beard took me in
> his arms and brought me down to the harbour. As we
> approached, I heard a wild beast sighing and roaring as if
> wounded or uttering threats . . . Suddenly the bitter odour
> of carob beans, tar and rotten citrons . . . a turn in the
> street — dark indigo, seething, all cries and smells — the
> entire sea poured into me frothingly . . . my head filled
> with laughter, salt and fear.

> 'One summer night I was sitting in our yard again, on my
> little stool. I remember lifting my eyes and seeing the stars
> for the first time. Jumping to my feet, I cried out in fear,
> 'sparks, sparks!' The sky seemed a vast conflagration to
> me; my body was on fire . . . Such were my first contacts
> with earth, sea, woman and the star-filled sky.'

The third characteristic, the disposition to empathy, is
likely to add to the aliveness of the internal forms — the images
and symbols: such a child is therefore likely to resist the
pressures from the so-called adults in our rationalist society

who discourage animation and anthropomorphising; the
more average child tends to yield early in his life to these
pressures.

The fourth quality is really quite self-explanatory. A person
without vocal talents cannot make a singer; a tone-deaf person
is debarred from becoming a musician; and where eye-hand
co-ordination is poor the visual arts will not be available for
the efficient expression of experience, etc.

When I speak of 'experience' I already imply that there
exists a vast inner world to meet, to match, to reflect or to
distort the information received from the outer world.

Imagery

The most closely relevant and related process to perception
is, of course, imagery. One might define an image as a
perception which occurs in the absence of an actual external
stimulus — be this perception of forms, of colours, sounds,
smells, movements or whatever. Though such external stimulus
may have presented itself in the past, it is not there at the
time when the image occurs.

Imaging is probably a mental process that functions
in all men. It seems to help him classify, abstract, to relate
present perceptions to past experience and it also helps him
bear present frustrations for the sake of future satisfactions.

Though a universal phenomenon there are many variables,
so that the image world of one person may be very different
from that of another. Images may, for instance, differ in
their degree of rigidity or flexibility, in the degree of voluntary
control a person can bring to bear on them, in their faintness
or sharpness, but above all in the predominance of one sense
modality in any one person. Which sense modality predominates
must inevitably affect the creative expression chosen by an
individual. Clearly one might expect that auditory imagery
predominates, or at least is very important in a musician;
kinaesthetic imagery is likely to be characteristic for the
dancer and perhaps also for the actor. Visual imagery will
occupy the foreground in the visual artist, but whether he
is a painter or a sculptor may depend on whether his visual
imagery tends to be three-dimensional, whether there is

fascination with this three-dimensionality and whether he wants and can in fact translate experienced three-dimensionality into two-dimensionality. Again auditory imagery is more likely to be important and to be valued by a poet, while in the novelist sensuous experience may be less prominent than thinking and other ego activities. I am of course not speaking of absolute absence or absolute presence of any one of them but only of their relative absence and relative presence.

Naturally there is a close link between 'images' and 'imagination'; in everyday language they are usually confused. But what we tend to mean when we speak about an image is the internal representation of a sensuous, but individual, object or experience, while imagination consists of a stringing together of images in the service of an unfolding story or drama. Thus while an image is like a still picture, a photograph, imagination is like a moving film.

Symbolization

One of the most important psychological processes and one of the most relevant to the creative process is symbolization. To symbolize means to be able to experience the existence of links between objects which are also recognized to be separate and distinct; thus without sacrificing uniqueness to wholeness, or wholeness to uniqueness one succeeds in experiencing both what is individual and what is universal in any particular object or situation. Essentially then, as Jung has suggested, symbolization is a process which involves an 'as if' attitude. While I was writing this paper I came across a note written by Lama Chime Rimpoche in which he quotes a Zen saying that seems to sum up what I am trying to convey when I talk about symbolizing:

> 'Before one practises Zen mountains are mountains and trees are trees; that is to say, there is only the reality of the reality of the relative world. But after one has practised Zen for some time mountains are no longer mountains and trees are no longer trees; one has seen the absolute, underlying unity of all things. But at the

completion of one's practice of Zen, mountains are
again mountains and trees trees.'

As a Westerner I find one of the most delicately symbolic
expressions in Blake's verse:

> 'To see a World in a Grain of Sand
> And a Heaven in a Wild Flower,
> Hold Infinity in the palm of your hand
> And Eternity in an hour.'

The capacity to symbolize depends on maturation and ego
growth. We may from early on experience potentially symbolic
images, the images that Jung has called archetypal, because
they appear so spontaneously and almost universally in men
everywhere and at all times; but we can only experience them
'symbolically' when enough ego consciousness has emerged
so that one can relate to the paradox of separateness and
identity. In other words, it is not the mental content but
the attitude of mind to the mental content that determines
whether or not it is symbolic.

There are in fact two earlier processes which one can
identify as the forerunners of the symbolic function. At
first the baby's experiences are made up predominantly of
sensations and of archetypal images, expressing instinctive
needs and wishes. (These archetypal images seem closely
related to what the more recent science of ethology has
named the 'innate release mechanism!).

After this develops an intermediate function which
Hannah Segal has named 'symbolic equivalence'. By now
the infant is aware of the separateness of objects and situations
but as soon as he recognizes some significant similarity the
reality of one of them is nullified and it becomes re-absorbed
in the identity of the other. It is the *'pars pro tuto'* reaction
which Arieti describes as characteristic of schizophrenic
thinking. In other words at that stage there is either total
identity or else total difference. No paradox can yet be
experienced. It is the stage in which, as in the Zen quotation,
mountains are no longer mountains and trees are no longer
trees.

It is only when finally symbolization has been achieved,

the 'as if' attitude, that recognition of the similarity of objects can co-exist with awareness of and respect for their separateness.

The mature individual does not necessarily slough off experience of sensation, archetypal images and symbolic equation; he does not necessarily rely entirely on symbolization. If he did it might actually impoverish his experience, much as if in adult love-making, stimulation of all the many erotogenic zones had been abolished and only the genital zone was allowed to remain available. In fact, symbolic equation has suffered much the same fate as the primary processes; that is to say, it has tended to be examined and discussed only in terms of regressive and psycho-pathological phenomena. Yet is is likely to play quite an important — even if transitory — part in artistic work and creation. The actor who has sunk all awareness of his own identity into the part he is to play, the painter absorbed in the object that has triggered off his fascination and inspiration, the poet, or the musician engrossed in the sounds that fill his inmost ear, all these are probably nearer to the experience of symbolic equivalence than to symbolization. And indeed this symbolic equivalence experience endows their work with that special flavour of conviction and emotional intensity that marks great and important work. But in the end the artist knows and acknowledges the co-existence of both external and internal reality. He symbolizes this awareness by accepting and ritualizing a boundary — a stage for the actor and dramatist, a frame round the picture painted which really makes the point that the reality inside the frame is different from the reality outside it.

The transitional object

A great spurt to our understanding of the nature and development of the symbolic function has come in recent years from Winnicott's concept of the 'transitional object'. This is the name he has given to any object — tangible or intangible, formed well or hardly at all, like a blanket, a sucking vest, a teddy bear, a tune or whatever — which the child, as it were, appropriates as his first self-chosen possession.

Winnicott regards the child's attachment to such an object
as the earliest expression of man's creative drive; for this
object is both given — it actually exists in the external world
and yet it is also made — it is the infant that invests it with
a meaning and significance which it has drawn from within
its own inner world. Thus the transitional object represents
both the mother — out there — and the infant and his inner
world, and the bond between himself and his mother. In
other words, the transitional object occurs at a moment in
time when mother and infant are no longer experienced by
him as fused; rather he is beginning to experience her and
himself as separate beings, but who can be together. And so
the transitional object acts as a bridge which connects the
inner world of phantasy to the outer world of reality and
thence — to culture.

This is how Winnicott wrote about it:

> 'It is usual to refer to 'reality testing' and to make a clear
> distinction between apperception and perception. I am
> here staking a claim for an intermediate state between
> a baby's inability and his growing ability to recognise and
> to accept reality. I am therefore studying the substance
> of *illusion*, that which is allowed to the infant, and which
> in adult life is inherent in art and religion, and yet becomes
> the hallmark of madness when an adult puts too powerful
> a claim on the credulity of others, forcing them to
> acknowledge a sharing of illusion that is not their own.
> We can share a respect of illusory experience, and if we
> wish we may collect together and form a group on the
> basis of the similarity of our illusory experiences. This
> is a natural root of grouping among human beings.'

Thus Winnicott thinks of the transitional object as the
first evidence of man's capacity to symbolize, which remains
at the root of his concern with meaning and with the
question 'What is life all about?' It functions as the germ of a
third area of the mind which relates neither to the outer
world of reality nor to the inner world of phantasy but to
a third area, the 'area of experience', an area where the
question, 'Is this real?' 'is this unreal?' is irrelevant and
where in fact, as Winnicott puts it, we never ask, 'did you

conceive of this or was it presented to you from without?'
because the important point is that no decision is expected;
'the question is not to be formulated'. It is this area of
experience which becomes the source of play, of imagination,
culture, religion and art. It seems to me that what Jung has
described as 'psychic reality' is that which is contained and
which is of the essence of what constitutes the area of
experience. But Winnicott has helped us discover the roots
and to understand more clearly its composition. We can now
see that in this third area sensuous experience meets
imaginative invention, cognitive activities are brought into
relationship with emotional activities and the needs for
order and for meaning find their expression in the discoveries
and in the creation of forms that 'embody' experience.

Play

Furthermore Winnicott points out that there is a direct link
between the development of the area of experience on the
one hand and play and the capacity to play on the other;
and so he suggests that there is

> 'a direct development from transitional phenomena to
> playing, and from playing to shared playing, and from this
> to cultural experiences.' (1971, p. 51)

The importance and seriousness of play has probably been
underestimated for a long time. It is a phenomenon that has
for long puzzled psychologists who have been trying to discover
its roots and its function. Some have thought of it as the
expression of surplus energy while the need to survive is taken
care of by others, e.g. the parents; some have followed a
biological model and proposed that in their play children
'recapitulate' the history of the main technical and social
skills. Others again have thought of play as a form of unconscious preparation for adult life and activities. Some have
emphasized the importance of the imitation of loved or hated
but important persons; some have emphasized its cathartic
function; others have seen in it a safety valve through which
repressed or socially unacceptable emotions can find
expression. Even the very definition of play and the

delimitation of its meaning has remained somewhat contro-
versial. When they speak of playing, some seem to think
exclusively of the pre-school child, when play is dominated
by phantasy and imagination, and is primarily solitary,
(though there can be a playing 'in the presence of others');
'playing with' is already at a new level of relationship to
external and internal personages. Some distinguish 'playing'
from 'playing at', the latter clearly involves imitation,
identification and role-playing. Some stretch the term even
further and include games, 'playing games' when the
collaboration with others is further complicated by the
existence and observance of known rules, jointly accepted.
And at this point we come to notice that play is an activity
no longer confined to childhood but engaged in also by
adults. What are they then doing, these grown-ups who
rush around on a cold muddy field, chasing a ball; or
climbing mountains — not in order to get somewhere, but
just in order to have done it; and those city dwellers who
emerge out of their centrally-heated houses and flats with
their refrigerators and dish-washers, what are they doing
sleeping in tents, washing in some cold stream and cooking
over a primus stove or a log fire? Mulling over all these
different activities, all of which could be called 'play', though
in other situations they are 'work', it seems to me that what
distinguishes play from other activities is its function in terms
of personality development and growth. This is not to say
that other activities, work, etc., do not contribute also to
personal growth, but in their case personal growth is
secondary to the actual purpose of the activity. This hypothesis
suggests itself particularly when one thinks of the various
play and leisure activities — in both children and adults —
which involve pain, hardship, anguish, even terror. Sailing
'for fun' on storm-tossed seas, sitting for hours fishing,
listening to ghost stories in the dark, playing 'cops and
robbers', and even 'bee-boo'. Surely essential to all these is
the attempt to increase experience — be it of the inanimate
world, of the animate world, of the world of one's fellow
humans or one's own private world. Thus play is any activity
which, I suggest, is primarily in the service of individuation,
in Jung's sense of that term. And as I understand this term,

it comprises readiness for even greater awareness of one's own nature, with its positive and negative sides, an ever sharper definition of who and what one is, which is then reflected in the clarity and appropriateness of one's self-image, a recognition of one's separateness and personal responsibility together with and in the context of an acceptance of the existence of patterns and processes which exist beyond our control or comprehension. In other words, individuation encompasses 'individualization' but moves a person beyond this essentially ego building process towards the search for values and meaning and self-transcendence.

Play and creation

It must be clear from what I have said about play that this activity is intimately relevant to creativity. Indeed my experience leaves me in no doubt that a person who cannot play is also deprived of the joys of making and creating, and is truly crippled in his capacity to feel alive. In a way this is really not a discovery of mine or even of my generation. In 1931 Jung wrote:

> 'The creative activity of imagination frees man from his bondage to the "nothing but" and raises him to the status of one who plays. As Schiller says, man is completely human only when he is at play.'

But is there any difference at all, we may now ask, between play and creation? Perhaps the difference is that in the act of creation man tries to transcend even this inner urge for ego growth and individuation in order to put himself also at the service of truth and beauty.

The arts' therapist is likely to be much concerned with the purpose and function of art so that he can reflect about the value of his skill and assess and re-assess any possible improvements or extensions. In another paper I have summarized as follows the psychological reasons why man makes art:

(a) The need to externalize internal images.
(b) The need to preserve his sensous experience by making

it gel into a form which exists outside and independently of him.

(c) The need to communicate to others — and so to validate further — his private imagery and experience.

(d) The need to give expression to what seems to be a fundamental impulse to make, and to make, whatever he does, according to certain quasi-universal aesthetic rules.

(e) The need to find meaning by relating disparate and individual objects of experience to wider, more generalized and more abstract ones. He does this by means of his capacity to symbolize. These needs are particularly closely related to the fact that having acquired consciousness man has also acquired knowledge of the existence of death. It is probably this knowledge which drives him on to ask about the meaning and the purpose of life, about his place on earth and in the universe, about the laws that govern the world and about the sort of existence that awaits him after death and that he might have experienced before birth.

And to these five I would now add the role of individuation, as I have discussed it in connexion with the function of play, restating here that I regard individuation as composed of the process of individualization *plus* the development of links and connexions between the ego and the self (or better the un-self), between the personal and the collective, the here-and-now and the transcendent and the awareness and acceptance of the 'mysterious' in the sense in which Einstein described it in my earlier quotation.

Self-expression and self-transcendence

In the last few decades art-making seems to have been viewed primarily as a mode of self-expression. But the 'self' in this formulation has tended to be limited to a pre-Winnicottian psychoanalytic conception of the structure of the psyche in which unconscious phantasies, and repressed unconscious wishes and needs play the most important part. 'Self-expression' has thus acquired overtones of catharsis, abreaction and the release of the rejected parts of the personality. On the other hand, the search for meaning, the testing of subjective experience against objective fact, curiosity, pride in skill and the need for self-transcendence — all qualities which Jung earlier on, and now Winnicott, as well as Rycroft, Milner *et al.*, have highlighted — all these have tended to be overlooked.

Concern with the unfolding of the unique, the individual, that is true individualism, regarded as the principal function of art, has evolved out of the tradition of Humanism. This was a very necessary rebellion against the predominance of the collective, with its disregard of the individual, and its established mores and traditions to which even the artist had to remain subservient. But like all rebellions Humanism had of necessity to remain one-sided. It probably needed a certain consolidation before one could review it to see whether there were any important areas which had been lost, unnecessarily. Perhaps it is only now that we are ready to recognize that individualization can be even further advanced — rather than hampered — through awareness and relationship to the trans-personal.

The concepts of the 'area of experience' as *originating* the art experience, and Jung's concept of 'individuation' as forming the primary *function* of art are likely to prove relevant to the approaches and methods developed in arts therapy. For these conceptual tools will point to the value in art-making of joining up as much as possible self-exploration and individualization with experiences that mediate transcendence of the immediate and the purely personal, perhaps through devotion to some non-personal goal — whether this be thought of as skill, technique, excellence, the Muse, Nature, Humanity, or as God or spirit, or just as faithfulness to a vision.

References

1. W. Blake, *Complete Writings*, ed. G. Keynes, p. 431. O.U.P. 1969, Oxford.
2. A. Ehrenzweig, *The Hidden Order of Art*, Paladin 1967, London.
3. A. Einstein, *The World as I see it*, 1956.
4. J. Field and A. Newick, *The Study of Education and Art*, 1973, London.
5. A. Findlay, *A Hundred Years of Chemistry*, Duckworth 1948, London.
6. S. Freud, 'Recommendations to Physicians on the Psychoanalytic Method of Treatment', in *Collected Papers*, Vol. II, 1912.

7. P. Greenacre, 'Childhood of the Artist', in *Emotional Growth, 1971.*
8. R. Gordon, 'Art: Mistress and Servant of Man and His Culture', in
    The Study of Education and Art, eds. Field and Newick, 1973, London.
9. C. G. Jung, 'The Aims of Psychotherapy', in *Coll. Wks.,* Vol. 16, 1931.
    ——Psychological Factors determining Human Behaviour', in *Coll. Wks.,* Vol. 8,
    1937.
10. N. Kazantzaks, *Report to Greco,* 1968.
11. P. Klee, *On Modern Art,* 1948.
12. D. W. Mackinnon, 'Personality Correlates of Creativity: A Study of American
    Architects', in *Creativity,* ed. P. E. Vernon. Penguin 1970, London.
13. M. Milner, *On Not Being Able to Paint,* Heinemann 1971, London.
    ——'The Role of Illusion in Symbol Formation', in *New Directions in
    Psychoanalysis,* ed. Klein, Heimann, Money-Kyrle, Holt, Reinhart and
    Winston 1955, New York and London.
14. E. Neumann, *Art and the Creative Unconscious,* Routledge 1959, London.
15. L. A. Reid, *Meaning in the Arts,* Allen and Unwin 1969, London.
16. H. Rugg, *Imagination,* Harper and Row 1963, New York and London.
17. H. Segal, 'Psychoanalytic Approach to Aesthetics', in *New Directions in
    Psychoanalysis,* ed. Klein, Heimann, Money-Kyrle, Holt, Reinhart &
    Winston 1955, New York and London.
    ——'Notes on Symbol Formation', *Int. J. Psychoanal.* 38, iv, 1957.
18. D. S. Winnicott, 'Transitional Objects and Transitional Phenomena' in
    Playing and Reality, Tavistock Publications 1971, London.
    ——'Playing: a theoretical statement' in *Playing and Reality,* Tavistock
    Publications 1971, London.

2

The importance of the body in non-verbal methods of therapy

SUE JENNINGS

This chapter will discuss the emphasis on verbal communication in our society, not only in the therapeutic situation, but at every level of interaction and living. My hypothesis is that man has an innate disposition to move in rhythmic patterns and that this is transformed in his various spheres of activity, such as play, work, symbolic activity. If this disposition is thwarted, then it becomes internalized, suppressed, distorted, and he loses touch with this basic area of his nature.

I want to investigate the notion that we are developing and fostering what I term 'non-physical' people. By this I mean that people are becoming less able to understand physical messages that they receive from others, and also have difficulty in using their bodies in positive, effective and creative ways.

This is evident in day-to-day interaction as well as in symbolic expression through the formalised arts, religion and ritual.

I shall discuss what we already know in these fields from recent research and will put forward my notion that man, in order to survive, needs to express his innate physicality in ways that are creatively and symbolically satisfying. I have already written on the importance of ritual in therapy.

This approach will be seen to influence our society both in education and therapy, and I will make suggestions for the implementation of an adequate preventative and therapeutic mental health programme. Apart from these specific suggestions, I hope to help the reader — whether a practitioner in

27

the field of the caring professions, an artist or a lay explorer — to challenge his own idea of physicality by expanding his intellectual awareness of unexplored possibilities.

I am writing from the viewpoint and experience of a trained therapist who uses dance and drama both in treatment and staff training, as well as that of a social anthropologist whose prime area of research is the human body and its use in communication. The body is a complex area of study, my examples are of necessity diffuse and varied.

My suggestions stem from many years' observation, not only in the therapeutic field, but also from my own findings and those of others in the wide field of non-verbal communication in society today. Obviously I have been influenced by my own creative expression through dance and more recently through writing.

Action and anxiety

There is a focus in Western society on verbal methods of treatment in psychoanalysis, psychotherapy and counselling both for individuals and groups. When non-verbal approaches are used they are seen only as a means to an end and not as having value in themselves. Psychiatrists will sometimes employ non-verbal techniques as a means of arriving at verbal communication, but the emphasis is always on the verbal expression or the verbal interpretation.

Not only is there neglect of non-verbal means of therapy, it also provokes much anxiety. This results in the creative arts often being relegated to peripheral positions rather than a complementary one, in a therapeutic treatment programme.

This anxiety concerning non-verbal means of communication is on two levels. One is concerned with symbolic expression; we do not feel comfortable unless we can understand through reductionist means, communication through art, music or movement. There seems to be difficulty in accepting them as other dimensions of communication. Also, there is a pressing need to make a verbal interpretation of symbolic non-verbal communication.

The other level of anxiety is mainly concerned with the physical action of the body. The body may be utilized in therapy provided someone else is 'doing' the therapy, or if the actions are very strictly controlled. For instance, we tolerate brain surgery, electric shock treatment and many forms of drug treatment where the specialist treats a relatively passive body. Many of these forms are intended to curb various displays of action such as hyperactivity. We have physiotherapy where movement is allowed and encouraged but very strictly-controlled. There is emphasis on the 'right' movement.

For example, working with a group of cerebral palsied children who were grossly handicapped, I was devising a programme of creative movement for the children in wheel chairs. This was being observed by their physiotherapists and many of the children moved, who had never voluntarily moved their bodies before. One actually got up and walked. The criticism of the physiotherapists was that the children were not making the 'correct' movements. My reply was that surely it was preferable to stimulate the *desire* to move in the first place; thereafter it might be possible to reinforce the correct movements.

I have observed hospital staff on the wards feel very ambivalent about allowing activities where their patients actually move around. Activity such as knitting, while sitting still is all right, but the anxiety seems to occur when people move their whole bodies around. I think some of this anxiety is due to the fear of loss of control; that someone with an active body could overwhelm. And since the staff and patients are uneven in ratio, there must be many unvoiced fantasies concerning potential physical violence in a patient group. When patients move around too, they are in effect being far less dependent and many of us (the same as many mothers with their children) find it difficult to cope with the autonomy of others.

This anxiety about physical movement in therapy is not only confined to institution settings; it can happen also in verbal group therapy sessions. I have witnessed extreme anxiety on the part of the group leader when group members wanted to move around, re-group the chairs or sit on the floor. It is usually interpreted as a display of some other kind of feeling, 'I wonder why you need to do that'; or 'what are you trying to tell us'; it would seem that in some cases a therapist has to diminish his *own* anxiety by a 'breach of conduct' interpretation. The action can never be seen as a counter-action against the often cerebral experience in verbal therapy.

However, I feel we need to look at society as a whole, and beyond the therapeutic situation, in order to understand this emphasis on verbal communication and the neglect both of body focus and body action.

Changing attitudes to the body

Never before has the emphasis been so much on verbal interchange as it is in our society today. Through every type of medium, through our education system, through almost every point on the job scale, verbal skill means status.

How has this come about?

There is no doubt that the industrial revolution played an enormous part in the re-evaluation of society and its norms. What we have not sufficiently realized is that the efficiency and productivity that the revolution hoped to achieve has in fact worked against some of man's most basic needs.

This century has seen the development of 'extensions' of the body; machines and instruments that can do the job 'better', i.e. faster, or with less physical effort. In the early days, man still had to operate the machines, and there was much body involvement. Man's physical dexterity was needed when machines broke down as the early prototypes often did. Recent technology is changing all this. Many technical advances need a minimum of physical supervision and in many cases it does not even require man's physical presence.

We have seen the dying out of the craft guilds which gave handwork status in the community. In terms of 'job satisfaction' one can scarcely compare the conveyer belt worker with the skilled craftsman. Not only did the craftsman have value in his hands, his activity was also part of the creativity of a small defined group, where an end product could be completed and admired.

With the increase of technology and the diminishing of body use we have undergone changes in attitudes towards the body. The status of the body has been outstripped by the status of the brain. This is most obvious in our education system where children who are deemed to be less academic are grouped to do cookery and car maintenance. I am not suggesting that this is intrinsically wrong, (although the range of hand subjects is very limited and confined to a practical career structure). What is damaging is the attitude of staff and pupils, of superiority towards the manual or practical worker as opposed to the brain worker. There is a wealth of research being conducted into reading schemes and literacy problems. The non-talker or non-reader is considered virtually a non-starter.

The problem starts even before school, with the lack of physical involvement between mothers and babies. Many nurses now encourage mothers not to try to breast feed their babies and suggest that bottle feeding is easier. In their attempt to assuage the guilt of the mother who cannot for physical or emotional reasons breast feed, they have gone to the other extreme of casting doubts on the breast feeding mother's own inclinations. Babies in our society tend to be handled only at feeding, bathing and at dressing times. Otherwise they are left to sleep in prams and cots.

I would suggest that we are conditioning a very early pattern of non-physicality in our children which later becomes reinforced in the schools, and continues into adult life.

Verbal communication has status either in verbal inter-change or for those who communicate through the written word. Again literacy is the important word here and the stress is on academic achievement. Since choice of jobs which give satisfaction is severely limited in the manual field, there is tremendous job dissatisfaction at the present time. There are now too many graduates for suitable jobs and a feeling of second best for those who do not make university.

With this decline in what I call body focus, or perhaps positive body focus, there are several resultant and related phenomena in our society today.

Firstly there are social statements being made through 'body language' in the way that the body is transported, decorated and held. One observations is that the words and body message often conflict. We can observe the clenched

fist behind a smiling dialogue or the hostile eyes when someone welcomes our visit. It is easier to be defensive in our
verbal messages than our physical ones, and there is often a
resultant brain-body split.

Secondly, there is the vogue for transforming the body.
This, of course, is present in many cultures at many times,
but it is interesting to observe the particular bias of our current
fashion trends. There is an emphasis on the extension of the
body; never have platform shoes been higher. There is a greater
inclination for the body to be encased, hence the tights and
the bodystockings. Gradually over the years knickers and
pantaloons have closed their apertures whereas at one time
they were purely decorative.

One could postulate that the greater man's emancipation
of his brain, the greater the enclosure of his body.

Furthermore, there is a great emphasis on the deodorizing
and disinfecting of the body. Deodorants are being encouraged
for men and women and sometimes children, not only for
underarms, but the whole body too; not forgetting the one
for feet! We lift our hands in horror at the woman who
makes ritual markings on her child's face but think nothing
of disinfecting our vaginas. We could be seen to be going
through a purification ritual in modern technological form
which occurs in the very distant past and the world over.

We seem also to have lost the means of satisfying group
body expression; in particular that associated with ritual.
Historically we have given expression to society's values
through the medium of dance and body movement. Sometimes this was of a social nature, at other times more of
a religious nature, but in Western society there is little opportunity for the shared group experience. I have written in
more detail elsewhere on changes in Western dances. Social
dancing has changed from group dancing to paired and then
to individual dancing.

This could well be a result of the individual focus that we
place in our society. Group identity could be said to be
breaking down in its attempt to establish and maintain
individual identity.

Platform shoes: an extension to the body.

So that at the same time as we have lost a satisfying means
of physical expression, the shared group experience, we have
also lost an important means of group communication.
Above all, we are denying the body as a means of non-verbal
communication and physical action.

What can we learn from the body?

(a) From social distance, signals, gesture and symbolism

In 1959, Edward Hall was writing on the different way that
societies organize their space and the bodies within it. Hall
defines 'proxemics', a term first used by him, as the 'study
of how man unconsciously structures microspace: the distance
between men in the conduct of daily transaction, the organization of space in his house and buildings, and ultimately the
layout of his towns.'

Some of Hall's experiments were concerned with cross
cultural interaction, and the effect of behaviour between
people from different cultures. The people themselves were
not aware of their differing attitudes towards spatial distance
between their bodies. There is great variation in tolerance
of nearness or farness. Within the culture itself, this 'social
distance' conveys various messages about the person with
whom we are interacting. We actually refer to 'keeping
people at arm's length'; extreme closeness can indicate
intimacy or conspiracy. These distances between people are
not arbitrary but are part of a society's non-verbal language,
and they have cross cultural variations.

We know from our own society that if someone stands too
near us we sometimes just back away; if we wish to assert
ourselves we stand tall, even to the extent of building up our
shoes. If we want to assert dominance we will place someone
else in a lower position, either in a lower chair or at the bottom
of a table. We place monarchy on a very exalted dais. Mehrabian
says, 'Greater relaxation . . . is associated with higher status
and a more dominant feeling. In contrast tension, which is
indexed by a symmetrical placement of the arms and legs, and
an upright posture, is more characteristic of the social
behaviour of those who are lower in status and who are more
subordinate.'

There are those with whom it is not possible to gain physical presence unless there is a letter first. In situations such as the ordinary person meeting the Pope, most people have to be content with very great spatial distances.

However, much research needs to be done into this type of body language, and in particular to the variations both between social groups and between cultures.

Ray Birdwhistle has also developed his own methodology concerning 'kinesics' which he defines as the 'science of body behavioural communication'. Birdwhistle has worked out an analysis of body communication similar to that used by linguists for language. It is based on a division of the body (head and neck, face, shoulders and trunk etc.) which does not hold up cross culturally, as Birdwhistle himself points out. Quite apart from understanding the messages we receive off the body, we know little about how societies classify their own bodies, and also how they use body terminology when classifying other phenomena.

However there have been some interesting anthropological comments on certain aspects of body focus. For example, in the early part of this century, Hertz discussed right- and left-handedness in *Death and the Right Hand*. He suggests that total right-handedness is frequently culturally conditioned. He says, even if there is physical evidence for the superiority of the ability of the right hand, why don't people train their left hand to compensate for the lack of ability. There are, in many cultures, specific tasks for which the right and left hands are trained, which are often based on oppositional beliefs in the society. The right hand is connected with the sacred, with the offering of gifts, (often holy places are entered by the right foot first); and the left hand is associated with the seamier side of life, with magic and with sorcery.

We now make allowances for left-handed children in our society, though in the past they have often laboured under great difficulty, and it is usually felt that right-handedness, at least in some degree, is something to be encouraged.

Steiner tells us that in Polynesian belief, the head of the chief was hedged around with the strictest taboo practice both concerning things that enter the head and things that were done to it. For instance, if the chief had his hair cut, the cutter would not be allowed to use his hands for anything else, even feeding himself, for some time.

Mary Douglas goes as far as saying that the relationship of the body parts of the person reflect those of the pattern of hierarchy of the society;

'The relation of head to feet, of brains and sexual organs, of mouth and anus, are commonly treated so that they express the relevant patterns of hierarchy.'

She suggests that interest in the body's apertures depends on society's pre-occupation with social exits and entrances, escape routes and boundaries. If there was no concern for social boundaries, she would not expect to find any concern for bodily boundaries.

And in Shakespeare's *Coriolanus*, we find an analysis of the interdependence of bodily functions in Menenius Agrippa's speech to the rebelling citizens of Rome:

> 'There was a time when all the body's members
> Rebel'd against the belly; thus accused it:
> That only like a gulf it did remain
> I' the midst o' the body, idle and unactive,
> Still cupboarding the viand, never bearing
> Like labour with the rest; where the other instruments
> Did see, and hear, devise, instruct, walk, feel,
> And Mutually participate, did minister
> Unto the appetite and affection common
> Of the whole body. The belly anseer'd, —
> . . . with a kind of smile,
> Which ne'er came from the lungs, but even thus,
> . . . it tauntingly replied
> To the discontented members the mutinous parts
> That envied his receipt; . . .
> "True it is, my incorporate friends", quoth he,
> "That I receive the general food at first,
> Which you do live upon: and fit it is;
> Because I am the store-house, and the shop
> Of the whole body: but if you do remember,
> I send it through the rivers of your blood,
> Even to the court, the heart, to the seat o' the brain,
> And through the cranks and offices of man,

The stringest nerves, and small inferior veins,
From me receive that natural competency
Whereby they live: and though that all at once,
. . . Though all at once cannot
See what I do deliver out to each:
Yet I can make my audit up, that all
From me do back receive the flour of all
And leave me but the bran.'
                    (*Coriolanus*, Act I, Scene i).

I have mentioned some of the ways in which the body is
used to 'make statements' within a cultural context, both
in the way bodies are grouped and the spaces between them,
and in attitudes towards various body parts.

Birdwhistle also draws our attention to the hazy thinking
regarding body gestures. It has often been thought that
because gestures do not use words, they can be understood
cross culturally. People tend to use the phrase 'natural gestures'.
However, after many years research, he suggests that there are
no gestures which hold the same meaning in every society.

Since there is cultural variety regarding gestures, we must
be careful when we try to interpret gestural meaning. Even
within our own society there can be differences. For example
in some areas children in young teens greet each other by
thumping each other. Yet what is a friendly communication
can be deemed to be 'violent and aggressive' by the observer
who does not understand the specific body language.

We have many practices in Western society, often tied up
with etiquette, concerning the right way to hold one's body,
to shake hands, which parts of the body must be covered
(the head when entering church, for instance, but only for
women, not men,) and a reading of Mrs Beeton's book will
yield many rich ideas. Many of these are still adhered to.

We also have beliefs concerning babies' bodies, especially
when they are small; concerning the cord dropping off, or the
closing of the fontabelle. Many mothers, for instance, still
insist on cutting their babies nails by biting them — at one
time they would also swallow the nail as well. We have no
systematic understanding of these beliefs in our own society.

Raymond Firth has written at some length in his recent

book on symbolism, on the various ways the body is used as
a symbolic vehicle.

He says there are four main areas where the body has
symbolic value. There is the use of the body as an abstract
means of communication such as kneeling to a god; we even
use the phrase 'bowing to authority'. Then there is the
more general application such as describing a man as being
big-mouthed, broad-shouldered, weak-kneed and so on.
Thirdly there is the use of the body to describe corporeal
units such as the body politic.

Then there is the symbolism concerning a piece of someone else's body, such as a lock of hair, teeth.

Even from these brief descriptions it is possible to see the
rich variety of material we are looking at when we are studying
the body and its varying messages. What we must be careful
to do is not to confuse the social statements of a society and
groups within it, with the private symbolism of the individual,
whose code may need much attention before we can understand
it.

(b) What can we learn from the body in action?

I mentioned in the early part of this chapter that there appears
to be a tendency in our society to negate physical movement.
There is unease when people move around, for instance, in
institutions and schools. However, this seems to be the attitude of our society as a whole.

Physical movement in public is very largely controlled.
Marches are ordered and supervised; movement from one
place to another is carefully controlled, or sometimes not
allowed at all. The gathering of large groups of people can
provoke feelings of insecurity and has recently been the
subject of new legislation. Some degree of social control
is indeed necessary, for reasons ranging from public safety
to the smooth running of the social environment, but this
control must be overt, not manipulative, unconscious control.

It is curious that moving from one place to another on
wheels is allowed, and we may even do this at great speed.
We may travel at amazing speeds in cars and aeroplanes,

Do we understand this body language?

What are they controlling? (Note contrasting stances.)

but it provokes comment if we run very fast down the street. Even an athlete training in public draws attention, and very often physical action in public apart from walking can lead to arrest.

There are other factors which would seem to be fostering this notion of staying in one place. Mail order catalogues encourage us to do our shopping at home. Theoretically it is possible to do all our shopping from our own sitting room. The range of door-to-door sales representatives selling anything from household appliances to make-up could mean that we do not need to set foot outside our front door. With the firm establishment of television we can have a full range of entertain-ment in our own homes, as well as up to the minute news and full sports coverage. We can bring beer home in ring-pull cans, and the local pub is disappearing as a meeting place, now becoming a place simply to drink. Thus we can begin to understand how movement is being controlled in our society.

There are other phenomena in our society which work against the physical use of our own bodies. This century has seen the rise of the body specialist. Dancing and sport are things that we tend to go and watch others do rather than do ourselves. Far more people watch sport than actually do it. Recent years have seen the rise of the sport star system, where footballers, for instance, are now able to earn sums that were at one time only associated with Hollywood filmstars.

Recently too, we have seen an increase in spectator dance spectacles. Dance companies coming from abroad increase each year, and the emphasis is on the exotic and bizarre. More and more dance is something that belongs to the domain of the specialist for our passive enjoyment.

The body specialist who can provide this spectacle of physical display is not only keeping the body of the masses still; the message is also that the ordinary body isn't capable of this type of achievment. Just as the deodorant undermines acceptance of the state of our own bodies, this vicarious experience takes away from our own inclinations and confidence to participate actively in sport and dance.

Critics would say that perhaps the reason for discouraging body movement in our society is because there is less space now that we are a heavily populated country. I would make two comments on this. Firstly, we have a choice about what we build and therefore how we use our space. Secondly, rather than having to build smaller housing units due to lack of space, perhaps we are building housing units in order to contain people — yet another way of giving people less room to move.

Authorities would also point out that movement control is necessary for public safety. However, this argument doesn't always hold. Recent events in Portugal have shown just the opposite. There were many fears that the 1974 May Day celebrations, the first for many years, would provoke unbridled behaviour in the processions. This was not the case. Despite the fact that there were thousands in the streets in a state of euphoria, there were no casualties, nothing got out of hand, and no troop reinforcements were necessary.

However, it is possible to see some very disturbing results of this curbing and containing of the body. Recent instances of football crowd violence have challenged popular support for the 'therapeutic' effect of watching. Cricket, and even tennis matches have been less orderly than usual and it could be suggested that too much passive participation could provoke physical assertiveness. There has been a rise in 'crimes against the body'. There has been an increase in baby battering, wife battering, child murder. Certain kinds of violence have become means of social identification: vandalism of railway carriages has become generally synonymous with football fans; mugging with skinheads. We could look at this as body destructiveness. The very thing we are trying to prevent in our society by control, is in fact happening in a very destructive way. Physical energy is becoming negative and inturned. Perhaps we could see this as a desperate attempt to express the need for a legitimate means of body recognition and body expression.

This destructive expression again can be seen in the therapeutic situation. We only have to look at the physical destruction of those with severe mental handicap and mental illness; the persistent rocking, head banging, finger rubbing, skin picking that goes on. There is also the 'frozen' body of the catatonic schizophrenic.

I am using these examples to support my hypothesis that man needs legitimate means of satisfying physical expression.

I would suggest that this need is an innate disposition, necessary for not only man's biological survival, but for influencing his mental and emotional survival as well.

Recent research into techniques of psychodrama, role play and action methods suggests that if a person can actually do something, rather than just sit there, he may well have more insight into his own difficulties and those of others. Apart from all the forms of treatment concerned with therapy working from the outside in order to effect change in the inside, there is a need for complementary, or alternative work which functions from the inside, from the person's own innate dispositions.

I am suggesting that the increased use of movement and dance therapy can have a direct impact on biological man and his own internal resources, rather than imposing this from the outside. Also by mobilizing this physical energy one is establishing a cultural framework within which learning and personal growth can take place.

Man's basic disposition to move rhythmically

In suggesting that man has a basic disposition to move rhythmically I am reversing the present thinking which tends to say that man needs to dance in order to express himself, or children need to play games in order to channel their aggression; i.e. the justificatory approach for physical recreation. These overtones reach out into therapy, too, when one hears the comment, 'drama is good to occupy the patients' — this notion of keeping them busy or diverted!

Again I am asking the reader to look at this the other way round. If man *needs* to move rhythmically then this will be how he orders his universe, i.e. he will work, play and worship developing these patterns and this will vary between different cultures.

John Blacking, in a recent RCA lecture, put it another way; he said that it was frequently said that dance was a mirror of society, that we looked at movement *because* of something else it did; but he said: 'Aren't music and dance important in themselves? Isn't culture a product of sharing, not of individuality? Therefore can't we look at movement and dance as a formal expression of order which is the basis of humanity?'

Blacking goes as far as suggesting that, rather than follow Marxist thought, where dance and music are part of the superstructure, and a *consequence* of production, we should look at them as the *cause* of production; that human attitudes and human ways of thinking about the world are a *result* of music and dance.

I would suggest from my basic hypothesis that from man's need to move, he then transforms this movement patterning into various cultural situations which can incorporate his work, his social interaction, his ritual and other forms of collective expression.

I use three categories which are a useful way of examining this proposition; they are functional, social and symbolic patterning. They are not to be seen as totally separate and exclusive, but overlapping and complementary.

Functional patterning occurs for instance in the execution of a productive task, such as the felling of a tree, pulling a rope; social patterning occurs in a shared expression of group movement; in our society it can be seen when we all join hands to sing *Auld Lang Syne.* It is an experience of group feeling and solidarity of the particular group that is together, and historically it can be seen in many dances which were not of a religious nature; it can also be seen in certain ceremonial happenings around the monarchy, Parliament and other social institutions.

Symbolic patterning is the shared rhythmic movement expression which reinforces the cosmology and belief system. It enters into many areas of religious worship.

If we look at all three areas in Western society we can see that there has been a change in body expression; as suggested earlier, in the work area the machine has largely taken over from the body which has brought about a decline in functional patterning; dancing has also changed and has grown from group dancing and now the emphasis is very much on individual dancing — when dance occurs, that is. Although discotheque dancing amongst the young can be a group experience, it can also be a very isolatory one. A group of people moving in a room together does not necessarily mean that the experience is shared; there is not necessarily any communication. The shared dance of the village green is very much in the historic past.

In symbolic expression we only have to look at Christianity as it is practised today to see that we have one of the most static of religions. There is no swaying or movement and little chanting, the procession in church is measured and the rhythms are similar for both weddings and funerals. In this respect it will be interesting to see the growing influence of the immigrant forms of religious expression; West Indian pentecostal meetings are attracting a lot of attention, where people sing, dance and trance. There is a rise in the number of Afro-Caribbean dance groups, steel bands and black cultural centres.

However, the very physicalness of the black man can cause suspicion and mistrust; myths regarding sexual potency and physical violence, and the 'primitiveness' of black people abound. There is the notion of orgy and loss of control. Yet what can be more repetitive and controlled than most ethnic dance? The importance of it for this argument is that it is meaningful movement, it is enjoyed and *experienced.*

Having discussed the three main areas where physical expression takes place and its current decline in Western society, I want to discuss the changes that are beginning to take place in our society, and to suggest how these must be fostered in order to develop the whole physical person, both as an individual and as a member of a group.

The winds of change

In education there is an increase in the number of physical educators who are also trained in movement and dance and who are introducing this into the schools. Much of the dance being done develops from the pioneering work of Rudolf Laban on 'modern educational dance' and forms the basis of most of the dance work being done in schools and colleges. It is now possible to take dance 'O' level, and evening classes are increasing which provide movement, dance and many ethnic varieties of movement expression.

However, many head teachers and educational specialists have to be convinced of the primacy of importance for this type of expression.

We are beginning to build local sports centres, local amenities for all ages in many types of sport. The problem is that many centres charge prices for admission or membership that limit it to too few people. There is outcry in local papers that these various centres 'don't pay'; perhaps we should look at it differently; if we could view this as a necessity instead of a luxury then we could feel justified in financing it from official sources. We need to convince local government as well as national, that centres of these kinds are providing the opportunity for training positive movement patterns instead of negative ones. If we have to judge it in economic terms, we could treat it as an investment and one which could save many millions spent in repairing vandalism, spent in the courts, hospitals and custodial care for young offenders.

Not only in sport but in many forms of art, creativity and movement of various dimensions do we need to provide facilities for the young and old. In therapy there have been some very important influences during recent years. Certainly Ronald Laing has contributed, despite much criticism, to a re-appraisal of *perception* in psychiatry. Through his writings and research, Laing has helped us look at mental illness as a symptom of something much more complex which resides in the family and in the society, rather than being the manifestation of an isolated sick individual. Laing has helped us to look at what the signals may be saying, exhibited by patients, both verbally and non-verbally, and to see that there is in fact often logic and order in these 'messages', not confusion and nonsense. Raymond Firth, the anthropologist, suggests that other societies display more tolerance of mental abnormalities, and more attempt at entering into a dialogue with patients rather than sub-categorizing them. Dr Marion North also points to possibilities in this field: 'One of the special advantages of movement as a therapeutic means, (or educational and recreational for that matter) is that people can work out in a positive way their experience of human contacts and relationships. As relationship problems are

usually associated with any kind of malfunction this kind
of movement therapy can contribute a great deal to treatment by helping the patient with new or difficult situations.'
I would point out that dance therapy is much more
advanced in the United States than it is here: postgraduate
training courses and research programmes are pursuing the
concept of therapy through dance and movement.

Recent years have also seen the gradual acceptance of the
place of the creative arts in therapy; we now have the
establishment of training courses in art and music therapy
and recognized training in drama therapy is being planned.
Placements are growing in hospitals for the art therapist
though this is as yet not widespread, and their frame of
work and pay is often far from satisfactory. There are many
consultants who still put the arts into a peripheral category
in treatment.

Another recent impact which has to a certain extent
changed the face of therapeutic treatment *and* the notion of
prevention has been the rise of the 'growth' movement in
America, now becoming established in the U.K.

Hailed initially as a licence for licentiousness, and
scoffed at by traditional psychiatrists and educators for
being non-scientific and self-indulgent, the growth movement
has begun to challenge the frozen physicalness of Western
man. Encounter and sensitivity groups provide opportunities
where people can encounter each other, confront, touch,
discover, play and explore areas which have for so long been
repressed in favour of cerebral expression or only allowed
in the area of play of the young child. People can find out
about their own bodies, can rediscover basic physical needs.
Despite opposition, the influence of this is being felt throughout psychiatry, and the growth movement itself is already
beginning to be institutionalized. Some training sessions by
traditional therapists already include techniques borrowed
from the encounter groups; classical psychodrama is beginning
to explore the non-verbal side in greater depth, and many use
body techniques in both 'warm up' and action sessions. Many
psychodrama leaders are being trained in both psychodrama
and other approaches.

How can these changes be most effectively developed both

in preventive mental health as well as in therapeutic treatment programmes?

Firstly, we must **recognize this need for physical movement** in man and provide opportunities for it both in work and leisure; then we must also look at our planning and see how we can more effectively arrange our environment in terms of housing, wide open spaces, work areas, sports and dance centres.

However, before such an ideal is ever achieved, whereby the emphasis is on prevention, we must look at therapy now and see how we can most effectively help.

We must become more efficient at understanding **the body**; far more research needs to be done on this and the analysis of body language within cultures in the same way that verbal language is being researched.

With this we can more effectively understand and differentiate between individual and private expression and group and public expression.

Secondly, we need to develop **the creative arts as therapeutic** forms both in re-education and treatment, remembering, of course, that movement and dance are not the only ways of using the body; that the body is greatly involved in painting, sculpture and music making. By developing these we are giving our patients other forms of communication and expression, nor merely data for verbal interpretation. We need to examine, for instance, the use of dance for discovering and sharing new forms of ritual.

The third area which is of great importance is that of re-education. One of the greatest difficulties in any form of insight therapy is that the behaviour does not always carry over into everyday life outside the treatment situation.

However much we get in touch with ourselves in an encounter group or gain insight through psychotherapy, for this to be truly meaningful, it has to make an impact on our daily lives outside and on our interaction with people in our homes, our work and our day-to-day contacts.

If a client through therapeutic help has gained insight into his difficulty in personal communication at home, he will be unable to automatically return to his domestic situation and adjust.

The adjustment has to go on at different levels and perhaps help would be needed in the family situation as well as the possibility of joining a small social group such as an arts group where 'growth' could be a continuous process. Through such a group there is the possibility of rediscovering *experienced* culture, not just receiving a passive and often processed observation of culture.

This is concerned with the whole field of re-habilitation, and if it is to become a real concept we must have communication between all the helping agencies. Too often the client is left to rehabilitate himself.

Another example should clarify this possibility. A patient may be able through psychotherapy to gain access to memories and achieve insight into why her shoulders are permanently hunched in a frozen posture. This may have been due to early conditioning when her father always had his hand raised in threat of assault against her. Although she understands the problem, the symptom will not be automatically cured because after many years of faulty posture it will have become a habit. Therefore some kind of physical re-education programme will be necessary for achieving normal posture and confidence in the previously cowed body.

This is where we must have links between the many therapeutic agencies and creative resource centres so that we are helping the whole person; and as far as possible, the whole person in their social group; we should not be just treating the symptoms of an individual out of their social context. These aims sound ambitious but are essential I feel, for the continued survival of man in society. For his mental, physical and emotional well being, man has to rediscover his cultural roots by actually experiencing them in some form, and being able to recreate them himself and not just observe this from others. The most important medium for this is man's own body. By recognizing and acting upon this, we shall not only become more effective helpers and healers, we shall be helping to build a healthier society where everyone has the possibility of achieving a sense of fulfilment and equilibrium.

References

1. R. L. Birdwhistle, *Kinesics and Context: Essays on Body-motion Communication,* Allen Lane 1971, London.
2. J. Blacking, 'Music, Dance and the Growth of Man', RCA lecture, 1974.
3. M. Douglas, *Natural Symbols: Explorations in Cosmology,* Barrie & Jenkins 1970, London.
4. R. Firth, *Symbols Public and Private,* Routledge 1973, London.
5. E. Hall, *The Silent Language,* 1959.
6. R. Hertz, *Death and the Right Hand,* Routledge 1960, London.
7. S. Jennings, 'Anthropology of Dance', *New Society,* Dec. 1972
    ——*Remedial Drama,* 1973.
    ——'Ritual and Performance and their use in Therapy'
    unpublished paper 1st Drama Therapy Conference, 1973.
8. A. Mehrabian, *Silent Messages,* Prentice-Hall 1971, New York and London.
9. M. North, *Personality Assessment Through Movement,* MacDonald & Evans 1972, London.
10. F. Steiner, *Taboo,* Penguin 1967, London.

Self-protection of the body amidst machinery and signals.

3

Creative play with babies

ELINOR GOLDSCHMIED

'It is in playing and only in playing that the individual
child or adult is able to be creative and to use the whole
personality, and it is only in being creative that the
individual discovers the self' (D. W. Winnicott).

Play and work

Play, as it is commonly thought of in our present day
industrial society, carries a sharp distinction from work. Work
is considered as a serious matter, for adults, since physical
survival and social responsibility are at stake. Play may have
its place, as something for which time and effort are
admissible after the demands of work have been satisfied.
Even the old precept of 'work hard and play hard' means
that there lurks the idea that play, if it is to be indulged in,
has certain strings attached.

A definition of this important word 'play' fully eludes us,
but a closer study might suggest that a change of view is
underway and that play is more likely to be accepted as
being necessary for psychological survival, both for individuals
and for groups, as is work for physical survival. Maybe this
acceptance is becoming more possible because of the
knowledge that machines could relieve us of so much of
the effort now involved in work. It is clear that much anxiety
surrounds this prospect and grave doubts are frequently
expressed about what might be called 'the threat of leisure'.

It would seem that if our noses, or most peoples' noses,
are not kept to the proverbial grindstone, then who knows
what highly pleasurable or frightening visions might emerge
for exploration, when we might truly have to come to
grips with each other! Perhaps at present it is only the pre-
school child, the mad, the aged and the very rich — in short,
the non-producers — who have to tackle this. Living in the
social climate of today and giving thought to what life in
the next decades may be, it is worth considering how best
we can equip our infants, who will be adult then, to
develop and to value their capacity for play.

How then can the infants of today have our 'permission'
to enjoy and to grow through their experience of play, unless
it is we, the powerful and directing adults, who are willing
to release this part of ourselves to interplay, warmly, generously,
and affectionately with them?

That play is an ever present element in daily life, deeply
reflected in our common speech, needs only a moment's
thought to understand. From this will flow our recognition
of the meaning and the value which it has, not only for the
young and 'irresponsible', but as a source of nourishment
throughout our lives — even if we feel we must make it
safe and respectable by giving it the name of recreation.

The phrases and the sayings which are used of play are
so varied and so manifold, that it is worth calling to mind
a few. Many are to do with social situations — 'playing it by
ear', 'playing it up, or down', 'playing for time', or 'playing
second fiddle' to someone. In the area of thought we 'play
around with an idea', we give our imagination 'full play' and
play with a ring or a lock of hair while we allow ourselves a
moment's respite in a daydream.

There are plenty of negative connotations too — of a child's
activity 'oh, he's only playing', or of someone's handling of
a piece of work, 'she only plays around with the job and
nothing gets done', or of the man denigrated as a 'playboy'.
So the list extends, and the boundaries of work and play
are constantly redrawn as we examine the content of how
we spend our time.

In much educational writing 'the importance of play'
for young children has become almost a **boring cliché,**

i.e., devoid of feeling, which only ceases to be boring when the adults who are supposed to respond to this idea, find that this phrase burnishes some deep and valued areas of their own experience, and that play has genuine meaning for them too, whatever form this may take in their daily lives.

Here lies the crux of the matter, for if it is true that you cannot give of something which you have never received, then we might have pessimistically to conclude that those who have not enjoyed childhood play experience will be gravely hampered in enabling a child, for whom they care, to flower in experience of play himself. Any public discussion of this theme nearly always produces the sad comment afterwards, from some adult present, that they were 'brought up in an institution' and have little or no memory of play. It is possible that they are also referring to their lack of memory of a close adult with whom they would have wished to share their early play.

It is important to keep in mind that later life can go on providing ways of gaining this experience. It can never be said that it is 'too late', though the missing of early experience *is* crucial, it is not final.

More optimistically perhaps, there is a chance of most babies having had some measure of loving interplay from someone central to their early lives, even if later childhood was lacking seriously in this experience. This reasonable chance may lie in the fact that the almost total dependence of the baby demands the attention of one person and of one pair of hands for his feeding, his washing and the changing of his clothes. Because of this, much of his very early waking life is liable to offer him some satisfying interplay, even coming from an adult who may be almost unaware of his deeper need. It is a little later on, when a baby's waking spans extend beyond the time required for this bodily care; then it is that he will have 'time on his hands', and the need for wider stimulus has growing urgency.

Interplay in early infancy

Between the caring adult and the baby, there lies the possibility of a continuing world of interplay of a new and complex

nature, after the first great qualitative change of birth. Throughout life, this area of bodily experience changes and deepens,
or may be restricted and denied, but in early infancy all the
elements for growth are there, open and apparent.

This interplay in the early months of life, which goes on
between the infant and whoever cares for him most intimately,
can be thought of in four ways, stemming from four sources —
from touch, combined so closely as it is with smell, from voice
and sounds, from sight and from the shared exploration of
objects. All these are closely interwoven naturally, but to
think of each in a separate way serves to identify them and
so to re-relate.

Touch

The language of touch, so well known to lovers and aggressors,
remains through life a means of communication infinitely
varied and capable of great subtlety. Both at the beginning
and the end of life, it is through touch predominantly that
feelings are expressed — towards the very young and the very
old. What then are the ways in which mothers, fathers and
others initiate and mutually enjoy these playful exchanges
with their infants? The baby's intent and serious business of
feeding himself at the breast or bottle will change as his
mother holds him up nestled over her shoulder, facing him
this way and that, patting, stroking, rocking him, nuzzling
into his small neck, entwining a finger in his fist, wrapping
him tightly in the comfort of a cradling arm, or holding him
securely while his unco-ordinated threshing movements may
be accompanied by those air-rending yells whose strength
and persistent power we never cease to marvel at.

The baby is exposed to such a total impact in this physical
handling that the 'messages' of loving, of anxiety, and at
times the veiled hostility which his very dependence can
arouse, all this will be communicated to him unerringly in
interplay with the adult who daily cares for him. Just as
we try, sometimes vainly, to read his signals, so it seems he
learns to pick up ours, and so in this total kind of learning,
adapting to stimuli outside of, and independent of himself —
thus the definitions of himself begin to be created.

As this definition begins to grow the close adult is aware of qualitative change of some significance. Donald Winnicott wrote: 'First, surely, it is the mother who plays with the baby, but she is rather careful to fit in with the baby's play activities. Sooner or later, however, she introduces her own playing, and she finds that babies vary according to their capacity to like or dislike the introduction of ideas which are not their own. Thus the way is paved for playing together in a relationship'.

To many adults the strain of this dependence is considerable, and it seems probable that the energetic play which adults often enter into with a baby — holding him tightly at arms' length up in the air, vigorous rocking or bouncing games seated on the knee — these may be some of the ways in which the adults are exploring, within the bounds of safety, their own aggressive feelings, for unquestionably in later life we all make use of play for this very purpose. The infant, in his turn, gains experience of the impact of adult feeling, and it is easy to detect when he finds this impact too sudden or too strong, responding with distress. In this connection it is worth nothing that the use of teasing at a later stage can form part of this aggression.

We have all been aware of the fun game which turns into a destructive thing when teasing gets out of hand. Perhaps the 'practical joke' of adults is an instance of where aggression oversteps the fine limit between humour and hurt.

For the baby, this experience of being held will have the widest range of feeling. 'Let me hold him for a bit' says the older child, or friend, or relative, for they know quite well that looking at the baby is one thing, but that it is not until you hold him that the interplay of hands and arms round his small body and his wobbling head takes a new dimension. The holder and the held are partners in a fleeting moment of experience which holds involvement and strong elements of tension. We have all heard, and made quips about our own, or the father's or the Vicar's risk of dropping baby, and the quality of feeling is then quite clear. As the growing infant puts out efforts to create his own bodily control, so he is helped in this way by the sure and vigorous handling he may receive from his close adults.

In the joy of reunion, embracing a loved person, or holding tightly in our arms, rocking to comfort and control, a distraught child, instinctively we use our bodies as communication. With murmurs and with gentle movements and all the expressions of affection and concern we will have once received as infants.

We have all used our bodily presence to stay watchful with a friend in sorrow, knowing that they must not weep alone, and how much more true of babies this would seem to be. It is only that the limits of our tolerance are not so very great, and fatigue sets in, that we leave babies to 'cry it out alone', while feeling guilty about those surges of exasperation at their inability to tell us, as the adults usually can, what is the cause of their crying or their despair.

In understanding the significance of loving and aggressive touch, it does not seem too much to claim that we create for him a body of profound experience, upon which the baby, as he grows to adulthood, will draw, add to and use in his own way. He will have learned that touch is also a language.

Sight

So closely linked with touch is looking, and all the richly varied messages which eyes convey. The intensity of this unwavering interplay of eyes is of sufficient significance to need a special term to describe it which I call *The Primal Gaze*. When we begin to think round the quality and the nature of this exchange of gaze between the adult and the infant, we realise that neither of the partners has inihibition or difficulty in sustaining and enjoying it.

The idea might not be too fanciful that adult difficulties in giving and receiving communication from the eyes might stem from an absence of experience in infancy of just this affectionate and accepting gaze.

In thinking of the significance of sight some of the many common sayings and poetic references come to mind immediately — 'a feast for sore eyes', 'beauty in the eye of the beholder', 'to drink to me only with thine eyes' and endless associations of food and touch and nearness. Also the many hostile and rejecting ones 'Get out of my sight!' 'I can't bear the sight of him', 'a guilty or an accusing glance', 'a withering

stare' and the bank manager who 'reaches for his glass eye' as
the client asks for an overdraft! We speak jocularly of 'blinding
people with science' as one of the protective or aggressive
onslaughts which we sometimes use deliberately, and we are
all aware of the hostile and frustrating experience of trying
to get into effective communication with someone who
persists in wearing dark glasses inappropriately, or refuses,
in conversation, ever to look directly at us.

The poetic description of 'the eyes as windows of the
soul' underlines the fact that the expression of the eyes is the
one thing which it is almost impossible to dissemble. This
is perhaps the reason why we sometimes choose to use the
telephone or write a note, so that in some difficult situation
with another person we can avoid direct eye contact, and
allow only our voices or the written word to 'speak' for us.

Watching a baby and the person who is mothering him,
it is the unwavering and exclusive quality of their looking
at each other, which is a most striking feature of their
relationship. It is the kind of looking on the adult's part
which absorbs the tiny details of the baby's face. A visual
exploration sometimes accompanied by gentle touch. The
movements of the surface tension of his skin, around his
eyes and mouth, the puckers on his brow, are a focus for
the minute observation, as are the subtle shades and tones of
colour change on eyelids, cheeks and chin. Holding an infant
in our arms we put the baffling question to ourselves 'What
is it that he sees — the impressions that he receives, what
do they mean to him?'

It is not for nothing that the question when the baby smiles,
and at whom, is one which arouses strong and often competi-
tive feelings in the near adults, which clearly indicate our
deep interest in being recognized. Just as we smile, perhaps
only with the dilation of our pupils and very little other
facial movement, the baby 'smiles' with his whole body, as
when he feeds or cries, all of him is involved in a response
which is total.

We would not question that in our relationships, that trust
and confidence both in oneself and in the other person, or a
group, is crucial to the understanding of the feelings and ideas
which we are trying to exchange. The all too common state of

'talking at cross purposes' would seem less likely to occur
when the discipline of eye exchange is there. Tracing in the
baby how the primal gaze develops and extends in range and
meaning, it is clear how this look, created first in the arms
or lap of the caring adult, lengthens like an invisible thread
which bridges room or garden space. The baby, when he can
use a toy, to hold out or to wave at others, is satisfied with
an answering look of interest and encouragement from the
close adult, without the need of actual body contact with
which to back it up. So it is then that part of the confidence
in separating begins. The range extends in time, as the image
of the other becomes part of the 'script' we are always
writing for ourselves and which accompanies us through
life.

Photographs, ranged upon the mantelpiece or carried in
the pocket-book, form part of the possessions stored safely
in the mind's eye. 'Out of sight out of mind' does not apply
to those things which we really care about.

Babies, busy with looking to their own security and the
forming of attachments central to their own survival, make
their most urgent demands for our attentive presence. All
the daily occasions where bodily caring are involved — the
struggles to fix the nappy comfortably, to clean his nose,
to negotiate his fists and arms into his sleeves or fiercely
beating feet into the garment's legs — all these activities are
shot through with possibility of play with eyes and hands,
if we have the time and the serenity to participate and
enjoy. Too often the conditions in which care and rearing
must take place are of gross inadequacy, for as a society
we have relatively small concern for the nurturing of our
infants, or for the well-being of the adults who undertake
this most demanding task. This does not mean that we must
keep silent on these matters, rather the reverse, for our
infants cannot do this for themselves.

Perhaps it is the quality fo commitment implicit in the
primal gaze which underlies its creativity, and which affords
a kind of springboard from which to move off into life.
Certainly in any enterprise there is no question but that
risks and effort can be successfully sustained where the base
is broad and well established. The looking which is exchanged

between the baby and his parent in their early days together
is part of this.

Sound and voice

The lullabies, the love songs, the songs of work and protest,
are part of the reminder that where there is feeling and
involvement, there are songs. There is 'the feeling that is too
deep for words', but generally our spontaneous response in
handling infants, as well as the touching and looking, combined
with exclamations, murmurs, crooning of indeterminate sounds
and often our own imitations of all the varied sighs, gulps, burps,
moos, and little mewing sounds, the squeaks and shrieks
which make up a baby's first 'vocabulary'. Much of this is
done in private, for we, as 'sensible' adults, can so easily be
made to feel, under cultural pressure, that expression of this
kind is foolish or to be laughed at.

 Until more recent times, the men in our society were not
allowed the expression of this kind of tenderness, but now that
rigid adherence to previously accepted roles is undergoing
change, our babies can hope to have more fun with father,
and he with them.

 One of the things which is most noticeable about this kind
of 'conversation' which we exchange with babies is that it is
often rhythmic and generally repetitive. There seems to be
a kind of enjoyable suspense to do with 'waiting for something
to happen' which we generate. The baby makes a sound
which is perhaps new for him, and we immediately copy it
back to him, often in the process turning it into a recognizable
word, accompanied from both sides with nods and smiles,
pursing of the mouth and wrinkling of brows — in fact with
the whole range of facial expression which 'speaks louder
than words' in every daily interchange in adult life. This
handing back to baby a word coined from the sound he
gives to us, is a fine example of what much of later education
is about, summed up in the phrase 'start where the learner
is and take him on from there'. Much of the time we readily
go with the baby at the simplest level of his earliest sounds,
and only some of them do we take, transform and so teach
him in a creative way. We can sense the delicate boundary

between the adult's, sometimes anxiety-laden need to guide and to instruct, keeping as best we can a fine balance between his own 'here and now' and what *we* may perceive as his next step. Within the range of this fine balance lies the creative and the pleasurable experience of learning — at any age.

The caring adult and the infant grow to be available to each other through the medium of sounds and words, and there is established the immediate reality and the future promise of enjoyment.

This delicious kind of 'wasting time' in play with babies, means indeed that we must have time to spend, and not only that, but also circumstances with lack of pressure, serenity, and health, which are the background in which this kind of creative experience can most easily take place. Most parents with the responsibility for the upbringing of the very young, suffer and bear such high degrees of stress and strain, that it is not surprising that our infants must frequently go short on this kind of play, even when we know the real significance it has both for them and for ourselves.

I do not think that there is any parent, however secure in themselves, who has not felt some deep anxiety in their under-standing at times like these, of how some others come to ill-treat their babies. That dependence of an infant and the utter importance we feel as we try to understand his wails, our energy worn down with our own fatigue, makes the severest test, which few can bear alone. Perhaps it is here that our understanding has increased and we know that if we are upon the edge, we must seek help and share the strain before control should break.

We have all passed through those wretched hours when nothing that we do seems to soothe the yells and screams, and we find ourselves unwittingly making more noise than the infant in our desperate efforts to bring him comfort, and to ease our own anxiety.

It is no accident, perhaps, that in later life we all have used the doubtful technique of 'shouting down' the others, who arouse in us some high frustration by their attitudes and the noises that they make.

By our quality of tone, continuing talking to our infants, as we handle and feed them and change their clothes, not only

do we encourage them to explore their own abilities in
making sounds with meaning, but we also give them their
first experience of that great dimension of human relationship
which lies in the use of speech. In our care of infants it
sometimes seems to be ignored that a growth towards a
mastery of language, and the capacity for abstract thought
which stems from this, is nourished and developed only
by such a simple thing as talking!

Inter-play with objects

Three ways have been suggested in which interplay takes
place — touch, sight and voice — and then the fourth, the
interplay with objects which leads on to areas thought of
more conventionally as play. This play finds its focus
in the loving adult's body, breast, hands or face or hair, for
these are constantly to hand, safe, familiar and available
if the adult is content to share. Then a little further out
to his own fingers, thumbs and toes as his own body
boundaries are better understood, also the common phrase
that a child is 'playing with himself' gives recognition to the
fact of masturbation.

So his experience goes outwards to the raw materials
for experimental play — the water in the bath, food upon
the dish — in so far as the adults will allow this.

When the grip and eye co-ordination is achieved, then
common household objects — a spoon, a peg, a brightly
coloured tin are useful for this kind of handling, as well as
toys whose scope is fairly well defined, such as rattles and
teething rings.

From the baby's first touching of his mother, her breast,
his bottle, the clasping of his fingers round the finger of
the close adult who holds him, his own fingers entwined in
the soft meshes of his shawl and gently disengaged by adult
hands — these are all part of his daily contact with objects
outside himself, which have their own existence and their
own validity, but which are only gradually perceived as such
by him.

From the random threshing movements of arms, legs, hands
and fingers comes the discovery of his own body and his own

control of it. Where previously it was the direct interplay of
adult and infant which was dominant, just as soon as he
is able to grasp a toy and bring it to his mouth for his 'inspec-
tion', learn about its nature from his lips and tongue, then
this new element becomes a vital factor in creative play, and
the adult's role has also changed in relation to the infant's
new found skill.

His mother will encourage him and curl her baby's fingers
round a wooden ring or rattle, watching for the moment when
his eyes, his hand with toy, and mouth move in unison and
the enjoyment of sucking any object which is now accessible
begins. Though it may appear to be a very tiny step, this
mastery of hand to mouth, means that another area of experience
is opening for the baby. Now, 'under his own steam' he can
grasp and wield a toy — his first tool, with which his work
and play begins. Not only can he do this for himself, perfecting
with each movement his skill in co-ordination, but he is also
able, and is indeed forced, to face something of the nature
of the items which he grasps, exerting their own reality by
reason of what they are. The wooden cube which is too
large to be pressed through a restricted space will *not* go in,
and so his magical powers receive their challenge. For him
the rub is this — unless the close adult will co-operate and
understand his own creativity in offering these objects
appropriately, the infant will be left quite high and dry, unable,
as yet, through his own exertions to go out and to get his
play material himself. We can almost hear him mutter, 'you
just wait till I get going!' Three toys are better than one or
two, for when there is an object in each hand and yet there
is a third which arouses interest and curiosity, then a choice
will, at some moment have to be made. This simple opportunity
to make a choice — which to put down and which to pick up
can be the very early start of that ability to choose which is
one of the hall-marks of maturity.

Since there are two hands and three toys, we can often
watch an infant come to his minute decisions, which are
for him, however, quite significant and demanding of his
thought and action.

And so a new dimension in his play has entered in with
objects which can be grasped and sucked, handled and

learned about, if the infant has the good fortune to have
a thoughtful adult handy who will see that varied things,
which are both safe and interesting, are well within his
reach during all his waking hours.

We are all so familiar with the 'conversation' which takes
place with unfailing regularity when the toy or teddy is
thrown out of the pram to be retrieved by the friendly adult
for as long as their patience lasts! Yet this throwing and
receiving back can also be a vehicle for smiles and words
undertaken at a little distance, a kind of new communication
which requires a toy so that it may take place.

Just as soon as an object or a toy comes into use then all
the myriad games which flow from this come into play. All
the 'here' and 'not here' as the adult initiates 'peeb-bo' along
with smiles, surprise and repetition — the appearing and the
disappearing of a rattle, first hidden and then suddenly
produced 'Where has it gone! Why there it is!' Things can
bang on other things, make different noises, or be thrown
to drop or roll and be retrieved. In this way the adult's part
becomes more complex, as provider of play material which
is suitable and safe, a stimulus to curiosity and experiment,
sometimes an initiator, one who takes part in play, but also
an interested and applauding audience for small triumphs,
a role which can quite well be played from a distance,
bridged increasingly by eyes and voice, and carried out
while other chores are carried on.

In finding objects of interest at this time, all that is
needed is the adult's imaginative eye, which sees that common
household things, like a tea strainer, a wooden spoon, a
piece of crinkly paper provide the focus and the pleasure
upon which the infant's own activity can ride.

The roots of sociability

We have explored these four means through which the adult
and the infant create their interplay. Through this mutual
knowing of each other the infant moves from his first base
to an ever-widening range in his experience. So he lives at
any one moment, as indeed does each of us in that state of
play where inner life, and all that belongs to other people,

other things, meet in a continuing stream. Of each new day
he can surely say: 'Today is the first day of the rest of my
life'. If within our close relationships we offer to our babies
the widest experience that we feel we can, they will select
and use as much as they are ready for. One thing is certain,
that you cannot 'hurry' babies. As adults we would sometimes
do well to learn again from them, what it really means to
'go at your own pace', unflustered by demands of daily
circumstance.

It has often been thought that very young children in
their first year of life do not have an interest in each other,
and do not have anything that we would call play going
on between them, and rather that it is only the caring adult
who is the focus of all of their attention. Could it be that
we as adults find it hard to accept that foretaste of the
fact that children, in their own peer groups, have times and
moments when they really have no need of us?

My observation, amply borne out by many parents, suggests
where there is a little group of two or three infants, settled
down upon the floor and with their mothers or their caring
adults close at hand and within sight, it is quite clear that
an almost continuous interplay goes on between them – if
we care to watch for it.

Observations of two such inter-changes between infants
come to mind – Robert, of eight months lying contentedly
on his stomach, elbows bent, hands and eyes and mouth
busy with exploring some toys. He wore bright blue bootees
and his feet were beating gently up and down. John, of eleven
months crawling competently close by, first fixed his eyes
upon the bootees, moved near and gently lifted and let drop
each foot in turn (thus in this instance the first contact was
made through the moving feet). John's eyes moved up to
Robert's head, who turned. Glances, smiles, wagging of the
head and small noises were exchanged. John crawling forward
laid his cheek upon the floor close to Robert's face, looked
at him intently, still smiling, stretched out his finger and
gently stroked his cheek. Another instance was with Robin,
thirteen months and twins of ten months who were seated
near him on the floor. He gazed into their eyes smiling, they
smiled back, made noises, waved their hands in the air and

moved their toes in response. Robin crawled to a small low box close by holding their attention with his eyes, sat himself upon it, bent forward and rolled himself in front of them — laughing and making bubbling noises, closing and opening his eyes. When the twins laughed he repeated his rolling act seemingly intent in evoking a response from the twins. They jigged up and down, nodding their heads, making chirping noises and keeping their eyes fixed upon him.

Infants playing on the floor together will, of course, need ample play material at hand, of the simple, safe and stimulating kind that I have described, which furnishes the 'island' upon which they lie if they are not yet mobile.

It may be that generally infants of nine, ten or eleven months are not found grouped together in this way, except in institutions, and so our opportunities for observation have been limited. Now that groups of mothers are tending, in an effort to break down their own, often serious, isolation, to meet together for periods in the week, their infants too will have a better chance to explore and so develop their own interchanges.

The preliminaries of later sociability may be experienced here within the orbit of the presence of the caring adult, which holds the anxiety about dependence satisfactorily at bay, allowing interest and curiosity the freedom to flow and feed.

Observing infants of this early age when they find themselves grouped together in this way, it comes out very clearly that they are making use, as tools, of their earliest communication with each other, just those same means of interplay which they have learned and continue to experience individually with their caring adults. Their use of eye contact, of touch, of 'pre-verbal' conversation and the offering and the acceptance of play material at hand, would suggest to us that in a very direct and immediate way, infants do begin to use the skills which creative play with adults has enabled them to start to learn.

As we walk about the streets and shops, or travel in a bus where infants are being carried or being pushed along, we can frequently observe how infants, often only for fleeting moments, 'signal' to each other, responding to each others presence with enjoyment which is evident, if mutual smiles and squeaks and wriggles are to mean anything.

It is with these beginnings that we may set the scene for the creation of a body of experience which goes to make up the 'textbook' of memory to which we always add, and which each one of us in varying degrees possesses. In adult life, we can make constant reference back if we allow it to remain available for use, both to ourselves and to those infants whose lives, in any measure, we may share.

Summary

Interplay between the caring adult and the infant has many dimensions and through his bodily experience the baby grows to know himself developing his relation to the outside world.

Through touch and smell, sight, sound and learning about objects — these are the ways in which play begins with the close adult.

Using these experiences the infant acquires his 'tools' of communication upon which patterns in his life are based. Given the opportunity to relate to his own age group, also within the first year of life, the infant shows us his earliest elements of sociability.

References

D. W. Winnicott, *Playing and Reality,* Tavistock Publications 1971, London.

4

Movement for retarded and disturbed children

VERONICA SHERBORNE

My experience of working with retarded children began in
1958 when I taught for the National Association for Mental
Health on one of their regional courses for teachers of
mentally handicapped children. I now work on a similar
course in a College of Education. My job is to prepare the
student teachers to teach all aspects of physical activity;
this includes movement education (the child's relationship
to his body and to other people) physical education (work on
and with apparatus, games and swimming) dramatic play
(which develops out of movement play) and dance.

Over the years I have noticed that children can make
progress in certain fundamental areas as a result of movement
experience of different kinds. It is possible to help developmentally retarded children to relate to their bodies, to
become more self-aware and more confident. It is possible
to help them to form relationships, and it is possible to
help them to focus attention, to concentrate. This progress
can be brought about by work with a teacher who understands
the processes by which bodily experiences affect the child
developmentally. It is this aspect of my work that I shall
describe.

The severely retarded child

The children my students and I work with range in age from
five to sixteen years; most of them function at the level of

a two to four year old child. Children in Special Care and in hospital ward classes are at an even younger stage of development, perhaps as young as six months old. Although retarded mentally a large number of mentally handicapped children can develop socially and emotionally to almost a normal level. The teacher of mentally handicapped children has to cope with a wide range of physical, mental and emotional abilities and disabilities. For example, one or two children in a class may be hyperactive, agile, excitable and noisy. These children avoid physical, and eye, contact; they appear to understand everything said to them, but rarely speak. Other children in the class may be over-weight and physically nervous; they may be friendly and co-operative, and use a limited vocabulary. The class may include a child who has come from an Educationally Subnormal (moderate) School because of behaviour difficulties, and this child will be brighter and more verbal than the others. Some children in the class may suffer from different degrees of spasticity; one or two may be in wheel chairs, or in calipers; one child may have impaired sight, and one child might be incontinent.

It is difficult to say which bodily experiences will be most useful to all mentally handicapped children, but all children need security, and the teacher's main job is to build up the children's physical and emotional sense of security through bodily experiences of different kinds.

First of all the teacher must know this bodily based security herself (it is mainly women who work with these children) because she can only communicate what she has herself experienced.

Experience of weight

A child who is secure is confident in himself and trusts himself. This self-trust is expressed in the way the child relates to the weight of his body. The experience of the body which seems to me to be fundamental to the child is that of his dependence, his weight. The child's attitude to his weight is expressed physically in many ways, for instance in the way he lets his body rest on the ground, in the way he lets himself fall on to a mattress, or the way he lets an adult carry him or swing him. A nervous child will not readily let go of his body weight, he will not give in to the pull of gravity, and he will not let his body rest on the ground. He cannot trust himself to the support of an adult, and he will resist the flow of his body weight on a swing. The degree to which a child will, or will not, commit his weight, is an indication of his self-trust, his self-confidence.

Gravity has been described as the architect of the body; like the air we breathe, we cannot exist without it, even though most of the time we are unaware of it. I think it is an essential part of the development of the young child, whether he is normal or handicapped, to gain a concept of himself, his weight and strength, through bodily experiences which go with the pull of gravity and which go against the pull of gravity.

The baby or young child is fundamentally affected by the way his mother supports him and plays with him. It is possible for the adult to 'feed in' to the child the sense of his weight, and by the way in which she does this, if she has a feeling of concern and affection for the child, she will also 'feed in' a sense of his value. I have seen many retarded and disturbed children develop self-confidence and self-trust through movement play with an adult. The child accepts himself and relates to himself more readily because the adult supports and accepts him. The child enjoys being lifted, swung and carried so much that he begins to forget his anxieties. By reinforcing experiences in which the child finds it safe, and enjoyable, to commit himself, the adult builds up the child's self-trust. There are many ways, too, in which the adult can demonstrate his trust in the child.

Experience of the flow of weight

Commitment to the pull of gravity is one expression of confidence, commitment to the flow of weight is another. Here the body initiates a movement, and helped by the pull of gravity, the body is allowed to move with the momentum thus caused. The simplest version of this is seen when a child who is lying on the ground begins to roll. I find it helpful to roll a child from lying on his back to balance

on one side of the body, and then fall back onto his back
again, and then roll onto the other side of his body. This
is a kind of rocking, and it is also the smallest 'falling' that
one can experience.

The floor is the best place for the handicapped child
to explore and discover ways of experiencing the weight of
his body. Handicapped children need regular opportunities
for playing with weight and finding out how to use it in
constructive and positive ways. They need to be able to let
their bodies roll, opened out or curled up, they need to slide
to wriggle, and they need plenty of opportunities to swing,
either on apparatus, or with the help of an adult. If possible
they should have some experience of bouncing, and sitting
on a trampette is the simplest way of getting this. The
children also need to find out how to fall and roll without
hurting themselves, and for this either gymnastic mats, or
grass, provides a soft surface. It is useful to fall and roll from
a sitting, and then from a kneeling position, before standing.
The more confident children will run and fall and slide, or
roll.

Babies and children respond instinctively to being rocked,
which is the earliest experience of the flow of body weight.
Babies also enjoy being gently bounced up and down on an
adult's knee. The rocking and the bouncing are rhythmical
weight flow experiences. In rocking the gentle swing of the
whole body has a calming effect and can become hypnotic
and sleep inducing. Bouncing has a stimulating effect.
Rocking, bouncing and swinging give the child a whole-body
experience which has a harmonizing effect, a whole-making
effect on his being.

Swinging can be indulged in by emotionally disturbed
children to the point that they become so intoxicated by
the free flow that they are unaware of danger. It is interesting
that the emotionally disturbed child will commit himself
to the flow of movement to the point of complete abandon,
whereas he will not readily commit himself to sitting or lying
on the floor. His love of the wildly unstable experience, and
his rejection of the stable, earthed experience is a reflection
of his emotional and physical state.

The hypnotic effect of rocking is seen in its extreme form

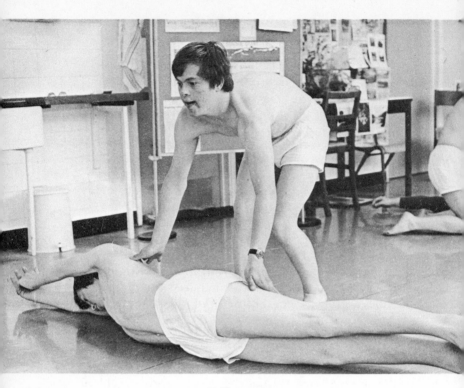

Rolling a partner.

in obsessional rocking. The movement may be a swaying
forwards and backwards in a sitting position, a swaying of
the head from side to side, or a sideways rocking of the
whole body with a shift of weight from foot to foot. In
extreme forms this rocking isolates the child from any form
of experience either of himself, or from the outside world.
It is a self-defence and a solace.

It is important to realize the benefits that can be gained
from the free flow, or momentum, of weight, and also to
recognize the extreme forms into which free flow movement
can develop. One of the favourite experiences for any child
is to be swung by an adult. There are many ways of swinging;
gripping the child round the waist, facing away from the
adult, so that the legs swing freely; holding the child by wrist
and ankle, allowing the whole body to swing round. The child
can also be curled up, if he is small, and swung in a compact
shape. Whatever method is used the child enjoys both the
free flow of his weight and the contact with an adult. Highly
disturbed children who do not normally tolerate physical
contact with an adult will be more inclined to accept it
because of their delight in being swung. One has to realize,
though, that swinging, while achieving some relationship will
probably add to their excitement.

A useful bodily experience for the child is that of being
pulled along the floor; here the child experiences free flow
while keeping contact with the ground. Like rolling and
swinging, this is an enjoyable experience for nearly all
children. It is possible for children to pull each other, either
by the legs or the arms, and they can pull an adult. This is
one of the ways that the adult can commit himself to the
care of one or more children. Children are more likely to
trust an adult who has trusted them.

Experience of body weight in water

It is very important for developmentally retarded children to
experience the buoyancy of the body in water. The children
learn to trust their weight to this medium, and water imposes
a flow of movement which is beneficial. As with all the
experiences I have described this opportunity to play in

water must happen regularly. A few children will react to water by becoming more tense and excitable, but given time they will settle down. The water must be pleasantly warm, and the children should be in their depth sufficiently supported by buoyancy aids. The quieter the noise level and the calmer the water the better, but unfortunately this is not always possible in many swimming baths.

I encourage children to use the floor as if it were a swimming bath, and for this I need a clean slightly slippery floor. I try to encourage in every way I can fluency of movement and confidence in allowing the body to move by virtue of its weight.

Experience of the body as a whole

In the activities I have described of rolling, bouncing, swinging and playing in water, the child experiences himself as a whole, and I think this should precede movement of parts of the body. The sense of his wholeness, of his totality, gives a child a sense of well-being and harmoniousness. It helps to establish the child in his body. I believe the sensation of being an entity, although initially unconscious, prepares the way for the child to become more aware later of the parts of his body as belonging to him. The unconscious bodily experiences precede the development of the more conscious sense of identity in the child.

Experience of the centre of the body

When the child's whole body is supported on the floor he becomes more aware of the back, shoulders, hips, stomach and chest; he experiences these parts against the resistance of the floor. When the trunk is supported on the ground these central parts can move more fluently and in a more mobile way than when the child is standing. It is very important for the child to experience movement in the central parts of the body. He can initiate a roll or a spreading out from

A severely handicapped child enjoys a swing.

the centre of his body and can begin to experience the
continuity of movement from the centre to his knees and
elbows, neck and head. As the limbs are not bearing weight
they can move in response to movement in the trunk.
Unco-ordinated and unself-aware children rarely experience
a harmonious flow of movement through the different parts
of the body. Some mongol children have an impressive
capacity for an easy soft continuity of movement which is
seen when they roll on the ground. They seem in their
element here.

There are two ways in which one can increase a child's
sense of security, one is by helping him to have confidence in
the base on which he is sitting, standing or lying, and the
other is by helping him to discover the centre of his body
as a place from which he can move, as a home which he
can come back to, as the middle which connects his
extremities. It is relatively easy to help retarded children
to become more well-based, more anchored, more earthed.
It is more difficult to help them feel centred. It is helpful
sometimes to tickle them at the waist and stomach as one
might a normal young child, and to pat their backs and
stomachs and 'feed in' body sensations which help to strengthen
their realization of their bodies' existence.

A clear indication as to whether a child has any awareness
of his middle is seen when he is asked to curl up. Some
children do not know the meaning of the words and will lie
flat on their stomachs on the floor. An important part of
self-awareness is the ability to pull the whole body together,
to feel all the parts of the body close together. Children can
be helped to experience this closeness in several ways. The
adult can curl the child up inside his body and rock him, or
make a 'house' into which the child can crawl and hide, or
swing him tucked up in a bundle. One can help some children
by curling them up on their side so they are holding their
knees, and then gently tug at this 'parcel'. They experience
this closeness more by having to maintain it against resistance.

There are some children who can curl up but dare not tuck
their heads in, they need to maintain a look-out. They feel
everything of interest and value is outside them, and there
is no security to be found inside. The child who is secure

within himself will curl up, head and all. Tense, nervous
children who dare not tuck their heads in can be helped by
doing a somersault over an adult. The adult can be on all
fours, the child leans across the adult's back, tucks his head
under the adult's body, takes his weight on his arms, and
slowly rolls his body onto the floor. The adult can help the
child by using a spare arm to enfold the child's head and
shoulders. Another way the adult can help is to sit on the floor,
legs out-stretched. The child stands behind the adult and
leans over one shoulder. The adult curves the child's body over
his shoulder tucking his head in towards his chest and
stomach. The child, helping himself with his arms, rolls
right over, finishing sitting between the adult's legs. Skilful
children can reverse the whole process so that they swing
themselves back into the adult again and return to where
they started. All kinds of somersaults and rollings involve
commitment to the free flow of weight, they emphasize the
wholeness of the body, and in the case of somersaults with
an adult's help they involve trust in the adult. All these
experiences build up the child's confidence in himself.

Anxiety is usually most clearly expressed in the shoulders,
head and neck; through careful somersaults a child can be
helped to allow his head and neck to be a continuation of
his back. He cannot see what is happening, he can only
feel what is happening.

The capacity to allow movement to happen, to let body
weight go, are indications of the child's self-trust. It is also a
sign of self-trust if the child can integrate his head and neck
with the movement of the rest of the body. It is also a sign
of trust if the child can shut his eyes. The child can be helped
to close his eyes if he is in a safe, contained, supported situation.
The containing, supporting adult can strengthen the experience
by rocking the child and humming or talking softly. The more
one can help the child to take in what is happening within
his body the better; he needs constant encouragement to discover
and to value his own resources, to 'listen to' himself.

Awareness of parts of the body

It is best to begin working on awareness of parts of the body

with the child well supported in sitting or lying on the ground.
In the total body activities I have described the child has
acquired some knowledge of his body at a fairly unconscious,
level. When working on parts of the body such as, for instance,
hands or knees, one is hoping the child will consciously realize
that these parts belong to him. The knees are a good part to
start with; hips are too central and fixed; feet are too far away.
The knees are half-way from the centre to the periphery; they
can move freely, they are close enough to the child for him to
feel they belong to him, and they can be seen easily.

A child who has had his knees patted, bent and stretched,
who has crawled on his knees, walked on his knees, who has
squatted with his knees near his shoulder, who has straightened
his legs and seen his knees flatten and vanish, who has
hammered on his bent knees making a percussive drumming,
will perhaps one day say 'my knees'. Even if the child cannot
speak he may realize they are part of his body and recognize
them again. A lively class of mentally handicapped children
will ask 'can we do knees to-day?'. They get a lot of fun from
finding out how they can stick their knees together, how
they can walk with their knees stuck out sideways, how their
knees can take them for a walk, jump them up and turn
them round. As one of the main weight-bearing joints in the
body the knees play a vital part in maintaining balance, as
shock absorbers and in all activities involving management of
body weight. They have the added advantage of being
expressive and comic which appeals so much to the
children.

I have seen children at the developmental stage of about
one year who are only able to focus very briefly on their
hands and fingers. It is helpful for the child to clap his hands,
rub them together if possible, and to touch fingers and hands
very lightly. One tries to build up the child's awareness of
his hands through touch, using light, delicate sensations
contrasted with stronger, hard sensations. Changes of tempo
also bring in a game or play-like quality; children naturally
enjoy sudden movement after very slow movement. Awareness of feet is important as they are the child's main contact
with the ground. For those children who cannot walk awareness of the body is particularly important, and they need

constant encouragement to make use of, and to discover, the movement possibilities available to them.

Through helping the child to become aware that his knees, hands, face, are part of him, one is strengthening, reinforcing, his body image, his body concept. The moments of self-realization are often tantalizingly brief. The capacity to focus attention is the key to body awareness. If the adult can interest the child in play which is absorbing and fascinating, the child becomes absorbed. This means the adult must be absorbed, and he has to be skilled in discovering what each child finds engrossing. Through the kind of play which emphasizes awareness of the body the adult can make a vital contribution to the development of the ego in the retarded child.

All the activities I have described, which could be called awareness of the ground, and awareness of the body, come naturally on the whole to normal children and to develop-mentally retarded children, and are normally much enjoyed. The psychologically disturbed child, who has suffered emotional damage, is so occupied with his anxieties and with erecting defences against any further damage, as he sees it, to himself, that he finds it almost impossible to commit himself to a relationship with another person, or to relate to himself. It is often very difficult to anchor these children on the ground, they feel vulnerable and threatened at ground level and prefer to be high, and perhaps out of reach. Some of these children are able to relate to things, to objects, and they may play incessantly, and even obsessionally with one particular thing. This becomes their security. Some of these children are often very skilful in the way they manage their bodies, on apparatus or on bicycles, for instance. For some of these highly disturbed children the degree to which they reject human contact is an indication of the degree to which they fear it, and yet crave for attention and affection. The conflict in the child between fearing human contact and desperately needing it is very great. Disturbed, hyperactive, children need special understanding and help with how to cope with their extreme energy which sometimes drives them in a way which could be described as demonic. Working with emotionally damaged children requires a

different approach from working with developmentally
retarded children, although both groups of children have
the same basic need for security. I will return to the problems
of these children in the section on Energy.

Locomotion

Normal young children go through important stages in
locomotion before they manage to stand. A child who
cannot yet sit may travel by rolling; another, who can sit,
may travel by propelling himself along with one leg while
sitting on the other; another, lying face down, will discover
how to lift his body away from the floor on hands and
knees and will begin to crawl. Whatever method is used the
child discovers how to manage his weight, how to use his new
found strength, and how to cope with parts of his body.
Handicapped children need constant opportunities for discovering how to manage their weight from these simple beginnings.
They are very inventive in the variety of ways they find for
themselves in getting around close to the floor.

They will shunt themselves along on their backs, pushing
with their feet, they will wriggle and pull themselves along
on their stomachs. Children should be encouraged to crawl
on their stomachs, pulling one knee at a time as far up to the
shoulder as they can. This kind of crawling, with the body on
the floor and the limbs working to propel the body forwards,
or backwards, produces more mobility in the body than
normal crawling on all fours. Children will discover ways of
travelling by rolling curled up or spread out, and again it is
helpful to draw attention to the knees and elbows. All children
love spinning on their bottoms, and they also enjoy spinning
on their stomachs. It is the free-flow element here which they
particularly enjoy.

Squatting and walking with short legs is valuable, the
weight of the body is close to the floor and the knees are very
much in evidence. Children will discover ways of travelling
using hands and feet; they can hop (in a squatting position)
on both feet; they can take weight on their hands and put their
feet down in a different place, producing a little twist in the
body and the beginnings of a crouched cart-wheel turn. The

varieties and ways that children will find for getting about
close to the floor are endless. These activities can be likened
to the movement of snakes, lizards, tigers, ducks, birds,
rabbits, monkeys, even caterpillars and snails. Movements
like those of sea anemone, starfish and octopus are also
valuable if the children have seen these creatures.

I think it is important for the child to re-experience the
stages of locomotion which the baby goes through, and to
experience some of the stages of evolution out of which
man has developed an upright stance. One of my reasons
for encouraging this is I want to keep the body as mobile
and supple as possible, and I can only do this through
activities·such as crawling, slithering, wriggling and squatting.
As soon as the body is upright the child has to maintain
his balance on the comparatively narrow base of his two
feet, he does not want to risk falling and a certain stiffness
often develops.

The legs and hips are the main weight-bearing apparatus of
the body, and the more the handicapped child knows about
his feet, knees and hips the better. One can help the child to
experience stability in standing by showing him how to plant
his feet wide enough apart to give him a broad base (but not
too wide), how to bend his knees slightly so that he has muscu-
lar control over his knee joints, and his centre of gravity is
lowered. The feeling of steadiness can be tested by gently
pushing against the child's knee or hip. The taller the handicapped child becomes the more he has to safeguard his
balance and the fewer risks he will take with his weight.
The more insecure children will not be able to let their
weight go in an activity such as spinning a partner. They
will walk round each other, but will not lean away from each
other.

It is a significant moment when a child jumps both feet
off the ground, and for the normal child this happens
normally between two and three years old. Having been
through all the confidence-building experiences which lead
to being able to stand, the child then wants to take off,
and having experienced the joy of jumping he will then
extend the height, depth, or length of the jump to his limit.
I worked with three and four year old children in a play

group for two years and found they never tired of jumping from a table onto a mattress, finding endless variations in flight and ways of landing. At the same time I worked with mentally handicapped children of ten years and found they had the same satisfaction from jumping and landing using apparatus in a gymnasium.

In jumping, bouncing and swinging the body is momentarily weightless. The adult can help the child to jump higher so that the free flow of weight lasts longer. The child's expression becomes more animated, and often a child who normally shows no emotion will smile.

Energy

The children I work with vary very widely in the way they relate to their energy; some are lethargic, others are over-active, and others withdraw into an inner world. It is important for a child to let his body go with the pull of gravity and with the momentum of his body's weight, but it is equally important for him to experience his strength, his resistance to outside forces, his stability and firmness, and his power and energy. Many mentally handicapped children like normal children, have boundless energy and need plenty of opportunity for using it in satisfying and constructive ways. There is a tendency to restrict the opportunities for physical activity for these children both at school and at home, and they may be expected to sit quietly and move in a controlled way at all times. If anything the handicapped child needs more opportunities for physical play than the normal child; there is so much to learn through the play. Some adolescents lose not only the ability to be lively and energetic, but also the desire, and some of them put on a great deal of weight.

The baby's first strong grip is the reflex clutching in the hands which can be seen immediately after birth; his first strong push is that of his feet and legs against his mother's lap when she holds him facing her. As the child discovers how to lift his head when lying on his stomach, how to sit and crawl and stand, the force he is working against is gravity. He develops his strength and uses his energy in a purposeful way. Movement which is forceful demands the focussing of

A schoolboy helps a child to experience strength.

attention and the focussing of energy. If energy is canalized, directed, it involves the focussing of attention. The capacity to focus attention is essential if the child is to develop. The experience of pulling against someone, or pushing against someone helps the child to relate to his energy and helps him to concentrate on what he is doing. His power of concentration increases with his capacity to organize strength, and these experiences contribute to the development of his sense of his identity.

The retarded and the disturbed child can become more aware of himself against another person. He can experience his energy best against the resistance of an adult, and although the force is directed against a person it, paradoxically, creates a relationship. An adult provides the best counter-strength because he can adapt the degree of resistance most sensitively to the needs of the child. The adult can do a great deal to help the child relate to his strength, or lack of it, and to help the child focus his energy and concentrate on what he is doing.

There are many ways of pulling people along the floor, of 'rescuing' people, and it is important for the child to pull the adult if he can. Children enjoy sitting on the ground back to back and pushing hard against each other. They use their hands and feet against the floor to help them push. This use of the floor to provide anchorage and a base is physically and psychologically valuable. The adult or child can experience this anchored or earthed quality by crouching and gripping the floor with hands, one knee and one foot, or by sitting and using hands and feet to maintain stability. In these positions the individual can withstand pressure from different directions, and this testing of strength and immovability is much enjoyed.

There are retarded and disturbed children who will not push an adult partner but will happily pull him. Pushing demands greater involvement with the partner. There are disturbed children who enjoy tugging against an adult, but only for a short time. The adult has to be sensitive about the moment to let go. Having been released the child will often return for another tug, and this may be the first sign of willingness in the child to make contact with an adult.

I am interested in the degree to which children will cling
to an adult. Some children are so hungry for attention that
they cling like limpets; others cannot grip the adult at all.
The strongest test of holding on can be seen in normal six
to nine year olds. The adult is on all fours with the child
slung under his body. The child holds on by using his legs
to grip the adult's waist and his arms holding on round the
adult's neck. The adult can crawl and the child is like the
baby ape who clings while his mother moves. The handicapped
child enjoys riding on the adult's back and clinging on.

Mentally handicapped children are able to work in twos
in pulling each other along the ground, or in pulling and
pushing while standing. They can push from the shoulder,
the hip, or from the back. The children get a sense of achievement from **organizing and** focusing their energy, and there
is a playful element in the pushing. There are always more
boys than girls in special education classes, and it is not
always easy for women teachers to understand the need for
the children to relate to their energy and learn **to organize**
and control it through strong movement.

If children have satisfying outlets for their energy, and if
they have good relationships with their teachers and with
other children they are less likely to be frustrated and
aggressive. If they have help from their fathers from an early
age in rough and tumble play, and if they have opportunities
for 'against' relationships at school they are more likely to
know their own strength and use it in a more mature way
than children who have not had opportunities for experiencing
their energy. The older children grow the harder it is to help
them, but it is still possible to help them come to terms with
their strength, or lack of it. The child who has withdrawn into
a fantasy world and who has 'lost' his energy is actually in
greater need of help than the child who is obstreperous and
destructive. Understanding and experiencing the positive use
of energy is perhaps the most important part of the teacher's
training.

It is possible for retarded and disturbed children to achieve
an experience of centred strength in their bodies; this gives
them confidence in their bodies and confidence in their own
resources. When children have experienced strength and

determination in pushing and pulling relationships against each other, and in gathering their energy to make a firm 'rock', they are ready to try the opposite way of using their energy in movement which is sensitive and gentle.

Sensitive delicate movement requires a refinement and control of energy which shows that the child is able to be in good relationship to the feeling, the emotional, side of his nature, and indicates a certain degree of emotional maturity. It is often only possible to explore this caring and gentler side of the personality after the child has felt secure and confident in his strength. However, one sees gentleness occurring spontaneously sometimes in children's imaginative play, in the way a child dresses a doll or puts it to bed, or in the way some children show delicacy and fine touch in painting or handling materials. Mongol children often have very good fine touch in their hands and fingers, and some can manage their body weight very lightly even though they may be overweight.

Movement to music which is both gentle and slow can be much enjoyed by retarded children; they can respond with a concentration which may be rarely seen at other times. This calm, absorbed, movement is achieved after children have used their energy in more out-going and vigorous ways. In fact I often build a lesson towards sensitivity, so that all the early movement experiences pave the way for the children to get nearer to this aspect of their natures. I am very interested in the degree to which a child can be strong and the degree to which he can be gentle. Strength and tenderness are part of our emotional equipment and it is in this area that the adult can help particularly the emotionally disturbed child. Mentally handicapped children enjoy relationship plays 'against' a partner and 'with' a partner, and often show warmth of heart and good feeling in the way they take care of each other in rolling a partner, rocking a partner, and leading a partner. This is particularly true of mongol children.

The experience of the opposite ways of expressing energy gives children a sense of well-being and satisfaction. I think

One child contains and rocks another.

this arises because the child is totally involved in what his body is doing, and so his movement has content and has meaning for him. Movement which has little or no dynamic content, which is neither energetic or sensitive, feels empty, and looks empty. If a child who is dissociated from his body does movements which are superficial and mechanical, which lack involvement and meaning, which do not seem to belong to him he will become more dissociated.

If the teacher is to help the child to organize energy, to focus energy, and to discriminate between the different ways of using energy, she needs to have experienced and understood these attitudes to energy herself. She also needs to be able to recognize qualities of strength or fine touch in the children she teaches, even if the quality of movement is not at all clearly defined and is also perhaps very briefly expressed. The way a child moves is a truthful indication of what is going on inside him and teachers need to read these signals. Most teachers read these indications instinctively. Children certainly read the teacher instinctively, and disturbed children are particularly sensitive to their teacher's ups and downs.

On the whole retarded children are neither particularly strong or particularly sensitive so that one tries to help them to extend their experience towards both ends of the spectrum of energy. Disturbed children often show an exaggeration of one aspect of energy; one child may be hyperactive and aggressive, and another may be totally withdrawn. In this case one tries to help the child to be less lop-sided, but first one must help the child find his security in what he does best, and then slowly help him to find the neglected part of himself.

A child who is in good relation to his feeling will be able to relate to another person with sensitivity and concern. A child who is emotionally damaged may be able to relate with some degree of concern only after he has built up trust in an adult and trust in himself. It is difficult for emotionally damaged children to work with each other. They are in such great need for security and affection themselves that they cannot feel concern for anyone else. Their deprivation, their sense of rejection, and bitterness, often leads to vicious attacks on other children. Some disturbed children cut themselves off from the outside world and take refuge in an inner imaginary world. These children have opted out, and are often more difficult to help than the children who actively express their resentment and destructiveness. The teacher's best way to make contact with the child who has escaped from reality is through dramatic play in which she can participate and share the fantasy world with the child.

Work with disturbed children is extremely demanding and the adult will be tested to the hilt. The disturbed child is damaged in a way which the retarded child is not, and the teacher who works with these children will be under greater strain. Although emotionally draining, the work can be very rewarding. Teachers of disturbed children need physical and emotional stability themselves; they need to be in good relation to their own strength and firmness, and to know something of their own aggression. They need to be secure enough themselves to be able to trust the children, and they need to be in a good relation to their feeling. Perhaps above all the teacher needs to have a sense of humour and to be able to play. We can help the emotionally damaged child more by what we have to give them as a person than by what we say or teach.

Teachers who work with these children particularly need the support of other adults and to be part of a team. They also need the chance to re-charge their batteries regularly.

Play

All the activities I have described are ones which most children do normally and enjoy doing. They are normal play activities which the adult encourages the child to explore a little further, and they are activities which can be as much enjoyed by adults as by children.

I think the enjoyment comes because people feel more at home with others and more at home in their own bodies. They also discover some new aspect of themselves that they are not aware of before. People participate because the play is enjoyable and rewarding, so the motivation to join in comes from the individual. The starting point for a group will be an activity in which most of the members will feel

secure, or the starting point might be an activity which one
disturbed child is likely to find non-threatening and so
will join in. There is no competition, no right or wrong way,
everyone is successful in his own way, nobody fails. The
members of the group contribute to, and share in, the play.
How the session develops depends on the reactions of the
group and on the teacher's degree of security, knowledge
and experience. The teacher depends a great deal on her
capacity to observe the children and to select from them the
most useful activity to try next. Or she may initiate a different
activity altogether which she sees the children need to experien

A movement class is the result of the teacher and children
working together. The teacher guides, taking movement ideas
from the children and offering them to the class. She gets
down on the floor with the children, and participates as much
as she sees the children need her to do so.

I have described something of the content of movement
classes for retarded and disturbed children, and I have briefly
referred to how one communicates the content, the method of
teaching. The content of a lesson can be presented in a
mechanical or a meaningful way. How the teacher teaches is
just as important as what she teaches. I can only describe
how one teaches as constructive play, and every teacher has
to find her own way of doing this. Success depends on the
relationship between the adult and the children; the better
the teacher knows the children and the children know her,
the more she will be able to help them.

Movement play can develop very easily into dramatic
play, and into dance, into movement and singing, and into
sound making; all activities which the retarded and disturbed
child need, and which all children enjoy. I feel the movement`
experiences provide the core from which the child can
develop in many directions.

Note

The first three illustrations were taken at Church Hill House Special School,
Bracknell. The fourth at Baytree Road Special School, Weston-Super-Mare.
Photographs — Cedric Barker.

5

Games and creative therapy

LARRY BUTLER

I want you to play a game with me. A word game. I write
with difficulty and indecision, so I invite you to participate
creatively in the gaps. Using just words, I hope to share
with you a few ideas about play, lots of questions, and a game
approach to working with people.

Who are you? What do you believe in, what can you give,
what are you good at, what are your strengths? How much
do your beliefs and strengths match up to what you actually
do? These are my first questions.

I am an artist, and I look for an artist in every person I
meet. I'm good at writing poems, dancing, swimming, painting,
cooking, asking questions, . . . and I'm good at encouraging
other people to do these things. I believe in feeling alive and
wide awake, in change and growth and the magic of everyday.
I also believe in a bibliography at the beginning:

1. Larry Butler, *A Book of Games*, 1974.
2. Cid Corman, *A Language Without Words*, 1972.
3. Erving Goffman, *Encounters*, 1972.
4. Johan Huizinga, *Homo Ludens: A Study of the Play Element in Culture*,
   Paladin 1970, London.
5. Mike Pegg, *A Handbook for Group Leaders*, 1974.
6. Jerome Rothenburg, *Shaking the Pumpkin*, 1972.
7. Anthony Storr, *The Dynamics of Creation*, 1972.
8. Robert Townsend, *Up the Organization*, Coronet 1971, London.
9. Lao Tzu, *Tao Te Ching* (trans.) Penguin 1969, London.

Who can create magic? Draw a circle anywhere. Beat the
drum. Speak the word. What you want to happen will

happen. Jump! Follow your stomach, breathe deeply and
fly! . . .

Be alive — *your* way. Eat an elephant, smoke gold dust
behind the moon. Shout your name while *Shaking the Pumpkin*
then give yourself a new name, run around the city acting
out your dreams. Swallow the ocean, then listen to your
blood. Smell the sky. Once upon a time words were like
magic; they still can be.

> a child smiles
> climbing the tree

> a tree smiles
> the climbing child

> smile climbing
> the child tree

> laughing
> the leaves shake

I am beginning to write 6,500 words. I want to create
magic. If you're not interested in magic, but more interested
in theory, skip to the end of the chapter and read backwards.
Do you want to create magic? Put down this book, go outside
and play, go do something you really enjoy but never allow
yourself time to do, close your eyes and daydream, do nothing.
Say hello to a stranger, ask him what he most enjoys doing.
I often meet people who don't know how to play. Playing goes
against the grain of our puritan ethic that says learning is
painful, that we are all sinners who need forgiveness, that
medicines taste awful, the more it hurts the better it is. That
man is contained in the laws of nature. The Clock. Bacon,
Newton and Locke promoted the puritan ethic in the guise
of 'natural religion'. I don't deny that pain is an almighty
teacher as well as time. What I do deny is the denial of joy —
which is what I live for. I say yes to Blake when he sees 'a
world in a grain of sand'. Joy is often lost, but as with any
treasure hunt, there are maps, clues, signposts; and there are
mountains of goodies for everyone.

                    left-over
                    from a cat's feast,

                    the child holds
                    a pigeon's foot

Homes, schools, factories, shops, hospitals, streets, docks,
suburbs, offices are sometimes sad places. Cinemas, bingo
halls, amusement centres, sports grounds, theatres, holiday
camps are sometimes sad places. Ruled by the clock, injecting
a flash of entertainment to ward off boredom and gain some
sense of satisfaction. Not many people have enjoyable jobs.
In my work a day seldom passes without someone asking me:
'Do you really get paid for doing this?' Yes, I get paid to enjoy
myself, to play games, to facilitate enjoyment in others, and
sometimes it is hard work, and sometimes it is not satisfying,
but it often is. In the last 150 years Western man has been
slowly unlearning parts of his puritan upbringing (that) (1)
splits work from play, (2) encourages self-denial, punishment,
and minimizes reward, (3) polarizes people into good & bad,
clean & dirty, rich & poor, sober & drunk, (4) promotes
competition rather than sharing, and (5) builds barriers to
change and growth.

It would be presumptuous of me to add to the existing
theories about the importance of play. For the moment, I
am supporting the biological view put forward by Anthony
Storr in his book, *The Dynamics of Creation*:

> 'In order to mate satisfactorily, it is necessary to learn
> to ritualise or suppress hostile patterns of behaviour;
> and animals which have had little opportunity to play
> cannot do this.'

Storr says elsewhere: 'Both games and works of art stand
somewhat outside the ordinary course of life, and do not
appear to be associated with the immediate satisfaction of
wants and needs . . . People look forward to parties because
they find their sense of self-esteem enhanced by such
encounters.'

                    watching
                    the bird
                    watchers

a cow
in the bog
chews his cud

Games can create magic. 'Organized games have rules to
which the players must adhere, and a game is spoiled if the
rules are broken. In this way a game is a microcosm, set apart
from ordinary life, and much better ordered than our habitual,
chaotic existence' (Storr).

The incentive for play is to gain insight into how games could
be used in different therapeutic/educational settings, with
different people: one other person, family, peers, or a mix.
In my work I use hundreds of different games: chasing, tagging,
role-playing, writing, painting, modelling, mimicking, fantasi-
zing, dancing, fighting, hiding, sculpting, racing, talking,
balancing, games. No two games are alike, no one game is
played twice the same. In a play session I often make up games
as I go along, and I usually play games that I enjoy. Each game
has a different incentive or goal; it may exercise a feeling, develop
body-awareness or team spirit, it may be an opportunity to be
aggressive in a socially acceptable way; the goal may be just fun
and enjoyment or playing with a problem by looking at it
through different means of expression, the goal may be to win
the game. Most games have several incentives for play, and
some of these go beyond words.

As we speak
now to each
other there

is nothing
being said.
We know the

place the words
fall into:

silences.   (cid corman
a language without words)

Reading is often criticized as being a passive experience.
This is partly the fault of the writer when he doesn't give the
reader space between words, where one can contribute to

the dialogue; and the reader when he doesn't read between the lines, when he approaches the words as only the receiver, not the giver. I want to give you space — freedom within the structure of the game. There is always the possibility that you might cheat or opt out, and that's o.k. because you will only get out of a game as much as you are prepared to put into it.

Planning for Play is planning for an experience of spontaneity; and this is not a contradiction; I recently spent 12 hours planning 8 hours of play for 150 social workers. Most of the plan was chucked in the bin after the first 2-hour session. Planning is my way of warming up or getting in tune with the needs of the people I will be leading. The goal of playing is always enjoyment; it may also be learning or therapy or creating a work of art (or science), and it can be all of these.

Some questions I ask myself before planning the first play session with a new group:

* What is my goal?
* What is the group's goal?
* What is the group likely to expect of me?
* What model of the group do I want to run, e.g. dancing, talking, acting, drama?
* What do I want to give and what do I want to receive?
* How much time has been set aside for playing? What part of the day or year will it take place?
* What is the age-range of participants?
* How many people, balance of sexes? Open or closed membership?
* What range of skills and personal resources are these people likely to have?
* Any handicaps, labels, e.g. 'psychotic', 'disturbed', 'social worker'?
* What equipment and materials are available?
* Where will we be playing — indoors, outdoors, small room, school, or clinic?
* What's the weather forecast?
* What will these people enjoy most doing?
* How will I know they are enjoying it?

A telephone conversation with my employer usually helps me to find most of the answers to these questions. Then I draw a map of a possible play session, including goals, people and their resources, time and space boundaries, as well as activities.

The First Play Session. We re-draw the map and state our common goals in the here and now. This chapter is like a first session. What do you want for yourself? What do you want to learn from this chapter? If I am employed to work with a group of people for 2 or more sessions (as I hope you will read other articles, chapters or books that I may write), I often begin by asking people to share what they enjoy about their life. I might ask you:

* To describe three successful moments you have had in the past two weeks, moments when you've done something well.
* Describe the sort of games you enjoyed when you were a child.
* What are your strengths, what are you good at, what can you give?
* What do you most enjoy doing at work, home, on holiday, etc?
* Describe the good moments in your life — turning points, moments of joy and well being.
* 25 qualities you like about yourself — write them down beginning each with 'I am . . . '.
* Following your answers, look for the creative principle, then set yourself goals to become or do more of it.

Most of us get out of touch with our sense of joy, we forget how to play. My approach to work calls for a love of enjoyment, an attitude of openness and growth; I want to work with people's creativity whatever their 'label'.

Sample play session

The following commentary is based on an actual play session with a group of social workers on a one-year applied social studies course. At the time of writing, the group is still meeting once a week for 2 hours. My goals have been to give the group tools they can use elsewhere in their work with people; and to encourage the group to use the games to develop their own growth and creativity. Excluding myself, there are 7 people in the group — 4 men and 3 women. Two days of the week, they are on individual placements; the other three days they are together with 15 other students. While reading the commentary, try to imagine that you are another participant, that you have been coming to the group every week for the past three months, that you are committed to be there even though it is not officially part of your course, and that you have some empathy for each person in the group:

> I arrive at 1.30 p.m. to an empty room. Soon after, Paul and Tom come in and tell me that Pamela and Mary can't come, Don is in a tutorial, Rose should be here, but they haven't seen Dick. I say we need the whole group for the game I planned, so we will have to begin with something else. Disappointment expressed. Pamela sends apologies, she has to visit a sick uncle; Rose arrives saying Mary has an essay to do.

(On average six people show up every week. Can you identify with any of the group members? Are you more likely to be absent or present? How would you feel? While reading, play the game aloud to yourself, inserting your own name.)

> I begin the session by planning it with the group. I ask, 'How long do you want to work for?' Tom wants to catch the 3.45 train to London, so we agree to finish at 3.30. I ask, 'What do you want to work on today?' Rose doesn't want to be the centre of attention, Paul says he will wait and see what happens, Tom asks me to suggest something to start with, then we can play it by ear. Taking off my shoes, I say, 'Right, we've got 100 minutes — let's make the most of them. We can only speak to each other using our own names or other people's names in the room.' Silence. Tom stands up, hesitates, sits down again. I stand up and walk slowly over to Tom; Tom cringes but doesn't move. I say, 'Thomas'; he says, 'Larry', cringing. 'Thomas — Thomas — Thomas — Thomas!' repeated by myself and others. Then everyone exchanges names: 'Rose — Paul —

Tom — Larry — Rose — Paul — Tom', quietly, as I move
behind Tom and say his name, 'Thomas?'; he says, 'Rose',
who is sitting next to him; I say, 'Thomas!'; he says,
'Paul', pleadingly; I say, 'Thomas'; he says 'Larry?';
I say 'Tom', putting my hand on his shoulder; he
visibly relaxes and says, 'Larry', with a sigh. Rose and
Paul have also been exchanging names, but no-one has
moved from their original sitting positions. I stand on the
table where Paul is sitting; looking down on him I say,
'Paul'; Rose says, 'Larry!' in a reprimanding voice;
Paul says, 'Larry', moving off the table crouching, then
returns to sit on the table; I stamp my feet on the table
shouting, 'Paul — Paul — Paul — Paul'; Rose jumps up
and moves to sit in a chair further from me but next to
Tom. She says, 'Tom? — Larry? — Paul?'. I sit down next
to Paul, saying 'Larry'; he says 'Paul', and so on.

(Two other group members arrive about this moment in the
middle of the game. How would you feel having been involved
from the beginning, or how would you feel as one of the
late arrivers?)

Vic and Don walk into the room making excuses for being
late. We refuse to listen and try to draw them into the
game by saying their names. We shout their names whenever
they say anything other than the name of a person in the
room. Vic and Don settle into the game — slightly bemused.
Gradually the activity settles on playing with sounds and
splitting up the names: 'Ro — m, Pa — se, Di — ul, etc.'
and silence. The game lasted for 15 minutes.

(Whenever you read a question, before reading further try to
answer it for yourself.)

I ask: 'How do you feel now?' Paul says he is intrigued
by how much he was able to say, not saying anything; Tom
says he feels much more relaxed now that the game is
over; Rose says she found the game initially difficult and
somewhat threatening, as when everyone was saying one
person's name. We all agree. Vic and Don say they felt
uncomfortable not knowing what was going on, but it
was o.k. once they joined in. I feel like a pusher and say

so. Paul feels the game was a very good starter, a way of
seeing where people are at, how they are feeling, by the
way they say their own name or another person's name.

I ask: 'How involved did the group get?' Rose says
'We were all involved, but it became more absorbing when
Vic and Don came into the room.' Tom points out how
I was more active than the others: 'We didn't move, where-
as you did.'

I ask: 'Is that a pattern for this group?' Do I often move
first, while others follow or don't move at all? The response
is 'Yes'. Paul and Vic talk about how they felt about
other people during the game, asking questions like 'Why
did you do that?' The idea of feeling frozen is expressed.

I ask: 'Does feeling frozen happen elsewhere with anyone?'
'Not being able to move?' Don has to go to a tutorial but
says he will be back as soon as possible! Paul, Rose and
Pat say they feel like not moving quite often. Vic says he's
the mixer, the one who gets things moving. I ask: 'How
do you feel about not moving in this group?' Rose says
she doesn't like it and everyone agrees.

I ask: 'Can we do anything about it?' 'Seeing that we
don't like it?' Paul says: 'Well, now that we've seen it
and talked about it, we don't need to do anything, we're
aware of it and it will change.' Tom and Rose are silent.

I ask Tom: 'Is this a pattern for you?' 'feeling unable to
move?' Tom says yes, so I ask him to give us an example.
He explains that he doesn't like dancing at a party, he feels
clumsy and doesn't like being looked at; but his wife really
enjoys dancing, so he dances after having quite a few drinks.

I ask: 'Do you want to change?' Tom says 'Yes'. so I ask
who would like to help him; and we all want to help. So we
proceed to set up a role-play of a party. Tom plays himself,
Rose agrees to play Tom's wife; Paul, Vic and I create a
party with sounds and rhythm.

(Where would you be in this role-play? Do you identify with Tom? How could you help Tom feel more comfortable at a party, more able to move?)

Tom gives a bit of information to Rose about his wife, then we are off to the music; Tom sits back, wipes his brow fumbles in his pockets, smiles and chats to Rose. Rose asks Tom to dance, Tom hesitates, Rose coaxes Tom onto the floor. She jumps to it, in her own space. They are about 4 feet ápart. Tom shuffles his feet on the floor, head and chest held upright and hardly moving his hips, feet never leave the floor. Our music dies away.

I ask Tom: 'How did that feel?' 'Just like I usually feel at a party — uptight, especially since I haven't had anything to drink.' Then I ask Vic and Paul: 'What did you see?' Tom looked uncomfortable, etc., and that Rose was really moving. I ask: 'Can anyone suggest a better way?' Paul says 'Take your feet off the ground, bend from the waist . . .' I ask Paul if he can show Tom what he means by repeating the role-play with Rose. They agree. Tom says: "My wife wouldn't have coaxed me to dance knowing how I feel; I usually get half-drunk and then coax her, knowing that she enjoys dancing'. With this new information, we repeat the role-play.

The same fast dance rhythm. Paul hesitates, then coaxes Rose onto the floor; Paul is a bit stiff at first, but he holds Rose's hand which seems to help him get into the rhythm; he bends from the waist and takes his feet off the ground, and he keeps in eye contact with Rose.

I ask Tom: 'What did you see?' More bouncy, relaxed, feet off the ground. Vic and I point out the eye contact and holding hands. I ask Tom: 'Do you want to have another go, this time trying to change your style based on what you've just seen?' Tom agrees, Rose catches her breath.

Then we're off again with a fast dance. Tom takes less time getting onto the floor, Rose seems to lead first with Tom holding on tight; but gradually his body comes to

life, bouncing, twisting, turning, hips and shoulders
rippling. I've never seen Tom move like it before. We all
applaude. Tom is beaming; he tells us he feels a bit
embarrassed. We all say that he really looked absorbed and
enjoying it. Tom says 'It's not the first time I've moved
like that; it's the second time and the first time I was
drunk.' We further discuss how Tom will try out this new
style at a real party on Saturday night.

Paul says: 'I can identify with Tom, I've had similar
difficulties at parties.' I ask Paul to elaborate. He explains
that he finds it painful to go to a party or gathering, where
he vaguely knows some people and others he doesn't
know at all; especially when he is expected to be there for
some work reason. I ask Paul if he would like to look at
that situation using the group as before in a role-play. We
all agree.

Rose, Tom, Vic and I play four people at a party who
know each other. Paul leaves the room and comes back
in as if he's just arrived. We agree that Vic vaguely knows
Paul from somewhere else. Rose and I take off our shoes,
and talk about feet and how comfortable it is to have our
shoes off. We tell jokes. Paul stands at a distance, gets out
a piece of paper and starts reading.

(What do you do when you enter a room and don't know
anyone? How do you feel?)

We talk about Paul: 'Fancy, reading a newspaper at a
party . . . ' 'Who's he? Does anyone know him?' Paul
looks up occasionally, maybe sensing that he is being
talked about. Vic goes over to Paul and asks him to join
us. Paul comes over and introduces himself: 'I'm Paul
Lawrence'. Vic introduces us, formally. We ask Paul what
he does for a living. He says: 'I work'. I say: 'What we
really want to know is do you make a lot of money? —
Rose is looking for a rich man.' All of us laugh except
Paul. Joking continues. Paul leans back in his chair. Tom
says 'Your name's Lawrence, is it?' 'No, it's Paul —
Paul Lawrence.' After several more questions, and beating

around the bush to find out something about Paul, Paul tells us he's a social worker. Vic says: 'Ah, one of those!' Paul takes offence. Vic explains that he's a student and that he thought Paul was a student as well. Paul says he's not a student, but he's doing a course, 'an in-service training course.' Then Paul asks us what we do. We skirt around the question jokingly, just like he skirted around the question when we asked. 'I'm a zoo-keeper . . .'

I ask Paul: 'How do you feel right now?' He says: 'Very much out of it, an intruder, cautious . . . ' He goes on to explain that it was a real situation for him that has happened many times before, especially when meeting colleagues socially when on placement. We continue talking about the reality and difficulty of the situation for all of us.

I ask: 'How might Paul do it better next time?' Tom says he could be more straightforward, more open and willing with information; Rose says that it is off-putting to see a person 'pretending' to read, 'hiding' behind a news-paper. Tom offers to switch roles with Paul and repeat the situation. Paul agrees, but says he still feels out of it; then Tom leaves the room and Paul leans forward joining the group. Everyone has their shoes off, so again, we begin talking about feet.

(If you were Tom, what would you do to change the experience and make it more comfortable?)

Tom comes into the room. We are joking and talking intimately. Tom doodles on the blackboard. 'Who's he, does anyone know him?' We comment that he looks a bit fed-up, at a loss; and suggest that one of us asks him to join us. We agree that Rose should go because she's good at putting people at their ease. Rose fetches Tom over and introduces us. We ask Tom what he does, he says: 'I'm a social worker'; and we all laugh. Tom laughs too but obviously doesn't know why he is laughing. Then he asks Rose what she does. Rose says 'I'm a zoo-keeper', and we all say other silly things. Tom laughs along with us, looking confused. I tell Tom we are teasing him. He asks me what I do. I tell him I teach social workers about

creativity, and that nearly every person at this party is
a social worker . . .

I ask Paul: 'What did you see?' He noticed that Tom was
nervous, but didn't hide it, was more forthcoming with
information about himself and made an effort to be with
the group; that Tom looked vulnerable and yet this didn't
detract from how well he coped with the situation. We
all help Paul pick up other points like posture, leaning
forward, eye contact, that were different and seemed to
be more successful. Paul wants to have another go; he
leaves the room, and we re-create the situation.

(If you were Paul, what would you do this time?)

Paul comes in and stands near to our group, facing us. It
makes us feel a bit uncomfortable, someone standing
over us. He looks uncomfortable too, but he doesn't try
to hide it. Vic invites him over. This time there is no
formal introduction, the conversation, jokes, continue,
and Paul is gradually drawn in. Paul listens and contributes,
and laughs with us . . .

We all feel that the way Paul behaved this time was much
more successful. I ask Paul: 'In your own words *What
have you learned?* and what was different this time? How
can you use it in the future?' Paul feels that he's learned
that it's o.k. to be nervous, and that it helps if you don't
try to hide your nervousness. Tom says it's good to let
loose, even when you feel clumsy or shy, if you are with
someone you trust.

Rose asks me: 'How do you feel about your role as
questioner, mover?' I explain that my role is also to
identify patterns, and be non-judgmental, and to give
people tools they can use on their own, or with other
groups. Rose then refers back to the first game which
demonstrated the pattern that I move first, and the
group waits for me to lead and make suggestions. I
suggest: 'One of you lead the first game next week, and
I'll watch.' Agreed. Vic expresses concern about taking
so much from me. I explain that the group has given me a

lot by coming each week for the last 4 months, and using what they learned in a wider context.

(The group is in the far corner of the room in a close-knit circle. There is a window in the door; if you wanted to come in, how would you feel, what would you do?)

Don comes in from his tutorial. Walking towards us, he asks if he is interrupting and if he can join us. I say, 'No', (You're not interrupting). 'But . . . ', then I turn to check out with what the group feels. Don says: 'Alright, I'll go have a coffee and come back later.' Almost in unison, we insist that Don comes and sits down with us now. We begin to explain what we have just been doing, when suddenly we realize that Don coming into the room was another repeat of the earlier role-play. So I suggest that we talk about what we just saw, did and felt. Don says he felt o.k. coming in, but he had looked in the window first to see if we were in the middle of something. He was surprised when I said 'No'. I thought I said 'Yes'; and Tom says he thought I said 'Yes'. Rose and Paul thought I said and meant 'No', 'you can't come in.' Paul explains that he also said 'No', thinking that was what the group wanted, but he really wanted Don to join us. Paul also says that he often does what he thinks the group wants rather than doing what he wants. Tom then says: 'Here we go again, Is that a pattern?' . . .

It's about 3.30, so I ask: *'What have you got out of the session for yourself?'*

(What have you got out of the session for yourself?) A page has been left blank for your answer.

Before we split up, I suggest a bit of homework for next week's session: To write a long letter to an imaginary best friend (like yourself) whom you haven't seen for some time. Then Paul says: 'I want to lead for a half an hour next week.'

Beliefs and theory and definition

'Take a pile of old newspapers, magazines, etc., scissors, a large piece of cardboard, and paste. Then spend an hour making a poster stating what you believe in, but only using the materials available, e.g. cutting out words, phrases, pictures which illustrate what you believe in.' People enjoy and believe in and play at and talk about different things.

I believe in singing, shouting, dancing, laughing, feeling for what feels right with a person, not looking for what is wrong with a person, which so often seems to be the role of therapist or teacher. I want to find the artist, the creative self-fulfilling part of a person; I want to learn about what an individual enjoys doing, then encourage him to do more of it.

I believe therapy and learning can only be real when it is enjoyed, when the individual is positively absorbed in the activity of the moment. In his conclusion about 'Fun in Games', Goffman writes:

> 'As far as gaming encounters and other focused gatherings are concerned, the most serious thing to consider is the fun in them. Something in which the individual can become unself-consciously engrossed is something that can become real to him . . . '

Adults seem to avoid having fun at work. Therefore, 'fun', if considered at all, is not planned for by architects, governments or senior staff; and is seldom considered important enough to be integrated into an overall educational, therapeutic, or social programme. However many theories are written promoting the value of play, the 'proof is in the eating'.

Huizinga, in his book *Homo Ludens*, says:

> 'Play is an activity which proceeds within certain limits of time and space, in a visible order, according to rules freely accepted, and outside the sphere of necessity or material utility. The play-mood is one of rapture and enthusiasm, and is sacred or festive in accordance with the occasion. A feeling of exaltation and tension accompanies the action, mirth and relaxation follow. Seriousness is, most emphatically, not the opposite of play. Play can be, and very frequently is, of the utmost seriousness. Thus

the cheat is far less hated or chastised than the spoil-sport,
the man who somehow subverts and shatters the validity,
the importance of the game.'

Adults who have 'clients' are sometimes spoil-sports,
even when the game is not explicit. When playing with
people, I enter into the spirit of the game as participant,
leaving behind me for the moment, the adult world of
talking, thinking and theorizing.

The play process

> 'To lead the people
> Walk behind them.'   (*Lao-Tzu*)

I never know what is going to happen in a play-session (and
I never know what I'm going to write), but I do know *how*
it is going to happen. Like a football manager, I enthuse the
players to action; using my body as a model, I suggest the
behaviour I expect from the group. Through what I do,
rather than what I say, I try to promote an attitude of openness, implying that it's o.k. to laugh, shout, cry, to be
silly and to express what you are feeling in the moment.

As if each person is creating a new world for himself, he
begins alone. I usually suggest a few short introduction games
which enable people to meet and find out where they are
at in relation to others, to become aware of possible entrances
and exits, to find a direction for the play. I feel my way
making comments and suggestions as well as interacting
with the players. This rehearsal or warming-up period is ragged,
tentative, and even cautious; like a painter faced with an empty
canvas, hesitantly he makes a few marks, rubs them out,
makes a few bolder marks, before he settles into the picture.
The fumbling, starting and stopping, could go on for the whole
session, or several sessions. I encourage the players to make
a meal of each moment, to sustain the action and deepen the
experience, spotlighting the creative patterns with action-
replays.

Eventually everybody gets involved in their own time and
way. The players are confident, I'm confident, we trust each
other; then boredom! That may not be the right word, but
it describes the feeling like when the artist has filled the

canvas with colour and shape and is still dissatisfied. I see
boredom as the female side of the creative process, the
quality of waiting patiently for the action to develop. Dissatisfaction with the moment can lead to escape, opting out, or to
a creative leap in the dark, which I call the 'second breath' in
a group play session. The player(s) who takes the risk of a
second breath, does so for the whole group, leading the
action towards its conclusion.

I sometimes get confused or lost in the middle of leading
a play-session; my second breath or leap in the dark is to
share my feeling with the group, and to ask them what they've
enjoyed so far and what more do they want. If I hide my
confusion behind well tried games or by not allowing the
players to develop the game in their own way, the session
may appear to go well for some, but it won't be magic. My
stomach will feel tight, and I'll be irritable . . .

Creativity is what you 'make' of it!

After play people often talk about what they enjoyed and
didn't enjoy, they share feelings about each other; or there
may be silence and reluctance to part. Ending is as difficult
as beginning, and just as unpredictable. But with an ongoing
group like the one described above in the 'sample play session',
the play process accelerates; game time may decrease and
the end can become the beginning of another process:

> 'A person may get honest and accurate feedback about
> his patterns (of behaviour), because all have seen or experi-
> enced him *doing* something together with them. Feelings
> and teaching can be matched together, and new directions
> of personal growth explored, using the shared experience
> as a common starting point.'

A game is a lie

'Out of a pattern of lies, art weaves the truth' (D. H. Lawrence).
And I'm reluctant to finish this chapter. I read somewhere an
experiment that claimed to prove that words are only 7% of
a communication; the other 93% involves the body posture,
distance between people, vocal speed and tone, eye contact,
etc. This has been a difficult dance to write. Sometimes I feel

a game is a lie, it cons people into action, and pretends to be an opportunity not to be yourself, a separate reality unrelated to everyday life, a release of energy that can make the players and audience feel impotent. Playing games can become an incestuous way of working with people: one game leads to another game leads to another game leads to another game leads to another game leads to another game, bridge, football, Hamlet, blindman's bluff, are played over and over again.

Not what you play, but how you play it; bound by time and space and rules, a particular game is never played twice the same; there is freedom within it. A game is a toy, and toys can be tools for teaching. A game is a way in, a beginning, another way of relating to people without using labels. A game is a lie, until you win.

The artist wins when he produces and people ask him to produce more. The teacher wins when he learns and his students learn more. The social worker wins when he helps and his clients help themselves . . .

If you don't enjoy games, don't play them. Do more of what you enjoy.

> never before always after when it's all
> over at the end seeing the consequence
> of so much palaver that really could
> have been left out of the event had
> it not been for the upkeep of ap-
> pearances which always seem im-
> portant at the time if one is
> to consider the whole thing
> then it must be the begin-
> ning of this that will in-
> dicate why so much time
> was wasted on unimpor-
> tant procedure . . .

I haven't said anything new, nor have I arrived at an answer, solution, or theory about games in therapy. I've given you some words in promotion of a playful attitude to therapy, and I've asked some questions which have as many answers as there are readers.

What if you were me . . . what would you write about?

6

Improvisation — the basis of creativity in music therapy

JULIENNE BROWN

'The man that hath no music in himself,
Nor is not moved with concord of sweet sound,
Is fit for treasons, strategems, and spoils;
The motions of his spirit are dull as night,
And his affections dark as Erebus:
Let no such man be trusted.'   (*Merchant of Venice* v.

From our earliest records of man's history we have innumerable
examples of the therapeutic power of music; one obvious
example is David being asked to help lift Saul's neurotic
depression through playing his harp. Virtually all the writings
on the therapeutic effect of music describe only the changes
in behaviour and little information is available on the type of
music that was used or the way it was applied. Music therapy
has now become a recognized discipline, defined by Juliette
Alvin as 'the controlled use of music in the treatment, rehabilitation, education and training of adults and children suffering
from physical, mental and emotional disorder.'

In the same book Juliette Alvin describes very well the
two broad aims of music therapy:

(1)   To observe the patient's responses to certain musical
      experiences; responses that may be helpful to the
      diagnosis or to the treatment of the illness.
(2)   To deliberately provoke certain reactions, and then to
      control and channel them towards a specific thera-
      peutic goal.

Music therapy in this strict definition does not include recreational music, 'teaching' the handicapped or performing for them; though all these have their valuable place in the wider music therapy scene.

It is only in the last decade that the training and recognition of music therapists has been formalized. As with most music therapists, my own early experience was as a professional musician. In the early days of my career as a teacher and flautist, I had little specialized knowledge of the world of therapy. Yet, as must happen to many teachers, children with various problems and handicaps were brought to me for ordinary music lessons.

I now realize that in fact I was doing 'intuitive' music therapy, but soon found my own limitations and need for guidance musically and personally. However it was not until I began conscious experimental music therapy with severely maladjusted children that I became aware of my own inner disturbed areas.

Before I began work as a music therapist, I not only took a qualifying course in music therapy but also accepted therapeutic help myself.

This chapter will develop my theme that improvisation is the basis of creativity in music therapy. It is intended not only for the professional music therapist but also to encourage and facilitate those with limited musical skills and experience; as well as challenging and clarifying music for the musician who literally has his art at his finger tips.

Music improvisation of a particular kind provides the key to the inner life, yearnings and strivings of any handicapped child or adult. It is the direct and active expression of feeling, of individual rhythmic, pitch and dynamic levels. What follows is intended to provoke thought, discussion and experiment; and will show, among other things, what I mean by improvisation, creativity, music therapy; what are the needs of the music therapist in such work; how I see this form of therapy forming the base for co-operation with other therapies.

Let us start straight in with a visit to a psychiatric social club where the music therapist is trying out a most basic and primitive form of rhythmic improvisation. The club is provided

with a good piano, guitar, double bass, set of 'pop' type
drums, as well as bongo drums and various other percussion
instruments of the more sophisticated variety. There are also
descant, treble and tenor recorders, and a wide range of sheet
music. The music therapy room is medium-sized, and the door
is always kept open for people to move in and out freely. The
staff comprises psychiatrists, psychotherapists, psychiatric
social workers, art therapists, dance and drama therapists.
The club is run on very democratic lines with the members
having as much say in its management as the staff.

There are eight people in the music room. Two of them
are very ill psychotics — one schizophrenic and the other
manic-depressive — with little chance of any permanent
return to normality. The others share a variety of neurosis
with all the depression and self-centredness that accompanies
these personality and character disorders. Many are newcomers
to the group and to the music therapist. The overall atmosphere is one of nervousness, hostility and depression.

The M.T., taking in the atmosphere at once **and realizing this**
is not the moment to start off with a rollicking music hall
number, keeps initial chatting and small talk down to a minimum and picks up a pair of bongo drums. Because of the
way the chairs and divan are arranged, most of the people
are sitting in a rough semi-circle. The M.T. puts two chairs in
the centre of this semi-circle and invites anyone who'd like
to come and have a conversation with her on the bongos.
Puzzled looks, embarrassed glances, attempts at indifference
cover a rustle of interest. Who can resist the chance to beat
on a drum? A manic-looking girl comes and sits opposite
the M.T. and chooses the larger side of the bongos to clasp
between her knees. The M.T. looks at the girl and starts to
beat slowly and steadily on the smaller drum. The girl
interrupts with some loud and irregular beating and angry
glances. The M.T. replies with the same steady beat, if anything a little softer. The girl's beating becomes wilder and
more aggressive and the next thing is she is beating on the
M.T.'s part of the drums. Now the therapist joins the patient
in a welter of drumming with both hands, sometimes on one
drum, sometimes on the other, sometimes on both. The girl
follows suit, and as she becomes even more uninhibited, her

primitive beating begins to take on a more regular pulse, even
some signs of **recognizable pattern. She begins to look more**
relaxed and even smiles a little. Both she and the therapist
are now enjoying an amiable and sometimes teasing drum
conversation. And it ends with the girl laughingly pushing
the drums over to the M.T. and returning to her seat.

During all this there has been a marked arousal of interest
among the group. They sit forward in their chairs, are riveted
by the 'conversation', occasionally glance at each other in a
sharing sort of way, and form very quickly into a group. Meanwhile, a group psychotherapist and a P.S.W. have come into
the room and are watching the scene with interest. Spontaneous
clapping breaks out at the end of the conversation, the group
members start to chatter among themselves, and there is the
beginning of some sense of comradeship.

Now two others offer to 'come and have a go' and have to
take turns. The next patient to join the M.T. is a quiet and
very depressed man. He also chooses the larger of the two
drums and sits waiting for the M.T. to start. She does nothing
but sit with her hands in her lap, looking at her drum. The
silence becomes very tense and the sense of anticipation
almost unbearable. Eventually the man starts to fiddle nervously
on his drum with the tips of his fingers. The therapist does
nothing in reply and he tentatively taps out a few irregular
beats. This time she does reply — by scratching softly round
and round with the nails of one hand. He seems nonplussed.
She repeats the scratching, this time with both hands. It is
a maddening sound and the man suddenly smacks his drum
with the flat of one hand several times. Still no response.
He smacks with both hands, first his drum, then hers, and
fiercely. His eyes, usually shifty and evasive, are wide open
and challenging. The M.T. in her own time starts to beat an
interesting African rhythm alternating 2/4 with 3/4 bars. He
listens and then tries to destroy her beating with more
banging. She waits, and then starts again. She continues with
a calm confidence and eventually he joins in by beating the
main beats with one hand only. Gradually he becomes absorbed
by the rhythmic, primitive beating and slowly **contributes his**
own individual patterns within the pulse set up by the therapist.
The mutual beating comes to its own natural conclusion; and

the group applauds again — this time more quietly, but
warmly. Discussion breaks out — about the beating and how
different members of the group saw it, what the man felt
about it himself, how the therapist saw it all; and what did
the psychotherapist and P.S.W. have to say! For the rest of
that evening the man himself was much more outgoing and
confident.

This form of rhythmic improvisation in the group became
a regular feature of the weekly meetings. Soon the M.T. was
able to withdraw from the beating herself as the patients
became more sure of themselves. They looked forward to
'talking' to each other across the drums, and became increasingly
free in discussing what had happened afterwards.

The value of this form of improvisation will possibly be
surprising in its depth when we analyse it musically and
therapeutically. Musically it uses the elements of rhythm,
speed and dynamics. With the element of pitch left out,
there is no question of playing or singing in or out of tune.
This is not to say that pitch as a musical element is not of
therapeutic importance. It is often, as we shall see later, of
paramount importance in certain situations. But this business
of drumming reaches right down into the guts of the matter.
Primitive, an archetypal experience, pre-intellectual, are some
of the descriptive words that come to mind. No musical
technique is required to take part, brain power or otherwise
is of minimal importance. And it is non-verbal. Having to
express oneself in words can be very threatening, painful and
seemingly useless and frustrating. The offer of another means
of communication such as this bongo drumming is in my
experience welcomed with open arms, or rather with open
hands, by the neurotic, psychotic, subnormal, even autistic
child or adult, not to say by the 'normal'!

When a music therapist sits down opposite a patient with
a pair of bongo drums between his knees, he is about to tune
in to the patient's inner rhythmic and dynamic state at that
particular moment. He will also reveal something of his own
inner state. He need not fear this fact as long as he consciously
recognizes and accepts his feelings at the time, and *uses* them
either by control or release, depending on the patient's need.
Even if he is not always in this fairly advanced personal state —

and age and experience do count here — he will have his experience as a musician to call on in his drumming to provide variety and contrast. If he finds this difficult to express on the drums, he should practise at home before attempting this method!

The bongo drums themselves provide built-in materials for the therapist. There are two drums but they are joined together. They are of different sizes. They are easily held between the knees. The players are bound to sit opposite each other, face to face. Whether or not eye contact is made during the drumming is very revealing and important. The position and movements of the feet, the back, the neck and head, the arms, hands and wrists — all are telling to the trained observer, especially as they are completely unconscious on the part of the patient. And usually of the music therapist too!

Body states and the actual drumming will reveal feelings and attitudes more quickly and clearly than in many other therapeutic situations. For instance, aggression, hostility, desire to control, were very clear from the bent back, forward thrust head and jaw, and stiff wrists and hands in the manic girl's beating; but also a good deal of inner chaos and lack of self-control as shown in the loud banging and irregular pulse of her initial beating. The shy man, who sat slumped and well back in his chair, was someone who suffered very severely from lack of initiative and all the sexual and work problems which that implies. On the other hand, his hidden anger and violence soon erupted when the therapist tantalized and irritated him with her scratching and calculated lack of response. In later sessions he revealed compulsiveness and inner rigidity through beating consistently with a slow, monotonous and unchanging pulse.

The question of territoral rights is one of the more amusing aspects of this form of improvisation. Sometimes patients will not venture on to the therapist's drum area for a long time, however much provoked to do so. At the other extreme (but much more rare) are those who will only beat there, ignoring their own ground. Freedom to beat on either drum as the occasion demands, indicates a growing maturity and improved relationship with the therapist or other partner.

In this non-threatening situation of drum talking, the goal

of exploring and developing relationships is paramount.
Relationship to oneself, to one's opposite number, to the
whole group — and this applies to therapist as well as to
patient — is what this is really about. And it is possible to
deepen these relationships and help them to grow provided
they are taken seriously over a period of time. Getting people
to communicate individually and in groups where real points
of contact seem long since to have been lost, seldom fails
with this method. Like all methods and techniques, it has
its limitations. But it seems to me its main strengths lie in
the fact that though the activity of drumming is free, it
happens in a structured situation. This is supportive to the
individuals and to the group. People are often surprised at
how easily they can reveal and accept the dark and weak
patches in their make-up, and after sharing them with other
members of the group, even laugh at them. More unexpected
still is the revelation of one's strengths and joy and inventiveness. One man I worked with astonished himself and everyone
in the group with great rhythmic variety and contrast in his
beating, after weeks of self-pity and indulgence.

The more flexible of my group psychotherapist colleagues
agree that diagnostic possibilities of this form of improvisation
are considerable. Also that it may well facilitate the early
problems of verbal communication encountered when a group
is first starting. A warning here to music therapists who
might find themselves faced with more overt violence, hostility
and anger in a group doing bongo drum improvisation than
they are able to handle. If they plan to use this technique
seriously and over a long period of time, they should either
have had considerable experience in group dynamics themselves, or enlist the co-operation of a trained group psychotherapist.

I have said that music improvisation provides a basis for
deep and lasting therapy. As the following example will show,
it can be an effective prelude to establishing relationships
where these have broken down or have never existed. The
musical element of pitch is of prime importance here, and
atonality, which has been described to me by some so-called
non-musicians as 'music without a home' or 'music which
doesn't know where it's going'. This will also show how lines

of communication can be opened up without a word being spoken.

The scene is the same psychiatric social club, the same music room, but different patients. All of them are very taciturn and sullen. The initial improvisation happens when a very fine cellist — a deep, dark young man starts the evening off by taking up his position in the centre of the music room and absorbing himself in a Bach unaccompanied cello sonata, as if there were no one else in the room. There are in fact four other people, a very disturbed and angry-looking man who is sitting at the piano with his back to the keyboard and glowering. He is older, and so is the pale, depressed woman lying curled up like a child on the covered divan. Two other patients are slumped in chairs, and so withdrawn that they give the impression of only being alive because their hearts are still beating. The music therapist is standing by the piano with her flute close at hand. There are, as always, other instruments lying around.

Suddenly the cellist stops playing Bach and starts playing all sorts of different sounds without any definite rhythmic pattern, and over the whole wide range of his instrument. Very high harmonics, with their far away, ethereal quality alternate with great low, vulgar roars in the low registers. The world is turned upside down. Great sweepings of sound played at random make it clear to all that this man has got in touch with a very deep level of his complex psyche. All very well, you might say, but he is a trained musician, able to express himself easily through sound.

The man at the piano who has been listening to all this and watching, equally unexpectedly puts his arms down on the black keys of the instrument which the M.T. knows he has never played before. The cellist goes on regardless, and the piano man puts down his forearms again, this time more loudly and angrily. The M.T. takes his clenched fists and puts them on the black keys at the extreme ends of the keyboard. He starts to bang where his hands are lying, then suddenly plays very softly. Then he tries to play with his fingers stretched out on different parts of the keyboard, puts the pedals down and listens intently to the enriched sound. Meanwhile, the cellist continues his own improvising and appears to be becoming more and more self-absorbed. Likewise the 'pianist'. He is now leaping about the keyboard with index fingers only.

The music therapist is standing by, relaxed yet attentive. The woman on the divan has drawn herself up to sit listening. Propped up on one elbow, she looks dazed and puzzled. There are slight stirrings from the depths of the armchairs. One patient lifts his eyes with great effort; the other clasps and reclasps her hands nervously.

Unobtrusively the music therapist takes up her flute. She has been picking up recurring melodic lines from the cellist, lines which always start on a low note, leap up to a very high note, and come to rest somewhere in the middle register. Though the actual notes are not always the same, the melodic shapes are. There is very little rhythmic interest. She waits for the next appearance of the 'theme' and then plays a similar line on her flute. Slight pause in the cellist's over-active improvising, a cursive glance at the therapist, and he continues with his seemingly random playing. Turning slightly towards the still experimenting pianist, she plays the line again, and yet again. He looks up at her. By this time he has discovered high, low and middle areas of the keyboard. Suddenly with the index fingers only, he describes just such a low, high, middle curve. Total silence from the cellist. The music therapist repeats her line, and is answered promptly by the pianist. The cellist recovers from his surprise and interjects with an aggressive repetition of the 'theme'. Laughter from all three. He inverts the theme. More laughter. He has turned his cello round to face the flautist and the pianist. The divan lady is now sitting up with her back resting against the wall. The nervous lady has her elbows on the arm rests and cups her face in her hands — watching and listening. The music therapist has noticed that the other man has furtively drawn his chair round to be closer to her and the two other players.

As the excitement grows, the tempo of the musical conversation increases. The music therapist starts to add just a few notes to the line, and provides it with a sultry, rumba type rhythm. The pianist seems to get pleasure from trying to imitate this on the keyboard — atonally, of course. And the

cellist is away! Mild cacophony. Flautist and pianist let
him have his head. When it is clear that he and the others
have had enough, the music therapist plays an insistent
rhythm on a high D on her flute, and then stops and puts her
instrument down.

Remember that there have been various simple instruments
lying about the room. The divan lady has reached out and
taken up the pair of maracas. She shakes them in the basic
pulse of the music. The man in the chair has put the bongo
drums on his lap but does not play yet. The nervous lady
is snapping her fingers rhythmically. The therapist starts
to move around the room, helping the maracas player to be
more forceful and the bongo drummer to attempt a little
beating. She also uses her voice now, unself-consciously
returning to the first low, high, middle line provided by
the cellist. She does this softly at first while encouraging
the latest instrumentalists to join in, and then with a clear
crescendo standing close to the pianist and cellist, she helps
them also to return to their simple beginning, and to draw
the playing to a natural close.

The silence which follows is palpable. The sense of 'group'
is very strong. Several people sigh in a relaxed way. Gradually
the individuals begin to emerge as the divan lady says, 'I knew
exactly what everyone was saying'. Then a surprised remark
from the man in the armchair: 'I really understand that kind
of music'. And finally the cellist to the pianist: 'Did you know
that you could play the piano like that?' This was a great
breakthrough for the young man who had seldom addressed
any remarks to anyone, and was very lofty about his ability
as a cellist.

There followed some lively chatting about what had
happened, and what was most striking about this now eager
group interaction was a sense of *belonging* to the experience
they had just shared. The therapist was very much part of the
group enthusiasm, and was understandably delighted at the
suggestion that they continue with the improvisation the
following week. This did in fact happen — for several weeks
running. Already in the second week, one of the patients
complained that everyone was 'talking' too much and at the
same time. This was the therapist's cue to show the value of

musical silence, of not playing all the time, of listening to others in the group and then contributing to and building on what one had absorbed. Finally, when the group felt it was well enough integrated, it invited the movement/drama group to join it by improvising movement and mime to improvised music.

Musically speaking then, it was the experimenting with free ranging pitch which provided the basis for this experience. The fact that the therapist made no attempt to organize the sounds that occurred into any recognizable and accepted 'scales', freed the players from any sense of musical guilt or judgemental criticism. This is not to say that 'anything goes' when an atonal melodic line is being drawn. Far from it — and clearly a Webern or a Stockhausen would produce more meaningful and artistically satisfying melodic lines than you or I. But the cellist and then the pianist were asking to take part in a mutual experience of some kind; and offered pitch — the high and low of music, the ups and downs — as the materials to be used. Notice that although the music therapist joined them in their rather crude and random notes at the outset, she gradually helped them to refine and shape the lines, adding rhythm eventually to give more structure and support; and using changes in tempo and dynamics to provide variety and contrast. Also, the use of a rumba rhythm may seem incongruous in the atonal setting, but it was in keeping with the maracas, bongo drums etc. which were available to the non-musician patients, and very suitable to the sense of fun underlying this otherwise too serious experience. The free use of her voice in the improvising served as an encouragement to the others. In subsequent sessions they gradually used their voices wordlessly more and more to add to the music making.

A different scene now, and one involving work with children. Improvisation is still at the heart of the therapy, but musically it is toned down to the needs of very young and severely handicapped children. And the setting is far removed from the drama of the psychiatric social club.

It takes place in a special nursery for multiple handicapped children aged eighteen months to five years. There is a great deal of team work between the 'teachers', the nurse, the consulting doctor, the parents, and the drama/movement therapist and music therapist. But as will be seen, the individual music therapy approach is much more clinical, although the purpose of the nursery was primarily a socio/educational one.

This nursery was set up to give guidance, help and relief to hard pressed parents of very handicapped, very young children. And for the children themselves, it was planned to provide interest and stimulation, to help them develop physically and emotionally as far as their potential would permit, and to give them a social setting of acceptance and encouragement with other handicapped *and* normal children (normal siblings were encouraged to attend who incidentally, worked out a lot of their problems!) This remarkable place was the brain child of the local Medical Officer of Health. The local health and education authorities combined to pay for the staff and the necessary apparatus and equipment.

The short morning had a definite but flexible structure. After a general settling in time when the children were helped to play with a variety of suitable apparatus and with the staff, there was group music and movement. Everyone joined in, and staff members held those severely handicapped in their arms, involving them in as much of the actions and singing as possible. 'Juice time' followed. Then there was more play-work with the staff, and at this point the drama therapist and myself went into separate rooms to do our more specialized therapy with individual children, selected according to their special needs and what we felt we could offer them.

My work was based on the belief that sound, particularly musically organized sound, has a direct impact on the feeling and thinking life of the child, power to stimulate sensory — motor responses, and to establish communication at basic non-verbal levels. Before starting the work I was given the children's family and social backgrounds, medical history and neurological test results, and psychological assessment. The sessions were to last up to 15 minutes and were taped and noted in writing.

As examples I give you Graham and Paul. Graham — 2 years, 9 months, had multiple congenital abnormalities and severe mental retardation; barely any vocal sounds or

babble; very shy and sweet natured; physically very inactive.
Paul — 2 years, 6 months, was the only surviving triplet; born
prematurely; athetoid; severely mentally retarded; query
autistic; and query some central auditory imperception;
minimal babble — mum/mum, ttt, brrr, gu-gu; very withdrawn
and resistant; physically restless and active.

The aims with both these children were firstly(and most
importantly) to stimulate pre-speech sounds, secondly to
improve concentration span, memory and powers of imitation,
and thirdly, to improve motor control, manipulative dexterity,
and to help counteract compulsive movement.

Vocal and instrumental techniques were kept as simple as
possible. Boredom during essential repetition was eliminated
by frequent changes in pitch, dynamics and tempo. Each
session began and ended with a sung 'hello' and 'goodbye'
and the child's name sung to a rising 4th and a falling 5th.
Most other words were sung to improvised melodies based on
the pentatonic scale. Any cries, grunts, shrieks or groans
were imitated by me and eventually altered to create musically vocal lines. The rhythms used in the vocal work were
based on the natural rhythms of the words, e.g. Hello Graham

$$\frac{2}{4} \, \flat \, | \, \flat \, \flat \, : \|$$

The only instruments used were small drums and chime
bars — starting with middle C, G, and high C, and gradually
building up the pentatonic scale by adding D, E and A. The
black pentatonic chimes were sometimes used when a pitch
lift was required. The cymbal was only introduced later in
the sessions; the recorder likewise.

The following are some of the observations made of the
work over a period of three months. With Graham, who had
nine weekly sessions, there was a steady build-up of communication from the first shy, tentative responses in sessions 1 &
2, via a musical 'peep-bo' game to signs of happier responses
in session 3, more positive and independent action (he
initiated the games and wanted to beat on chimes and drums)
in sessions 4 & 5, to greater alertness and answering me
rhythmically on the instruments (session 6), followed by
the first signs of aggression (session 7). Smiles and self-

assertiveness came in the last two sessions where pipe and cymbal were introduced, even a little laughter. He had consistently shifted the focus from the greetings and games to work on the chimes and drums, where improved concentration, involvement with the instruments, memory and imitation all provided satisfaction.

Most striking was the early emergence of expressive pre-speech sounds — aah, mmm, overlapping with 'look'. For instance, there was a rising aah of pleasure to my playing very loudly then very softly on the chime bars, mmm to my dropping a mallet, and grunts of displeasure at having a drum put on his lap. In the last session the tape clearly recorded an attempt to say 'goodbye'.

Paul had thirteen weekly sessions. This boy was very withdrawn and responded initially only when the lower pitched chime bars were held against his ear; and then again when I sang in a low voice close to his head. Then his eyes flickered and he turned his head in response to changes of rhythm and tempo. But his autistic behaviour grew more pronounced as an abreaction to music in the first five sessions, though interest was there and involvement growing. In the 6th session, however, much of the hand flapping teeth slapping and gazing around was gone, and efforts to play on the drum more sustained.

He was a great dribbler. In the first few sessions he used the chime mallet knobs to suck and chew; but we soon made a game of this till he was aware that they were for musical playing and that he could make rhythmic patterns with them on chimes and drums. But the tension in his body, and his arms in particular, had to be reduced before this could occur. In session 6 he tried hard to play on the drum, but tensed up. The sensation of the mallet in his hand with me holding his arm, falling and vibrating naturally, brought the necessary relaxation. My recorder playing (7th session) and bird-like whistling (8th session) — all improvised — added to this easing up of tension. By the 10th session he was holding the beaters himself and playing rhythmically with both hands — and smiling!

As with Graham there was a steady increase in pre-speech sounds. But they were much more on a monotone (? some deafness) and more drawn out and slow when they came. Their speed started to increase after the 9th session, and in the 13th, in the presence of a doctor, he tried to say 'no' and 'yes'.

It is possible here to draw some conclusions and see pointers to future research. It seemed clear, even from this very limited period of time spent working with these children, that music as a therapy of this improvisational kind has a great deal to offer in the very early years of a retarded child's life. Most striking in the above cases and others was music's power to stimulate pre-speech sounds. Follow-up work by a co-operative speech therapist, and one particularly interested in the shattering problems encountered by such children when they attempt to express themselves in any way at all, would seem the logical and important next step. Just such work was undertaken by the drama/movement therapist who was working on the team, when the musical form of therapy had played its part in improving motor control, manipulative dexterity, and had helped counteract compulsive movement. And some of the little patients she had been working with individually, were taken over by myself when it became clear to both of us that music therapy was what the child would now derive most benefit from.

The direct result of this limited experimental work in music therapy was the setting up of a properly controlled research project at another institution for the multiply handicapped and severely retarded child. The findings of this project are shortly to be published, and may prove interesting.

An intelligent mongoloid child of eighteen months was referred to me by a consultant paediatrician. It had become his practice to enlist the help of speech, music, physio- or drama therapists after he had dealt with the medical problems whenever he thought that such work would benefit a little patient. In the following example I would like to show what can be done through improvisation, firstly in assessing the responses of such a child to sound, and secondly how the co-operation and support of the mother can be won and sustained.

This child was the last of seven. The mother had been in her late thirties at his birth which had lasted for three days.

She was an efficient and dedicated mother, but obviously under considerable stress with such a large family to care for as well as fulfilling the demands of her lively, small mongol. The child's arms were very active but not pushing up. From the waist down he was passive, however, with weak pelvic muscles. He was able to clasp his hands well. There was a query as to the condition of his heart, and some brain damage after such a lengthy labour could not be ruled out. His hearing was judged to be acute. His father was musical, his mother not.

When I first saw James, he had just come from his first psysiotherapy session (aimed at strengthening his pelvic muscles and legs) and he was upset and tired. To test his initial responses to sound and to myself, I had his mother hold him with his back to me. He was very sensitive to sudden sounds (what eighteen months old child is not!) but he liked my singing his name and greeting. He also enjoyed my moving his legs in cycling movements and saying 'chuff-chuff'. He almost smiled at that, and his mother expressed surprise that he had allowed me to touch and hold his legs.

He had apparently already heard several nursery rhymes played and sung by one of his sisters. So all testing of his response to sound was done through improvisation. As I was working with him privately, I had at my disposal a good cymbal, my flute, recorder, chime bars, small drums and piano. James opened his eyes wide and then narrowed them to little slits in response to soft sounds on the cymbal. There seemed to be barely any reaction to forte playing on the same instrument. When I improvised a sad, slow, legato melody on the flute, he relaxed against his mother, listened intently, and looked sad and thoughtful. A move from the lower to middle flute register and a gayer, staccato tune, and he sat up and smiled. To the chime bars there was some response, especially to dissonances. When I stopped suddenly he looked puzzled. Taking him on my lap to see how he would react to the sound of intervals, rhythms and chords upset him, even though his mother was sitting right next to us. All the same, he calmed down and seemed to enjoy gentle pentatonic chords played with a simple lilting melody to a rocking rhythm — with body movements to match. To changes of

dynamics and tempo on the drums, he responded vocally as
well as physically, and with rises and falls of excitement to
crescendo and diminuendo. His reaction to silence was a
special wriggle of his whole body; and without doubt it was
a command for me to go on. Any notes played on the recorder
stimulated a grabbing at the instrument which then went,
naturally enough, into his mouth for a suck and a blow.

It seemed clear to me that with such a young child and
with only six short sessions in which I could give any help
through music, (they were from abroad) the work would
have to be done with mother *and* child. The father, though
musical, was not making himself available in any way, but
the mother was more than willing to try any guidance I was
able to give. Based on my initial observations of his physical
and emotional responses to music, and on his developmental
needs I evolved a short programme of work for James and
his mother. She, incidentally, needed a good deal of loosening
up vocally and physically; but this was done unobtrusively and
with a sense of shared enjoyment. Much of the work was built
on extremes of pitch, speed and dynamics; for they both
needed 'stretching' and plenty of contrast and variety in an
otherwise rather flat existence.

Each session started with some physical movement —
swaying to slow, fast and moderate tempos; swooping from
high to low to middle positions to the tune of *Hot Cross Buns*;
my improvising on flute or piano to facilitate the exercises
he was being given by a physiotherapist to strengthen his leg
and pelvic muscles. I observed some of these physio sessions
at the clinic to make sure I knew what was going on. Then
work at the piano — with mother holding child on lap — the
March of the Black Keys, for instance, where the mother used
the flat of her hands at first to improvise a rudimentary
march on different parts of the keyboard in varied tempos,
and with contrasting dynamics. This would stimulate the
child to use his own active little hands on the keyboard; and
his mother would 'answer' him by playing again on the
keyboard, picking up his rhythms when she could. Sometimes
she would answer by tapping on the wood when she couldn't
think what to do next on the keys.

This work was the beginning of mother — child conversations at a sound level. The piano 'question and answer' effect would invariably be followed by some form of vocalization from James, which would be replied to by the mother in a similar vein. Or the vocalizing was stimulated by the mother improvising pentatonically on the chime bars or glockenspiel. She was taught which notes to use for this, and later how to add certain notes to create dissonance. To improve her uncertain sense of tempo, we used a metronome allegro, moderate, largo, etc. To improve melodic lines made on these instruments, we described with our mallets large arcs over the notes to make too much restricting stepwise movement impossible. Drumming on bongos and other small drums was discussed for future activity; and a simple bamboo pipe to follow up his desire to blow.

During all this time, the mother's musical and communicative senses were being sharpened and developed. And incidentally, greatly enjoyed. James was becoming more and more involved in this world of sound and rhythm; and was being stimulated and challenged in a way which was clearly meaningful to him. Before they left England, the mother was given not only a resumé of what we had done together, but clear guide lines for work she and James could enjoy for many months to come. Improvisation at her and James's level had created a new and dynamic bond between them, and between them and me. Less intensely, but none the less importantly, the team work had been extended to the paediatrician who had reports on all we were doing, and the physiotherapist who was very co-operative. Over the next year the mother reported in particular a great improvement in vocalization leading to good pre-speech sounds, and in general a sense of physical and emotional well being and confidence in herself and her child which she attributed directly to musical improvisation.

Musically speaking, what was done seems on the face of it, very simple and easy. Simple, yes; easy, anything but. In this therapeutic situation I found myself challenged to reducing all my previous musical training and experience to the most basic, uncluttered elements. Improvisation had to be almost primal — both my own and that which I was able to draw from this relatively unmusical woman. And in this reduction I saw more clearly than ever the relationship between the pitch, rhythmic and dynamic elements of sound and the psychological, physical and spiritual make-up of the human being.

From these four examples of music improvisation used in different settings, let us see what light is thrown on our original concern with

(1) (a) Improvisation (b) Creativity (c) Music Therapy
(2) The needs of the music therapist in such work.
(3) This type of therapy as a basis for co-operation with other therapies.

(1) (a) *Improvisation* here is clearly a mutual exploring and sharing of random sounds produced on musical instruments or by the voice. This random, free and at first, unstructured flow of sound provides the necessary release of thoughts and feelings and physical movement for any therapy to start. It is comparable to the cathartic experience which occurs between analyst and patient in individual analysis, and between group psychotherapist and patients in group therapy. It is the 'analysis' in terms of sound of a patient's inner life, and is followed by or alternates with the process of 'synthesis' in which the random element gives way to spontaneous shaping and organization of sound into rhythmic phrases. melodic lines, and controlled dynamics.

(b) *Creativity* and the creative approach conjures up words like on going, growing, changing and adapting, not static or secure, allowing chaos and confusion and then ordering it, variety and contrast. Atonality can gradually give way to tonality, or vice versa! Rhythmic and speed irregularity and disorder can become rhythmic phrasing and steady pulse. A death-like sameness in quantity or volume of sound (dynamics) or quality (tone colour) can be replaced by differences giving variety and contrast, and life.

(c) *Music Therapy* is the use of creative improvisation in sound which allows for the unlocking and development of the inner life and its potential, so that communication and relationships can be established, without guilt and in a non-threatening situation.

(2) *The needs of the music therapist in such work* are manifold. All music therapists need to be thoroughly good

musicians; and often it is the 'jack of all trades' type of
musician who is most successful. But the ability to improvise —
or to put it another way — to compose spontaneously, is a
rare gift (though more musicians have it than know it).
Anyone who wants to work in the way we have just read of
needs to discover his own creative improvisation potential
and then to work within it. He needs a sound knowledge of
the elements of sound, and the interest to explore, alone and
with others, how to use these elements separately and together.
And then to adapt them to the therapy scene. The better
his technique, the wider his knowledge of actual compositions
(as opposed to composers!) particularly those of the 20th
century, the more effective and varied will his improvisations
be. In addition he needs to be able to improvise in other
major styles of the past including Spanish, Old Time Music
Hall, *West Side Story*, etc.

As to the personal side of the work, he needs an extra dose
of self-awareness but not oversensitivity, and the ability to
be involved and yet detached. His 'watching eye' will help
him control the tricky boundary movements which inevitably
develop between himself and the patients, whether adult or
children. In my view, any music therapist working with
disturbed children or mentally ill people who is not genuinely
well balanced would do well to have some individual or
group therapy, or both. And while the demands of the subnormal and physically handicapped are different in this way,
the music therapist is always confronted with teamwork
with other staff. This can at times be difficult if one does not
understand the dynamics which exist in any group of people.

The dangers of working in this improvised way, especially
in the early days of being a therapist, are firstly, that therapist
and patients can be carried away in a welter of purposeless
noise; secondly, the therapist gets carried away by the drama
of the initial release, then to be discouraged by the hard
work and apparent nothingness following the honeymoon.

(3) *Improvisational therapy as a basis for co-operation
with other therapies.* The spontaneous and very creative
nature of music improvisation as a therapeutic technique
seems to lend itself easily to working along with therapists
in other disciplines. It is after all, the overlapping points of

similarity between the arts which make collaboration possible. As we have seen, it is at the improvisational, freer level that music, drama, movement, mime were actively able to explore and work together for the good of the children or adults concerned. At their many points of difference they have to work alone. Psychotherapy, whether individual or group, is, at its best, an art in its own right; and has many important points of contact with music. With most of the other therapists, including speech and physio, I have found that music improvisation as a therapeutic technique is most easily understood and accepted.

Conclusion

Music has in common with all the great forms of art different planes or dimensions. There is the horizontal (rhythm), the vertical (pitch), and depth (dynamics and tone colour). Its unique quality is that it moves *in time* (which gives it a fourth dimension.) This transient, ongoing characteristic is particularly striking in the creative process of improvisation. Anyone who has been involved, as patient or therapist, in therapy based on this process, will testify to its great value. I believe it to be the particular contribution which music has to make to the world of creative therapy.

Reference

J. Alvin, *Music Therapy*, J. Baker 1966, London.

Editor's note

Details of specialized and general training for both professional and non-professional musicians appears in Appendix 2. More extensive reading in music therapy will be found in Appendix 3.

7

Psychodrama, creativity and group process

ANNE ANCELIN SCHÜTZENBERGER

The place of psychodrama in society

Psychodrama is composed of elements which are implicit in the term itself: from the Greek, *psyche,* meaning breath, spirit, soul; and *drama,* meaning action. The word expresses the foundations of social interaction — individual identity and the personal action springing from it. Taking this as a starting point, then, psychodrama may be described as a form of group psychotherapy or training in which the patient (or subject or 'protagonist') enacts his problems or conflicts, instead of talking about them, in a kind of spontaneous sketch, role play or Commedia del Arte, with the support and participation of the group, and the help of the psychodramatist.

Psychodrama was first promoted by the late Dr J. L. Moreno (1890–1974) who started, as a medical student, to play out with children and with students, a 'living newspaper', dealing with events of the day and fantasy situations. In Vienna, during the Twenties, he observed and explored the idea of the therapeutic effect of catharsis on the actor in these fantasies. In 1925 he moved to the United States, where he initiated research into and understanding of action methods, and group dynamics, developing psychodrama from 1926–30, around New York, and *group psychotherapy* from 1932. Working to observe the relations and interactions of a small group of people living and working together, he developed the field of *sociometry.* He questioned them about their

131

preferences about who should do what (sociometric choices affected by the sociometric matrix); about how much or how little love a person gets in their group (*sociometric status,* expressed through its hierarchic range from 'star' to 'emotional proletariat'); about what constitutes the personal world of a person (his or her *'social atom'*) and how that is related to creativity, productivity, accident-proneness, health, and happiness. Through this research Moreno explored his theory that we continuously play roles (physical, social, professional, personal); the book that came out of the experience was *Who Shall Survive* (1934).

According to Moreno, we may survive in this changing, difficult world of the twentieth century only if we are able to perceive what is really going on in the 'here and now' and if we are spontaneous and creative enough to invent new solutions. Thus we will be fit and free enough to invent fresh answers to the new and difficult situations that confront us with what he calls 'spontaneity'. We are better enabled to play the roles that life asks from us, can more easily find new roles or new ways of play the roles of men, women, adolescents, old people, etc. – those roles that life obliges us to face, which nobody can predict at a time when the old, classical roles are outdated.

Living in the here and now can involve a great strain; many people live in and from the past by unconsciously reacting in the present to situations that have already confronted them in the past; their reaction is programmed by their past experience, and so they avoid the necessity of reacting spontaneously and properly to the present moment. People may also be so busy preparing the future that the present simply slips through their hands without their even noticing, without their being aware of how they breathe, sit, stand, walk, without their noticing the colour of the day or the faces in their family. For Rollo May and the Existentialists, this inability to live in the present is related to anxiety: the fear of facing death, of nothingness, causes one to overload, to fill up one's time with anything – television, light reading, even overwork or sickness. People play games and think in terms of 'passing time', according to Eric Berne just to kill time and so not be faced with themselves, the world and their fate.

In order to see what is going on in life, and to be prepared to face new and difficult situations in the here and now, it may be best to try out new roles, various ways of handling problems and this spontaneous approach to living in a sheltered situation. This could be provided by a small group of benevolent strangers, a small face-to-face group (called a training group, T-group, psychodrama workshop group or seminar), permissive and warm, as warm and secure as a womb; (Moreno calls it a *locus nascendi*) a place to be born or socially reborn in the group. With the group's support and involvement.

In this situation each person, as a group participant, may look at him/herself through the eyes of the others — in the 'social mirror' of the group: people may ask the others to give them feedback about how they look when they speak, sit still, exchange — during various interactions — information that family or professional colleagues either never give, or when doing so give uninvited in the form of counsel or scolding, the contrary of an invited, constructive feedback. Thus, people never know what they are really like; their friends like them while their enemies hate them. They do not perceive themselves as they are but rather with the 'halo effect' of that first good or bad impression.

Another point is that each person acts 'normally' without realizing that they are in a role, in the meaning that Shakespeare gives to it ("all the world's a stage and all the men and women merely players"). Goffman sees people as continuous actors, co-acting at the same time in everyday life a number of roles. He suggests that people prepare unconsciously 'backstage' — in bedroom or kitchen — to perform in public — the school-room, the living room with guests, or entering a good restaurant.

When we eat, for instance, we are in the learned role of eater as it was learned, either well or badly, with our first 'auxiliary ego' — our mother. Thus we have healthy food habits or suffer from indigestion, gastric ulcers, liver problems, diarrhoea or constipation; we either undereat (anorexia) or overeat (bulimia). It may be brought into the open by role playing or by conducting short psychodramatic scenes of family life until the repressed stress and suppressed memory

will bring back the baby's feelings of hurt and resentment
(still living in some part of the adult's memory or hidden in
some part of his body) and his way of punishing his mother
or himself by these food habits, this particular eater role.
Then the situation is rehearsed in psychodrama, enacted in
different ways, a new role of eater arises and the person is
often cured — even after many years of anguish and sickness.

In the same way we are breathers, sleepers, walkers, standers,
men and women, husbands, wives, parents, professors, doctors,
teachers, officers . . . in the way we have been taught the role.
Whether we have adopted a role through acceptance of a
certain pressure, or in reaction against it, neither is the result
of a free act. To be able to play our various roles in the manner
we want to, we have first to see ourselves — as we are — then
to adapt or change.

To be able to grow, to mature, to develop, to live as a person,
each human being, according to William Schutz, has basic
need of inclusion (in a group), control (over the situation), and
affection (as an individual).

My personal psychodramatic view of human beings is to see
men and women as defined by the following approaches:

The roles a person plays in his/her life

The present, past, future roles; physical, professional, social
personal roles, — the cluster of roles one assumes. The role
a person plays (his role as protagonist) is influenced by
the counter-role of the other (the role of the antagonist) and
by the role expectation of the group and of society. When
in interaction, A's role influences B, and B's role influences
A, without their being aware of it.

His/her sociometric status

One's love grade in the groups to which one belongs. For
instance, one may be very much loved (a 'star' or 'affective
capitalist' receiving too much love to use); one may receive
enough love (a normal figure in the group); one may be
circling on the outskirts of the group, receiving almost no

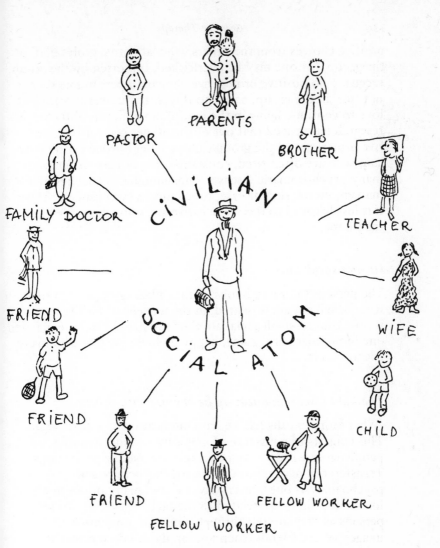

The Civilian Social Atom.

positive choices from the others, (the 'affective proletariat' of the group); or one may be overlooked, forgotten by the group, receiving no positive or negative choices (a person one does not 'see' in the group, and who therefore receives insufficient love to continue living in the group). Sociometric and clinical research has proved that out of the 20 per cent of the affective proletariat of the group came accident-prone people, persons who are often tired, constantly late or may suffer from many psychosomatic diseases — insommnia, headaches, rheumatism, ulcers, skin disease, tuberculosis, even cancers. Thus it is less harmful to receive negative attention from the group than none.

His/her social atom

The persons (animals, books, plants, ideas, groups . . .) to whom each person is related, in the nucleus of his life. It is sometimes a small social atom of shy people, or an expanded one of popular, easy-going, happy-go-lucky people who make friends easily.

The kind of communication he/she has with others

(What Moreno calls *tele* i.e. communication at a distance.) This consists of a mixture of empathy — understanding people from within — and transference-making projections. Transference occurs not only in psychotherapy and psychoanalysis but in everyday life; and many of our adult likes and dislikes are related to the fact that we do not see persons as they are but through a mist or 'projection of images' of old friends, enemies, family. We do not realize that we like or dislike Mary because she reminds us of a dear or dreaded Aunt Emily.

Real encounter between people, in the here and now

Happy are the rare persons who meet, encounter other persons on a human base and in a 'real' encounter. Too often, we see others as 'non-persons', — the children, the servants. There is a 'good sunny side' and a 'shadowy side' in groups, unless one pays attention to this, points it out, and sponsors therapy for the group. This is easier to do in a small face to face group than, say, in the whole of industry or the world at large.

In order to help us see ourselves as others see us, there is a very simple psychodramatic tool: *'role reversal'*. Person A (called the protagonist, or actor or subject) is in discussion or interaction with a person B (called the antagonist, co-actor or auxiliary ego). Then, by exchanging roles and places (psychodramatic identities), each can see himself/herself from the outside, as portrayed by the other, in this mirror. In every argument or difficulty between people, the situation is usually simply 'I (A) am right, and you (B) are wrong'. By role reversal in mid-discussion the situation is explored from the other's point of view, feelings are identified, and a more objective understanding of the situation may result. From that moment on, the situation is quite different and A is able to see the complexity of the situation, and even to understand both sides of it.

One of the major difficulties of life today is that there is no training for what is most important for living; there is no formal preparation for school, for marriage, for job applications; on the contrary, each of these often appears a hit or miss affair, with success or failure often apparently 'scripted' right from the start. One way of stopping this process before the point of no return is reached, is to rehearse socially and personally difficult situations on a psychodrama stage, with people with whom one feels secure enough to try and fail, and try again, and do better and better. The first such situation is often very frightening, even if it is approached with optimism. The resistance to change is strong and can be reinforced by the fear of making the situation irretrievably worse.

It is important, too, through group process and psycho-drama, to develop a perception sharp enough to see the dynamics of the interaction in which one is engaged, the role one plays, and how one reacts to the roles of the others, in an unconscious feedback reaction, and then in return create in others a feedback role reaction.

In this way one arrives, by role playing and role rehersal,

at an understanding of how one influences, by assumed roles
and by one's reactions, the role of others; how the antagonist
influences the protagonist; they are co-actors in the same
scene, on the stage of their everyday life as well as on the
psychodramatic stage.

There is a permanent interaction and feedback process
between co-actors related to roles, status, verbal and non-
verbal communication, status symbols, dominance cues,
(pecking orders) eye contact, body language, social distance,
use of territory, signals from clothes, hair, posture, facial
mask and its decorations. Even breathing: 'lungs-greek-up-
lift' breathing or 'belly-hindu-below-the-belt' breathing
gives a different posture, composure, deportment mobility,
grounding and human relation.

Role expectancy of others not only brings bias to the
situation of the co-actors, of each actor in the situation, but
transforms their behaviour. By-standers noted that once the
radio announced that John Kennedy was elected President
of the United States, the physical distance between him,
his guests, the journalists present in the room got greater,
as if by a given, unspoken order; showing to President John
Kennedy, by this greater distance, more respect and reverance
than to Senator John Kennedy; as if the strict rule of etiquette
regarding the Royal family, priests and Gods was obeyed even
in a modern Western industrialized democracy — without
word or thought.

These 'rules of the game' are taught, learned or inbred —
people climbing up the social ladder or changing status or
culture have to learn them, either the hard way or in a psychodrama session. Any change in role or status will involve this
process of adaptation based on understanding of the circumstances touching the role. Often status and role changes go
with a great change in social or family relations, of residential
area or even of religion: many immigrants, second generation
youngsters arriving as part of the first generation, later cut
their family ties so as not to be ashamed of their families who
do not speak 'correct' English and have the 'wrong' kind of
homes, outlook or lifestyle for the cities in which they live
and work.

Too much concern with the 'rules of the game' approach

to life may result in a kind of amputation from one's life of experiences and vital feelings. Self-actualizing people, in Maslow's words, live through 'peak experiences' — in which through religious, artistic, or even passionate experience — they live fully for the moment, suffusing the instant with its brightest colours and scents, a moment when time moves from future to eternity in an unforgettable experience. These experiences happen, too, in LSD trips, psychodrama groups, group therapy, encounter groups, — and often after a near meeting with death or a moment of illumination, as happened to Paul on the road to Damascus. Psychodramatic method is a major approach of our time involved with re-establishing contact between people, showing their relation to themselves, their 'real self', and their 'here and now' reality and may offer them peak experiences. It provides a catalyst for new developments in the fields of psychotherapy, management, training, education and factors in the human potential movement. Action methods, role playing, sociodrama (for social problems), ethnodrama, encounter groups, Gestalt therapy, group psychotherapy, all come from psychodrama. Psychodrama integrates factors of verbal and non-verbal communication, experiential learning ('gut learning') with the 'process of building coping skills in interpersonal relating', as Howard Blatner phrases it.

Psychodrama may be used to all these ends, related as they are, and in the following example situations:

- in *psychotherapy* with sick, neurotic, psychotic and even so-called normal adults and children.
- in *education*, in order to teach languages, history, and various skills.
- for *growth,* to help normal adults to develop their potential and personal growth.
- for *training,* especially of staff, supervisors, psychiatrists, doctors, psychologists, nurses, priests, social workers, salesmen, professors, industrial supervisors, custom officers, actors, teachers, to relate to others in their professional roles and improve their performance of those roles.
- to *prepare* people for new situations.

— to *cure*, e.g. tobacco or chemical addiction.

— for *therapy*, e.g. adjuctive therapy with physically handicapped, brain-damaged adults and children.

— to *prepare future mothers* for natural childbirth, and for skills in taking care of their infants.

— to help people in *transition periods* such as divorce, bereavement, discharge from hospital or prison etc.

— for *social-psychodrama*, to overcome problems of social know-how in social and professional situations such as a change of job or location.

— to *train people in spontaneity and creativity* by use of spontaneity tests, role playing of various standard life situations and unlikely situations. For example Moreno's classic test, where you are asked to sweep the floor, in a room without any further indication of who or where you are (i.e. usually you think you must be in your own sex and age role); then to be told that your wife is dying in a fire accident (i.e. you are male and married) then that it is *your* house that is on fire (i.e. you must try to stop it and call the fire brigade); then that the babies are crying (i.e. you have a family to save); then that your Ph.D thesis, nearly finished, is still in your study on the top floor (i.e. you are a student) and so on. This is but one way through improvisation to train

— and develop healthy creative spontaneity.

Liberating spontaneous creativity within society

Einstein states that 'the elements of creative thought and the underlying psychological entities appear to be used for reasoning; certain signs and images of varying degrees of clarity can be combined. This combination game seems to be the essence of productive thought.' André Breton, the French surrealist poet, speaks of the 'wonderful capacity for combining, for grasping two distant realities within the range of our experience' and of the 'spark that flashes when they are juxtaposed'.

Creative thought could be defined as a new combination of elements, associated not for any specific or useful purpose (though the final result may indeed be useful), but almost fortuitously; the more diverse or distinct these elements, the more creative the process or solution.

This creative process may be approached in the manner of the American school, through association of thought; it occurs:

By chance: the association of thought happens by chance, through mutual influence of perception or ideas, deriving from the surroundings or other appropriate stimuli. Two unconnected ideas may enter the conscious mind, because they occur simultaneously, by chance, in one's environment.

By similarity: the association occurs through contiguity; it becomes apparent either because of the similarity of associated elements or similarity of stimuli. This type of creativity is found in certain forms of poetry, music and painting — where the resemblance of sounds, forms or colours is very important — as well as in other kinds of work, where use is made of homonyms and rhythm rather than the manipulation of symbols.

By meditation: the necessary associative elements may be evoked through contiguity, by the meditation of common elements. For example, idea X and idea Z, which normally have nothing to do with each other, can be brought together by idea Y, which is associated with each of them. Thus, the series X, Y, Z, takes on a meaning. Poincaré related how he discovered Fuchsian functions (generalization of elliptic functions) in this way, simply by combining two different kinds of mathematics which happened to have the same model of transformation.

This theory of the association of ideas, (a flash, a spark, a new and fruitful combination) is generally followed up by constructive analysis, an examination of the structure of the ideas whose resemblances or similarities enable the research to progress. On the other hand, the flash of inspiration is usually born on prepared ground as much in terms of culture (general and technical) as of preliminary orientation of thought. The mental tool already exists for true creative work to be done and for the flash of inspiration to occur.

For the past twenty years specialists in group training, either using psychodrama centred on group work and liberation of spontaneity and creativity (Moreno) or 'group work' and 'sensitivity training' in group dynamics and human relations, centred on the self as well as on the group, contents, process and reason of interaction (as in the NTL 'T-groups' in Bethel) have turned towards creativity and related areas which can take man out of the rut, enabling him to see things in new ways and to overcome his resistance to change. Brainstorming, creativity seminars, initiative games, language-seminars and the various exercises in perception skills and verbal and non-verbal communication all work in this direction.

The setting up of T-groups (i.e. Training groups) provides an example of the direction that this area of work has taken during the last twenty years. Established as training groups for people working in industry, administration, commerce, teaching the army, the church, hospitals, the T-groups give sensitivity training and awareness about one's own and others' feelings. Working in small groups without a theme, participants are more concerned with the process than with the content of the exchanges. The leader is 'permissive', 'non-directive', co-operative and group-centred.

Moreno based his approach on the concept of the vital impulse of the creator; he linked creativity with the liberation of creative spontaneity, inhibited in the West by an urban, production-consumption orientated society.

Moreno states that in the evolution of man, spontaneity appeared 'before libido, memory and intelligence . . . . In effect it is generally discouraged and thwarted by our cultural mechanisms. Many of the problems of the psyche and social difficulties suffered by humanity are attributable to an insufficient development of spontaneity. For this reason the art of teaching people to use their spontaneity is the most beneficial thing to be learned in any of our educational institutions.' He also pointed out that anxiety indicates a loss of spontaneity.

A 'cultural conserve' (Moreno) is the end product of a cultural endeavour, the fixed conserve or preserve of culture, the contents of all the libraries, the teaching in all the schools, the knowledge acquired by a child in the home or at school, what is given by radio, television, the theatre, the cinema, books, lectures — all the 'conserves' of the past creativity of others offered to the intellect.

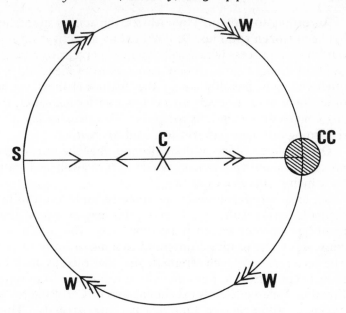

Canon of Creativity (according to J. L. Moreno).

Field of rotating operations between Spontaneity−Creativity−Cultural Conserve (S-C-CC)

S = Spontaneity, C = Creativity, CC = Cultural (or any) Conserve (for instance, a biological conserve, *i.e.*, an animal organism, or a cultural conserve, *i.e.*, a book, a motion picture, or a robot, *i.e.*, a calculating machine); W − Warming up is the 'operational' expression of spontaneity. The circle represents the field of operations between S, C and CC.

Operation I: Spontaneity arouses Creativity, C. S —> C.
Operation II: Creativity is receptive to Spontaneity. S <—C.
Operation III: From their interaction Cultural Conserves, CC, result.
            S—> C—> >CC.
Operation IV: Conserves (CC) would accumulate indefinitely and remain 'in cold storage'. They need to be reborn, the catalyzer Spontaneity revitalizes them. CC—> > >S—> > >CC.

S does not operate in a vacuum, it moves either towards Creativity or towards Conserves.

Total Operation

Spontaneity-creativity-warming up-act $<\frac{\text{actor}}{\text{conserve}}$

According to Moreno's hypothesis, the adult's spontaneity has been frozen and must be liberated by an activating and warming-up process which will thaw the perceptive processes and lead thought through new associations of ideas, along other channels, possibly along other neuron chanins, causing other 'memories' to come into contact with each other, thus enabling fresh perceptions to appear. This thawing out and reforming into new patterns will lead to creativity.

One could consider, as does Moreno, that the warming-up process awakens spontaneity which in turn awakens creativity for which it acts as a catalyst.

So, creativity responds to spontaneity, and from this inter-action is born a 'cultural conserve'; this may be a new development but may consequently become frozen (become a conserve) when passing from mind to mind or body to body. The very form of psychodramatic or other therapy may itself become frozen. For example, it is possible to misinterpret Freud or Melanie Klein's psychoanalysis or Carl Rogers' 'non-directive' group-centred approach as being 'passivity'. This misunderstanding may combine with a fear of deviating from the norm they represent and with a desire for a codified organization to reconstruct a cultural conserve around psycho-drama. The result is an orthodoxy which is inimical to the richness of spontaneity — creativity that Moreno saw as the *sine qua non* for psychodrama.

Ideally, then, a loose sequence is established: a warming-up, a starting of intellectual creative activity, a liberation of spontaneity — creativity resulting from the thawing out of thought patterns, and the generation of ideas which develop and gather momentum.

If we return to Moreno's definition, creative spontaneity consists of providing a new and adapted response for a new (or old) and difficult situation; creativity is linked with cultural patterns, cultural tradition and spontaneity (and with the drawback of cultural conserves and repetition).

Functionally, spontaneity is connected to two poles:

— Automatism and reflex action on one hand, and
— Productivity and creativity on the other.

We may ask ourselves how and why individuals give a

stereotyped response to a given situation or idea. Why should the drying-up of creativity occur? It is well known that a child discovers the world, remakes it every minute and lives in a state of creativity and spontaneity. Man's first universe of discovery is replaced during childhood and adolescence by a second, socialized universe where the learned image learnt has replaced the perceived thing. Education brings with it a social, normative perception dependent on fixed conserves or cultural patterns which paralyse fresh perception and creativity.

Stereotyped response can be acquired through habit and repetition and although habit has its positive aspects, enabling one to gain time and increase efficiency, it can set up a negative pattern of reaction. If the same indications always lead to the same conclusions, the same causes always produce the same effects, if the same orders are always received, always to be followed by the same actions (if we are continually blamed for what we do, or conversely if we never get any reaction at all), there results a habitual stereotyped response, habitual action and even thought, virtually a reflex action. This habit has not only a positive aspect, but also a negative one.

Far too often creativity is dormant, silenced, diminished or castrated. Various methods exist to re-establish belief in one's individuality, to liberate creative—spontaneity, to warm-up and so to produce work which is personal, creative, useful and productive. There must be motivation, re-activation of the cultural patterns to provide the intellectual tools and perceptual changes.

(1) When the creative faculties are blocked due to neurosis, *individual or group psychotherapy* may be utilized (psycho-analysis, individual or group analysis, psychodrama, non-directive sessions: psychotherapy for the 'normals'). This allows the individual to become aware of the obstructions, traumas and communication problems, to throw off the influence of parasitical thoughts and to halt the loss of energy caused by the weight of old personal problems or inability to cope with certain situations.

(2) *Resting* the intellect, when it is in a state of habit

following physical or intellectual fatigue or merely an excess
of tension. This is often achieved by holidays, rest, a trip,
a change.

(3) *Providing the conditions for creativity,* in an appropriate
atmosphere, where ideas emerge and are exchanged, where
the group morale is high and stimulating and the climate
vivid. This induces in the group members a desire to seek,
to work, to find, to create, to become useful and efficient.
Working groups of this kind often gather around scholars
or leaders who know how to put men to work, help them
develop, gain their trust, encourage and support them,
create healthy competition in a climate of tolerance, friendship, trust and exchange, with a degree of freedom and recognition of value of the others; they allow the researcher to
assert himself, to gain confidence in himself and in his ability
or talent, and to fulfil himself in his work.

(4) *A training group* in 'human relations', a 'sensitivity
training' using group-centred, 'non-directive' methods: group
dynamics, psychodrama, growth games, role-playing. About
fifteen members of staff of various industries or organizations
meet for sessions, with no programme or theme, for a few
sessions, with a permissive group-leader or conductor, who
lets the group feel free to discuss anything or nothing special,
while helping it to understand its inner dynamics, process of
decision making, fight for leadership, form of communications,
blockages in the communication, and helps the group members
to grow and become more mature and responsible persons.
'Feedback' of the 'here and now' feelings makes group
members understand what is really going on (content, process)
and allows them to compare what is felt by each and every
member, with what is expressed by the more talkative or
powerful, to compare and confront the message(s) sent to
the message(s) received, and the message(s) actually sent to
the message(s) a person intended to send out. Each member
may develop his awareness of the communication net set
up inside the group, the various leadership and membership
roles each one plays, his projections on the others,
transference on to the group leader and/or other members,
intercommunication, his reactions to authority figures and
his personal needs, roles, drawbacks, potentials.

One often finds in these sessions lectures, discussion sessions, observation training, role-playing of professional and personal problems, with free time for reflection, relaxation and exchange. Frequently, persons gain more awareness of themselves and others, insight into life, values, commitments, choices, roles, *being*. Many a member understands the difference between himself for himself, himself for the others, his ideal self, and the tranself of the group, between his being, doing, having (this or that positions, status, appearance), between expressing a new feeling (ecceity), distance from the experience, resistance, filling up the time.

Many participants have compared this experience with the happiness and new energy they find in a month's holiday, a religious retreat, the euphoria of love or rediscovered friendship, the exaltation of a 'trip' (LSD or other). Freedom from the usual routine at least results in reflections, a break which enables the individual to see his life and work in a new perspective; if often results in a renewed capacity for friendship, creativity, productivity, new ideas, ways of thinking, being, perceiving. So these sessions often trigger creativity.

Psychodrama in action

Having discussed the social applications and relevance of psychodrama, some description is necessary of its practical mechanics and how these may vary from group to group, and within different therapeutic disciplines.

Usually psychodrama takes place in a group; it is an action method used as part of a more general session in a verbal, psychotherapeutic or training seminar or workshop, or with various non-verbal or action methods. The commitment of the group could range from a one-day workshop, for instance, to the long-term commitment of an ongoing group for three weeks or three years. It may be used, too, for education and training.

In each psychodrama session there are three phases:

(1) *The warm up of the group,* breaking the ice amongst people or even participants who already know each other. An actor, 'main ego' or 'protagonist' will emerge, and act out a

particular problem, concern or difficulty that he wishes to explore or try to solve.

(2) *Action,* enactment, production or psychodrama par se: the *protagonist* will 'live out his life on the stage' (Moreno) with the help of assistants, therapists or co-trainers, or other group members called (once they are on the stage) *auxiliary-egos,* and will portray the other person needed by the action.

(3) *Feedback or sharing* of feelings by the group, after the action, once the actors have returned to the group: the protagonist, along with each participant and group member from the audience may express his feelings* and emotions about what just happened; many group and other participants* catharsis may then happen — not only the protagonists's.

In training groups, a fourth phrase is added:

(4) *Understanding the sociometry and the dynamics of the group,* the group process, and *discussion of the psychodramatic and action techniques* used in the action and warm-up.

There are five factors in psychodrama:

(1) A *protagonist* or main actor or main ego, subject, participant or patient client, sick or so-called normal person, acting out his life on the stage.

(2) *The Director of psychodrama* (a title given by Moreno to a dozen of the best specialists), or psychodramatist: a psychotherapist trainer, group-leader conductor in charge of the session.

(3) *An auxiliary ego:* any person who will assume the role of the antagonist or co-actor, acting with the protagonist, or any person who takes part in the situation acted out.

(4) *The group or audience:* generally psychodrama happens in a group, whose feedback is important to support the pro-tagonist, for him to share his feelings, personal identifications and various experiences in the 'then and there' or in the 'here and now'. By doing this, the group helps the protagonist to overcome his feelings of isolation. However, psychodrama may be performed with only one person and, say, his doctor, or with a therapeutic team as in French analytic psychodrama for children.

---

* Personal feelings but not advice or judgement.

(5) *The 'round' stage:* sometimes a real stage with three steps from the floor to the stage. It serves as the cradle, a *locus nascendi* or matrix, where the person may be socially born or reborn and seen in his *status lastendi* (Moreno). It may also be a symbolic stage, including a specified action area in a room, delineated by a carpeted area, a change of colour, or a small open space well defined by a horseshoe ring of chairs, for the group members to use while observing.

As Moreno puts it, psychodrama may happen anywhere.

The question of props is fairly fluid: none are absolutely necessary, though a few optional ones may be desirable, such as two or three chairs, a small table. Sometimes a mattress or light portable sofa or bed is used, and cushions or pillows may be useful. Normally smoking is forbidden in a psycho-drama theatre as it is in many conventional theatres; it may also be frowned upon as 'acting out', i.e. a transfer into the act of smoking of an unspoken feeling that could otherwise be expressed in the group. A carpeted floor with big cushions is sometimes preferred to a row of chairs, by people who are accustomed to informal, relaxed groups and like to sit on the floor; these seating arrangements make practically no difference except that people then tend to lean their backs on the walls, which may increase the size of the group and the distance between people and make it more difficult to stand up for action. Informal dress is important if participants are to feel free to take on widely different 'characters' as demanded by the action.

Psychodrama may be taken in a broad sense, or as having a more specific meaning, though it is basically for the investigation of personal problems.

Role-playing is a derivation of psychodrama, used mainly in industry or education, to try to find out more effective ways of dealing with situations, such as applying for a job, inviting important people for dinner, asking the boss for a rise, and learning how to intervene in difficult situations, stating with more ease a foreign language or seeing history and geography more vividly.

Action methods are either the use of various psychodramatic methods or techniques, in psychodrama, 'T-group', group analysis and various forms of training, either by the use of adjunctive group-action-activities, such as art, dance, painting, music, games, play, guided fantasy, sensory awareness exercises, some Gestalt therapy, or encounter group exercises, relaxation, meditation — many of which were rediscovered forms employed by psychodramatists and by Moreno in the past, and subsequently expanded under various denominations.

There are, classically, three schools of psychodrama:

(1) *American Classical Psychodrama,* created and developed by J. L. Moreno in the United States from 1921—25, until the 1960s. It is mainly described in Moreno's and his wife's books, *Psychodrama* I (1946), II (1959), III (1969) and IV (in press in America, 1975). In this form work is centred around the psychodramatic action at each session, which are run by various Directors of Psychodrama, invited to the Beacon or New York Psychodrama Institutes. Although sessions are usually therapeutic, there are also public sessions, in the form of live or recorded demonstration sessions, where people buy tickets in order to watch — or participate.

(2) *French Psychoanalytic Psychodrama,* (evolved by Dr Sege Lebovici, currently President of the International Association of Psychoanalysis, 1973, and, though somewhat differently, by Didier Anzieu). In this form work is usually with children, in short individual sessions of 10 to 15 minutes, with the help of a psychoanalysed team of assistants, generally graduate students, using Freudian classical concepts: transference, regression, as well as spontaneous play.

(3) *French Triadic Psychodrama* (evolved by Anne Ancelin Schützenberger, Director of Psychodrama from the Moreno Institute since 1955 in France, Europe and Latin America). It is an extension of group analysis, T-group or analytical and existential group psychotherapy, using action in a small group with a permissive climate meeting usually once a week for two years or for intensive sessions from time to time. Classical techniques of psychodrama are used once the action has moved on to the stage. Triadic Psychodrama brings togethe the approaches of J. L. Moreno, Sigmund Freud, and Kurt Lewin.

The psychodramatic action is related to group life. The dynamics of the group are seriously analysed, sometimes for several sessions after the psychodrama, utilizing the symbolism of the language, dreams, and the relationship of what is acted out in psychodrama to what is happening in the group process, and the relationships to the group leader, therapist or psychodramatist (transference). Thus the group discusses as much as it plays, and sometimes more. Psychodramatic action does not always take place at each session — some suggestions for action may eventually be considered a flight from group issues.

Psychodrama is an approach to the human situation *in* the group, *by* the group, *with* the group, in a relationship of mutual interaction between individual and group.

Many therapists, psychoanalists and trainers do not see the implications of this distinction between group psychodrama and individual psychodrama within a group, but it is a major one and changes the approach to the work. Psychodrama is a *group therapy* whereas Gestalt is usually *individual therapy in a group,* using some (but not all) psychodramatic techniques.

The distinction between psychodrama *in* the group, and psychodrama *by* the group, is subtle: a person may come to a public session, or to any session, to clarify his problems or situation, and will act out his life on the stage in front of an audience, with the help of a psychodramatist, auxiliary ego(s) and comments from the audience.

The audience may be moved by the action — as happens in actual theatre — and react to it, some by crying or leaving the room, others by taking part, dreaming, or thinking of something totally different. This will be psychodrama in the group, but not by the group, as action did not spring from group life and group interaction, and as what the protagonist acts out is not really related to what goes on in the group. The protagonist is in front of an audience rather than acting from within the group. Nevertheless, in the course of action a strong interaction may or may not develop between the protagonist and the group; the audience may be completely involved at the moment, but not related afterwards to the protagonist, nor feel responsible for him, which is incompatible with the case of psychodrama within and by the group, where strong group ties are built.

Even in a small, face-to-face group, meeting regularly, a psychodrama may sometimes start, involving only one person, with various degrees of interest from the group. Even if the action may seem good, often during the sharing other participants will admit frankly their lack of interest or of real participation.

This is an important issue, because it illustrates the danger of putting the protagonist in the situation of opening himself and his 'secret garden' in front of indifferent people, thus dividing the group into exhibitionists and voyeurs (peeping Toms). Both parties could in this situation feel uneasy afterwards. Thus it is important for the psychodramatist to be aware of what is going on in the group, and not to jump into action for the sake of action, or to follow the desire of the would-be-protagonist, without first having understood the dynamics of the group and what is at stake within the proposed action. Some of the uneasiness people have felt about psychodrama comes from what seemed to them to be the revelation of personal secrets. This may happen if the group is not ready to move into action and to hear and be with the protagonist

in what he may live out. The individual's past is only interesting and alive for the group if it is linked with what is going
on and if the protagonist is accepted and wanted by the group.

The situation is different when the action springs from group
interaction when what is acted out on the stage by the protagonist is the very problem or situation of the group, in which
the group was and is involved, the main feeling of the group
being embodied by one person in his personal life situation.
For example, the group may have been involved with problems of authority and leadership in the group; then it leads
them to relationships with parents, father and mother roles.
Some group members become very much involved with
their relationships back home, and then one person may
emerge, very much involved (with the support of the group)
with a problem with his mother . . .

The situation is acted out on the stage, and all the group
is with him, all the time. After the *action*, sharing of feelings
is important: comments and personal reactions emerge or
are called for by the psychodramatist, from all present,
which may lead to another scene, with another protagonist,
for example, about his problem with his·father, then returning
to the group, with everyone personally involved in the

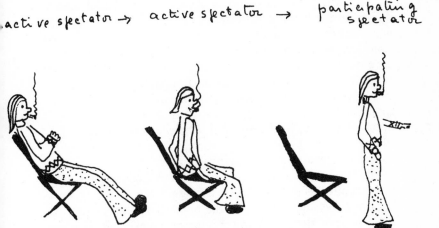

The Warm up of inactive spectator to full participant
(Claire Fontaine, aged 11).

action. If we then use the triadic approach, we can decode
this and understand it, in the 'here and now' of the group
relationship, relating to the trainer or group leader who,
because of his role, embodies the parental figures as well as
the authority figure. The group will then gain insight through
the action in order to understand better the 'here and now',
the complete and complex cosmos of relationships with
authority figures, fights for leadership, projections. All this
emerges through group interaction involving everyone, and
everyone's 'then and there' back home, as well as everyone's
'here and now', within the group. In this way, going with
the group and the feelings of every member, there emerges
respect for how the protagonist wants to work in that particular group situation. There is no suggestion of pushing him or
letting the group push him, but rather of letting him follow
his own rhythm and pace.

One of the important issues in understanding what is going
on in the group, during the seminar as well as during the
actual sessions, is to take into account the underlying flow
of feelings (the 'discourse' of the group), according to one's
knowledge of personal and group growth, laws of group
dynamics and group evolution, and not simply respond to the
group's sociometric choices, or its demands for a show or
action for the sake of action. Further, the phases of 'dependency' towards the psychodramatist, moving on to 'counter-
dependency and independency' (William Schultz) (when he
functions as an expert in psychodrama and no longer as a
parental transference figure) must be understood. This takes
time. It might take a few sessions to analyse, understand
and benefit from an active psychodrama session, where *all*
that was directly or symbolically said or felt in the scene,
on the stage and in the group during the action (including
silence, non-verbal communication, movement around the
room) is relevant. Psychoanalytical and symbolic decodings
of the language used are understood and analysed and taken
into account as much as what is role-played on the stage, or
dreamed the night before or the night after the session. All
the trends of the group and the major issues in the sessions
of that week or month, plus the relationships of the group
to leadership and power are also taken into account in the

understanding of group dynamics. For these reasons I prefer
not to start psychodrama as such immediately, but often
after the group has been through several sensitivity sessions,
when their relationship to the leader is clarified and a sense
of trust and group feeling is created.

What is happening in the session is understood in an
existential approach by the nature and 'colour' of the group
co-conscious and co-unconscious (the 'tranself') in a cluster
warm-up through what is lived out, said, felt — all is taken
up into the 'living present'; by this we mean *ecceity*: a direct
relation in the here and now, with no distance within the
person between what he feels, thinks and expresses — thus no
distance, for the individual, between self-expression and direct
encounter with other group members. Thus, when the speaker
discovers new feelings while he is speaking, and is in contact
with his real, present feelings, he speaks from his own deep
human nature; what he says becomes living and true for each
member or the group or audience, and not, as Eric Berne says,
a 'game' i.e. 'play psychiatry' as opposed to 'real' involvement
in the psychotherapeutic situation. By this process of being in
contact with their own deep nature, people re-establish
contact with their own individuality as well as with collective
humanity, and regain their spontaneous and creative qualities —
their *being*.

Learning to communicate well with others; living in the
present; inhabiting one's body; being lucid about what is going
on in oneself, in our relationships, in the world at large as
well as all the groups within which we work and live; understanding clearly the roles we play in everyday life, and the
interaction one has with others; feeling free to use imagination
and creativity in everyday life; being able to open our role
cluster and play many more roles, finding new interactions,
new answers to the new demands of life — all this is psychodrama.

Its philosophy and numerous techniques help children and
adults, the so-called 'normal' and the so-called 'sick' in their
personal and family life as well as in their occupations, to
grow and develop, with a 'surplus reality'. Spontaneity training, creativity training, born mainly from psychodrama, is
spreading out, with many psychodramatic, role-playing and

action techniques, in many therapeutic approaches, training and education.

If we want to survive in this difficult, changing world, we may learn from psychodrama's creativity — spontaneity approach and philosopy to learn now to be on the go and ready to face what may challenge us — what life may have in store for us. It is a training for life.

References

1. J. L. Moreno (1953), *Who Shall Survive*, New York, Beacon House.
   —— (1946), *Psychodrama* I, then Vol. II: III.
   —— (1959), Psychodrama II.
   —— (1969), Psychodrama III.
2. Anne Ancelin Schützenberger, *Precis de psychodrame* (a handbook on psychodrama, with history, 100 techniques, glossary of terms, examples) 2d. ed. revised 1970, Paris, Editions Universitaires.

8

Psychodrama with disturbed adolescents

ROY SHUTTLEWORTH

All adolescents in our culture face special problems, problems which become exaggerated for the child with a poor innate constitutional make-up or social environment. MacLennon and Felsenfeld describe adolescence as:

'a period of great change which marks the transition from childhood to adult life. During this time boys and girls have to establish their identities as men and women, to decide which roles they wish to play in the adult world, socially, sexually and occupationally; to separate themselves from their primary families, to become independent and to envisage the establishment of their own families.'

It is important to remember that adolescence covers a wide age range in which marked developmental changes take place. One of the difficulties of working with disturbed adolescents is that their stage of development will be not only very varied between individuals, but also invariably be retarded in comparison with their normal peers. Erikson characterizes adolescence as a period of identity versus role confusion, when the adolescent strives to establish a stable sense of identity against a background of physical change and the opportunities offered in social roles. During this period some role confusion must occur in all adolescents. Erikson believes that when that confusion is based on a strong previous doubt about sexual identity, delinquent and psychotic episodes are not uncommon.

157

Anyone who works or lives with adolescents — particularly with difficulties — will recognize these confusions. The adolescent can swing from acting like a small child to a mature adult, from treating an individual as a loved subject with hugs, to a hated enemy with punches. Sexual identity is one of the most marked problems. In the extreme, girls will proclaim loudly that they are lesbians and have grown a penis, while a little later on they will flirt openly with any available male. In institutions I have found outbreaks of self-tattooing which seem to suggest a need of physically impressing some permanent tangible identity upon themselves.

Most adolescents in a situation of reasonable security are capable of differentiating their roles and finding their identities. The small percentage who have to seek help, however, present perhaps the most difficult and challenging problems of all the age groups to the therapist. Therapy must be heavily orientated towards helping the individual resolve some of these confusions. As the vast majority of adolescents I see have delinquent tendencies, I usually assume that their most stable role is that of the 'bad' child. This role is not only the one that they feel most comfortable in but also the role that others, in particular their families, expect them to play. There is therefore a vicious circle between role expectation and role fulfilment. The therapist has to break into this vicious circle and change the roles and the expectations into others that are most positive. It is hoped that the new roles will receive positive reinforcements which will allow them to become a permanent part of the individual's behaviour repertoire. The same aim, of course, is adopted for the treatment of other maladapted behaviour, including bizarre psychotic behaviour, e.g., an individual who talks to trees may feel reasonably comfortable in this role as the 'mad' one with all the attention it attracts and the expectations it arouses. Hence no attempt will be made to develop more adaptive roles.

In recent years there has been an increasing interest in group therapy in the treatment of adolescent problems. I will look first at the rationale and problems involved in the use of conventional groups with adolescents before moving on to the theoretical and practical use of psychodrama groups.

Conventional groups share many of the aims as well as the

problems of psychodrama groups and I hope to show that in a psychodramatic setting we have a much better chance of achieving the aims and overcoming the problems. The most obvious advantage of groups, over individual psychotherapy, is economic. Most therapeutic units are limited in the number of trained staff available and may be required to help twenty or more children. Therefore the more people who can be included in a session the better. More important, there are sound reasons why deep interpretative individual psychotherapy is irrelevant to adolescents. Most adolescents lack the reliable ego structure considered by many to be the prerequisite for successful psychotherapy. Hersko in describing this difficulty, suggests that the adolescent will typically respond to a deep analytic approach with intense anxiety and increased acting-out and frequently by withdrawal from therapy. Hersko sees it as the prime role of the therapist to encourage ego develop-ment and the synthesis of conflicting identifications rather than to foster insight into unconscious conflicts. He uses a primarily supportive, educative approach and encourages identification with suitable adults. As group involvement is habitual with adolescents Hersko suggests that the idea of receiving help in a group is not too threatening and that the adolescent benefits from sharing problems with others as well as having allies when it comes to dealing with the therapist.

MacLennon and Felsenfeld suggest 'that small groups provide a miniature real life situation which can be utilized for the study and change of behaviour . . . the group, skilfully conducted, can provide a mirror in which the group member can evolve a new concept of himself, test this out in action with his fellows and find new models for identifica-tion.'

I have drawn from these two sources as well as Evans and my own experience, to provide the following catalogue of adolescent difficulties encountered in adolescent group psychotherapy.

Unlike most adult groups, adolescents do not often sit happily for an hour or so and attempt to sort our their problems in a mature and civilized way. More often than not they will be distracting each other by irrelevant chatter

or thumping one another or the therapist. This may be a
response to anxiety but is just as likely to be boredom. This.
means that the therapist has to be much more active and
controlling than he would be in adult psychotherapy.
Consequently a 'work' group, where problems are looked at
in depth is often of brief duration and will usually degenerate
into irrelevant activity. This can be very upsetting to the
inexperienced therapist. Group themes can be focused upon
but it is usually difficult because of the easily distractible
nature and lack of persistence of adolescent groups. Therefore
the therapist has to be much more active and make individual
interpretations, particularly in regard to 'here and now'
behaviour. The therapist can be lured into concentrating
on just a couple of the more powerful group members who
make the most noise, to the detriment of the quieter members.
Often the more powerful individuals will show great resentment if the therapist turns his attention to a quieter or less
popular member of the group. Ideally this aspect of 'here and
now' behaviour is better pointed out by another member of
the group than the therapist. Often the adolescent will not
have the emotional maturity nor the verbalizing ability to
be able to tell the group what is bothering him. There may
be a great fear that by saying something self-detrimental he
will show himself up or give ammunition to his peers to taunt
him with later. The adolescent may also have a strong need
to defend himself from secret fears of being mad or of being
thought to be mad by his peers.

Adolescents will often place the therapist in a hostile role,
if for no other reason than because he is an adult. This
hostility may represent some displacement from the anger
he feels for his parents or social situation. On the other hand,
he may be simply testing the 'safety net' that the therapist
represents to see if it is reasonably secure. The therapist
walks a fairly tight boundary between being over-flexible
and therefore causing insecurity, or too inflexible and not
allowing the adolescent any breathing space.

The group defences described by Bien will often be seen
with adolescent groups. These take the form of 'dependency
demand' which can be represented by helpless dependent
behaviour, complaining, asking for help, passive dependancy,

'flight and fight', where anxiety provoking situations can either lead to aimless fighting or horse-play or leaving the room (I have had individuals leave the session and return up to six times in an hour) and 'pairing', where two members take over and divert the group from its work. Often this will be done by two of the more powerful members, while the more passive ones sit back and enjoy the escape from involvement.

I have had reasonably broad experience with adolescent small groups, both within the institution and in out-patient departments, as well as in-patient psychodrama groups, and feel on balance that psychodrama groups offer far more scope in helping the adolescent come to terms with himself and his environment as well as allowing the therapist to handle the particular difficulties and challenges that have been described above. Psychodrama is more fun for the adolescent; allows him a better chance to examine his roles and practise new ones in a more realistic way, i.e., by actually *doing* it; does not rely so heavily upon the ability to verbalize his feelings and allows the therapist to utilize distracting and avoiding behaviour in a play situation. I have found that the best 'verbal' work groups have occurred *after* the particular problem has been enacted in some form. With psychodrama, however, goes the danger of greater involvement and catharsis because of its power and therefore must be used responsibly. My groups are voluntary and the individual is free to leave if he wants to at any time. Because it is done within an institution there is always the backing of colleagues if anyone becomes too upset. I should add, however, that in the three years that I have used psychodrama with adolescents there have only been two occasions when individuals have become visibly upset by a session and on both of these it was in a positive way and easily managed by the nursing staff.

I am using the term psychodrama in two contexts. One is the specific sense, where the individual enacts his conflicts instead of talking about them and the other in the generic sense which includes this specific form plus sociodrama, role-play and some forms of movement. Role play has been described by Mann as where a person is explicitly asked to perform a role which is not normally his own or is explicitly asked to perform a normal role but not in a setting where it is normally taken. Sociodrama is the enactment of some social situation such as a Court scene, where individuals are asked to play various roles within the total situation.

Although I use many of the concepts and techniques formulated by Moreno, the father of psychodrama, my orientation is much more towards the learning theory, in attempting to conceptualize what goes on in the group. My small group training is in the Foulkes tradition so that I try to emphasize what is going on within the group rather than concentrate mainly on outside material. I have described elsewhere the theoretical, practical and experimental basis to psychodrama [Shuttleworth, 1973 (a), (b)] but I think it would be useful briefly to recapitulate some of the work.

As with all forms of psychotherapy very few adequate studies are available to give empirical support for psychodramatic techniques. Those available have usually looked at one of the ingredients of psychodrama. Boies in an excellent review of the literature available on role play, states that in spite of a lack of concrete empirical demonstration of behaviour change, most who have worked with role playing feel that it is a successful therapeutic process. Bonarius in an individual study of a special form of role play — fixed role therapy — makes quite incredible claims for its positive value over a very short period. Krietler and Krietler rated the behaviour of psychiatric patients in sociodramatic situations and compared with ordinary daily life behaviour. They found a high concordance between the two and suggest that this supplies important proof of the concurrent validity of psychodrama i.e. that psychodramatic behaviour reflects daily behaviour and does not depend on the quality of acting ability. Zadik in a limited study on my own out-patient psychodrama group, found that there was an increase in self-esteem at the end of twenty weeks' treatment. The individuals who showed the most change also showed increased introversion and indications that they became more aware of the ways the others perceived them in the group. Bandura's experiments into Modelling Theory offer much which is directly applicable to understanding what goes on in a psychodrama group. He and others have found considerable evidence that quite

complex behaviour can be learned vicariously by observing
other people's behaviour and its consequences for them.
Within a psychodrama group the models can be both the
therapist and his helpers as well as the other group members.
Group members do not necessarily have to be directly and
actively involved in order to derive benefit from the psychodrama. Caplan has discussed some of the problems of identification with bad models primarily in an uncontrolled ward
setting. The psychodrama group provides a reasonably
relaxed setting where different forms of behaviour and its
consequences can be observed by the non-active members
in a controlled way. The therapist has to always be conscious
of inappropriate behaviour being more attractive than
appropriate behaviour and hence more likely to be used as
the model. This can be particularly acute when looking at
authority problems e.g. a rather aggressive adolescent showing
the group how he was insolent to a policeman may have more
appeal to the adolescents innate ambivalence towards
authority figures than a role play involving respect for
authority figures. The therapist must also be aware of his
own adolescent needs as in such a situation he may indicate,
even if unconsciously, a certain admiration for the anti-
authority figure. Adolescents can be very acute in detecting
this. This raises the moral and philosophical question of what
sort of models the so-called 'healthy' therapist wants to
present to the adolescent. I feel it must be a genuinely felt
model for the therapist as adolescents are very quick to
detect a phoney. At the same time it points to one of the
advantages of working with a number of adults who feel
comfortable enough with each other to disagree publicly on
some of the models presented in the group. On the other
hand, the adults must not be seen to disagree so much that
the rest of the group sit back, partly enjoying seeing the
'parents' squabble while getting thoroughly confused.

   Adolescents are extremely demanding about the quality
of consistency of their adult models and have very critical
views on any deviation from an often puritanical norm.
Anyone who works with adolescents has to be very thick-
skinned because of the constant criticism of clothes, hair-
styles, and physical blemishes as well as personal behaviour.

Psychodrama with adolescents

Authors writing about their work with adolescents and child-ren, stress the advantage of psychodrama in two main areas, therapy and diagnosis (Lebovici, Drabkova & Sullivan). Diagnostically one can work in a fairly rigid framework using psychodrama as a form of projective test as described by Hass and Moreno. This is a 'sociodramatic technique which allows the observer to follow the role behaviour of individuals through a planned series of real life or life-like situations. In doing so he may interpret projections of his subject's role and inter-actional and spontaneity processes. The observer may also discover how and how well the individual is reading himself and others, who co-function as co-actors in his life situation.' For example, a scene may be set in which a boy is home late and his parents (played by two members of the group) are very anxious and angry. The boy walks in to be met by their recriminations. The way in which the individual playing the boy handles this situation can tell you much about his attitude towards his parents as well as the way he deals with aggression, both from a reality and fantasy level. Hass and Moreno describe nine test situations for this form of projective test, the majority of which require the individual to use imaginary persons or objects to relate to in some way. In my experience, it is better, when working with adolescents, to use real objects and persons, as imaginary ones usually lead to confusion and anxiety. Hass and Moreno see this form of action projective testing as having an advantage over the traditional projective tests such as the Rorschach, TAT and ORT where the individual is shown cards, because it allows the individual to relate within the social matrix in which he lives. The major problem, of course, is to achieve some form of standardization of the stimulus offered to each individual, which will allow more accurate analysis of the individual's responses. I have found it useful to use this form of action projective technique in conjunction with the Object Relations Technique (ORT) — (a traditional projective test where the individual tells a story suggested to him by the objects on the card) — which looks at one, two and three person situations as well as group relationships. I usually give the ORT to new admissions as an initial assessment which provides some suggestions about the way in which the individual relates to his environment. In later weeks, when he has settled into the psychodrama group, I will set up scenes similar to those in his initial ORT stories. Not only does this allow for a greater case study of his difficulties but also gives a chance to work through the problems therapeutically.

Of course within the loose structure of any session, a great deal can be learned about the group members' difficulties. The therapist's major difficulty is unravelling the enormous amount of material presented to him in each session. Ideally one would like to work with a battery of visual and auditory recording equipment for later analysis. Apart from the prohibitive costs for most institutions, I cannot see how this could be done without much disruption to the session. Although our analysis is very *ad hoc*, it circumvents the problem of the group feeling that they are guinea-pigs who are being spied upon.

Therapeutically psychodrama techniques are flexible enough to be adapted to most therapeutic stances. Lebovici, for example, works from a psychoanalytic stance with a large team of psychoanalysts. He suggests psychodrama in groups with adolescents with psychomotor disturbances and individual analytic psychodrama of brief duration with adolescents suffering from severe behaviour disturbances and psychotics. My own groups are orientated more towards an emphasis on roles within a group analytic structure and it is only rarely that I can see the benefit of individual psychodrama.

The Adolescent Unit where I work is in the grounds of Long Grove, a large psychiatric hospital near Epsom in Surrey. On average we have 25 patients, the majority in-patients. Most could be loosely diagnosed as behaviour disorders with problems ranging from delinquency to extreme social withdrawal. There are usually two or three adolescents with clear schizophrenia or borderline schizophrenic symptoms. The average length of stay is six months. Much of their day is spent in a well staffed school attached to the Unit. Apart from psychodrama the treatment consists of medication where necessary, individual supportive therapy, family therapy, traditional small groups, a weekly community group and the chance to make relationships with stable accepting adults, particularly the nursing and teaching staff. I see each aspect of this treatment plan linked together, each playing an important part in attempting to allow the adolescent to return to the outside community better able to cope. Because of their psychological difficulties, most adolescents entering the Unit have some educational difficulties which the teaching staff will concentrate on rectifying. All have family problems which we help to sort out directly through family groups or indirectly through therapeutic groups and individual contacts made with the staff acting as surrogate parental figures. Insights gained in therapy have to be tested within the smaller community of the Unit. It is important that all members of staff are kept informed of what has happened in any activities that they have not been able to attend (although as far as possible all of the staff are encouraged to attend and participate in all of the treatment activities available). A number of case conferences are held each week to give general feedbacks as well as review individual cases. Because of the range of treatment it is difficult to assess objectively the individual benefit of each aspect.

Psychodrama is held once a week for an hour during the school lunch break. It is a voluntary group and the adolescents are free to come and go whenever they please within a session. Between half to two-thirds of the Unit attend each session. The majority of the group form a stable core who come each week while the rest is more changeable and their attendance might even depend on the weather. I am helped by two members of the staff who attend each session and they are often supplemented by up to five visitors or more transitory members of the Unit team. I encourage visitors because the more adults attending, the more security the adolescents feel and they can provide a freshness in role play and the models presented. I of course insist that outsiders come as participants and not observers. We work in a small conference room which is very unsuitable but as Boring and Deabler describe, one can be very adaptable in psychodrama in an institution. We use no special props although bits and pieces in the room are readily requisitioned when necessary (ashtrays on stands have been used as microphones, clubs, or guns in various sessions). Although it would be very nice to have multi-coloured lighting like the psychodrama rooms illustrated in the textbooks, we make do with simple curtains which can be pulled to represent night or a mood.

Classically a psychodrama has three phases — a warm-up, the drama and finally a feedback discussion of the drama.

Warm up

Although I have found with adult groups various forms of movement, trust exercises, dance and non-verbal encounter type techniques are a good way of warming up a group, I have usually had dismal failures when I tried these on the usual large group of adolescents. They become very embarrassed, self-conscious and abusive and do their best to sabotage the exercise. I feel that, although I probably bear some of the responsibility for this failure because of poor technique, the basic problem is that disturbed adolescents are very wary of anything that can be looked upon as childish games because of their flimsy ego structure. I have found the most comfortable way of preparing the larger groups for what is to follow is to simply sit around in a conventional group way and wait for them to suggest what they want to do or demand that I suggest something. Usually the group takes about five minutes to form itself. During that time the visitors will be sized up, insults will be thrown at the regular staff, people in the group will be jumped upon and wrestled with. This, if you like, is a form of spontaneous warm up which is possible because of the security of knowing most of the people present. Adolescents new to the Unit will usually sit quietly for the first couple of sessions and I usually do not attempt to involve them directly until they indicate that they are ready by asking for a part or agreeing when a member of the group asks them. Once all the group is assembled, I then take direct control by asking them politely to shut up. This usually gets the group's attention but if there is a particularly over-active adolescent we may get the group to hold him down physically while he attempts to escape. This has the very practical purpose of wearing him out and also the therapeutic one of non-verbally

conveying security through the physical contact. If the
therapist knows the group well (and has handy adult helpers)
this act of physical contact and trust can be reinforced by
getting the group to hold the therapist down. Boys will often
respond to this form of aggressive contact, whereas an over-
active anxious girl will respond to more direct physical contact
like a hand on the shoulder from one of the adults. This
approach with boys would probably lead to accusation that
the therapist 'is a poof'.

A very small group of two or three adolescents and at
least four trusted adults can have more success with trust and
caring exercises. Recently, because of the Christmas break,
most of the adolescents returned home for several weeks, we
were left with three who were staying on the Unit because
they have no home to go to. They are obviously among the
more emotionally deprived, two having spent most of their
lives in various children's institutions. They asked for a group
and specifically requested certain trust and caring exercises
which I had tried to use on the larger group some months
previously without much success. We first worked on an
individual who lay on the ground face down and was then
made into a cake. The group gathered round and simulated
the ingredients falling on to him with their hands — the flour
falling lightly, the nuts somewhere heavier. When all the
ingredients had been included, they were mixed together and
pressed into shape. Not only did this exercise lead to a feeling
of wellbeing from the physical massage, it also allowed a
safe form of physical contact and caring. We then did a group
rock where each member of the group is in turn lifted by
the rest of the group and rocked. Usually there is a spontaneous
singing or humming to accompany this exercise. Finally half
the group sat on the floor in a relaxed position with their
eyes closed and they were joined by an anonymous partner
who supported their backs and gently manipulated their
heads and arms until they moved only under their partner's
control. When this was achieved their partner was led around
the room, still with their eyes closed, first by contact with
the body and later at arm's length. When they had been
returned comfortably to the floor, they had to guess who had
been in control of them. This was repeated with another

partner and then the manipulators became the manipulated. This exercise allows the individual to not only feel himself in a trusting and dependent position but also to take a turn as the person to be trusted and take on the dependent responsibility for another. This warm up can lead to a drama involving a theme of rejection and loss which becomes safe to do because non-verbally the feeling of trust and acceptance had been expressed in the warm up. The presence of five adults not only helped to provide the security to allow the session to happen in the first place but also helped to reinforce the feeling for these deprived adolescents that not all adults are rejecting. It also meant that the dependency feelings were shared around and not pushed towards a single adult which would be unfair to the participants.

The drama

In an established group the theme of the session will normally be suggested by the adolescents because they will be used to the general format and know what to expect. If I move in too quickly with a suggestion then one of the group who wants to suggest a theme may give up. Only rarely does a suggestion not come from the group and this is usually because there is a lot of anxiety about some trouble in the community, such as someone absconding. In these circumstances the group will come in a very dependent frame of mind and demand that the therapist suggest something, probably of an escapist nature. *No* attempt should ever be made to coerce an individual into dramatizing some personal aspect of his life. If a problem is brought up then I will use my clinical judgement to decide whether to invite the individual or individuals to dramatize it if they feel like it. For example, Ron, a boy of 14, with a long history of violence towards his peers, had attacked a new boy, Steve, the night before. Several of the group were complaining bitterly that he always thumped anyone new. Ron sat looking sheepish and protested that it was unjustified but when asked whether he would like to show us what happened he readily agreed. As the major participants were present they each played their own roles first. It emerged that Ron had hit Steve on a very flimsy pretext. Ron was asked to step out of the scene and one of the adults acting as an auxiliary ego played Ron in a re-enactment of the scene, while Ron observed. The auxiliary ego was then asked to show us what he would have done to handle the situation in a more suitable manner. Ron was then asked to ego one of the peripheral participants and say why Ron had to act so violently i.e. Ron placed his hand on the shoulder of the peripheral participator and thus taking over his role and spoke to the auxiliary ego playing Ron's role. In this role Ron was able to say to the auxiliary ego that he had to thump new boys to prove that he wasn't weak and therefore win their respect and friendship. The group and Ron were able to appreciate his feelings of insecurity in a new light. The rest of the group was spent in attempting to show Ron that his actions were self-defeating as they just lead to hatred and rejection. The more suitable role as protector to the new boys was looked at. This session seemed to have an effect as Ron's violent behaviour became less marked after this.

On occasions, individuals will bring problems directly to the group. Bill, a boy of 15 with a long history of petty antisocial acts, was unaware that many of the staff felt that he should be transferred to a more closed and controlled Unit. He said that he wanted to have a Court case session and quickly suggested that we could dramatize the last time he went to Court. As I sensed that he wanted to look closely into this event, I used adults only to play the various parts, while the adolescents sat back as observers. In an anxiety laden, very personal situation like this the adolescent members of the group will tend to protect themselves by not taking their roles seriously and the session will probably disintegrate. If it had been a sociodrama Court case — which adolescents love to do — then the parts would have been played primarily by the adolescents themselves. Bill first played the policeman who prosecuted the case. He was then asked to ego each of the roles, showing us what they said and he then egoed his mother to show us what she was thinking. When the magistrates came to consider their verdicts, I made all of the group into magistrates, including Bill, and the group were able to discuss quite openly what was best for Bill. The overall feeling was that Bill needed more supervision. Bill agreed with this, saying that if he was sent to a place like the Adolescent Unit they would not control him enough. Difficulties which emerged in the session about his poor family relationships were left to later sessions. His own demands for control came out in a way which would have been very difficult if tackled more directly through a conventional group. The other adolescents in the group were able to share their own problems of control.

Role playing may occur on a simple level where one of the group is applying for a job and will ask to rehearse this with other group members playing the roles of boss, secretary, etc. On a more complex level, opportunities for role play may emerge from general discussions heard around the Unit. Betty and Judy had been describing the childish behaviour of two of the boys on the train when they were returning home the previous weekend. It seemed clear that the boys were keen on the girls and simply trying to attract their attention. An attractive French male nurse who had joined the group as a visitor was invited to show the group how he would get into conversation with a girl he fancied. The boys were greatly impressed by his ability to attract the girls interest without making obscene remarks or jumping on the seats. This form of adult behaviour is normally learned by the adolescent from stable male models but most of the boys in the group lacked these models in their own home life. The group then role played various male-female encounters and ended with a general discussion of what each sex looked for in each other. Often in this sort of group sexual anxieties will emerge which can be handled within the context of the group. Psychiatric case conferences are a popular form of sociodrama and will usually be suggested by members of the group who know they will soon be the subject of a real case conference which will decide their future. It is an excellent way of showing the therapist how they see themselves in relationship to the institution and helps the individual to clarify his feelings about his progress and future. The adolescents will often express much anxiety about their status as patients in a mental hospital, particularly when every day they see chronic patients walking in the grounds.

They understandably fear that one day they will end up in
the same position. I usually try to arrange for the adolescents
to play the roles of the staff i.e. psychiatrists, psychologists,
nurses, social workers and teachers. This often leads to
hilarious and startling insight into the way in which they
see us. Other members of the group play the patients. It is
important that the individual adolescents who are played,
should be present in the group as the group will usually
suggest defensively someone who is not there. Apart from
being unfair this means that much of the value of the group
is lost. The most useful confrontations occur when one of
the adolescents playing a staff member confronts another
group member playing himself and offers advice on what he
should do to make progress. This represents a simple form of
'role reversal'. When I want to get over to the individual some
special insight into his behaviour, I will ask an adult member
of the group to role play that individual. Once the 'patient'
has been interviewed, the 'staff' group will have a general
discussion to decide what is wrong and what can be done
for the 'patient'. The group may decide to interview the
'patient's' family and they will then be chosen and brought
in. Twelve year old Graham, who was a very aggressive boy,
had come to the Unit because his parents could not cope
with him. He had physically attacked his parents on numerous
occasions. He played his father in an interview with the
'psychiatrist' and showed the father to be weak and ineffectual.
This situation was aggravated by the fact that Graham had
been adopted at the age of seven and was very anxious about
being sent away. The aggression was seen as a means of getting
over the suspense of waiting for the final rejection by provoking it. We knew that although the father was rather weak,
both he and his wife wanted Graham. Graham was asked to
play his ideal father and this time showed a strong controlling
father who ruled his family very strictly. In this session we
were able to reassure Graham that his family loved him and
would not reject him and to build on this information in
later psychodrama sessions as well as in family sessions. These
were eventually able to help Graham accept his family's need
for him and strengthen his father's role.

The theme of power and control is a recurring one in

adolescent psychodrama. Providing the therapist can maintain control and has the help of three or four adults, a very useful session can be one where an individual is allowed to play out his fantasies. Pam, a girl of 14 who, after the death of her mother seven years before, had lived in a children's home. She was admitted to our Unit after she had run away from the home in an attempt to encourage her alcoholic father to let her live with him. When he had rejected this idea, she became very depressed and spent several days waiting outside his pub. During earlier sessions we had helped her work through her feelings towards her mother's death, together with another girl whose mother had also died recently. I will touch on this aspect when I describe the sessions we had with Hazel. Pam's major defence mechanism against her anxiety of being rejected and her understandable uncertainty about the world, was to be very bossy and controlling. She was particularly controlling in one session, telling group members where they could sit and ordering weaker and unpopular members out of the session. I suggested to her that she could be a very powerful person and run her own drama. She decided to become Queen of the Skinheads (a rather delinquent adolescent cult current at the time). She organized the group into a marauding gang who went around the country, robbing and killing. The victims were usually the adult members of the group with myself selected for special attention. She managed to have me killed three times in the most gruesome ways possible (one being boiled in oil). I eventually formed a rival group to combat Pam's group and the drama finished with Pam and me locked in full scale physical combat. This seemed to serve as a form of abreaction with myself being placed in the role of her father and bearing the brunt of the anger that she felt for his rejection. I eventually won the conflict and Pam relaxed. I announced that the drama was over. Pam was asked by one of the group if she would really like to be very powerful and she answered that of course she wouldn't. In later weeks we were able to tackle more directly her need to control others.

I would not attempt this form of fantasy exercise until I knew the individual concerned very well and had an adequate number of co-therapists.

Feedback and sharing

I discovered early in my experience with adolescent psychodrama groups that the best way to clear them out quickly
was to have a formal analysis at the end of the group. Although
the adolescents know that the group is therapeutically orientated, they come voluntarily because they want to enjoy themselves. Any attempt to make it formal takes it away from the
play element. At the same time it is essential to find some
way of consolidating any important things that have emerged
in a group. I usually attempt to finish the drama aspect at
least ten minutes before the end of the session, sit down
and wait to see if the adolescents spontaneously make comments. It is only then that I feel that I can direct the discussion
towards looking at the group itself. I have shown in some of
the preceding examples how, in the circumstances, the
discussion can arise by turning the whole group into magistrates considering their verdict, or a clinical team looking
at the patient's progress. Gradually from this situation the
therapist can direct the group towards the pertinent issues.
I feel it is important not to stick rigidly to drama if a discussion
emerges very early in the group and seems to be the way the
adolescents want to tackle a problem. Talking is often a much
safer medium. On occasions I have cut off the drama myself
and reverted to a safer discussion situation because of the
anxiety which has been aroused in a session.

The descriptions I have given so far have been concerned
with events in single sessions. Like all group therapy, the
benefits evolve from week to week. An individual in a group
may have to place himself in a non-participating role for
many weeks before he is ready to become a protagonist. I
see the group members growing in emotional strengths and
maturity each week and psychodrama is an excellent way
of monitoring this growth as well as hopefully playing a
part in furthering it. Hazel is a good example to illustrate
this growth. She came to us two years ago at the age of 14.
Her African father had committed suicide several weeks after
her English mother had left him. Her mother completely
rejected Hazel and she has lived in Children's Homes and a
variety of foster homes since the age of three. Most of these
foster situations were very unsuitable and Hazel has always

been an aggressive unmanageable child. Eventually she grew into a strong adolescent who could no longer be contained by the foster organization and after attacking one of her custodians she was placed in an adult psychiatric hospital before coming to the adolescent unit. On admission she was surly and aggressive, particularly towards the female and black staff. Her speech was monosyllabic, consisting mainly of expletives. Her acts of aggression were impulsive and consisted mainly of sinking her teeth into the victims. She showed marked cognitive defects but there were indications on testing that she was potentially of at least average intelligence. She found it very difficult to leave the Unit, refusing to go on school trips. Her only contact with the outside world was her social worker. Hazel was an extreme example of a deprived girl fixated at Erikson's oral dependency stage and whose role confusion was aggravated by her colour. Her major defence against a hostile world was by oral and physical aggression of a very primitive kind. It was several months before Hazel ventured into psychodrama. For the first weeks she came mainly as a disruptor. She would wrestle and fight with the rest of the group and would alternate between sitting on me and thumping me. The only way I could contain her was to pin my arms around her, which made directing difficult, to say the least. She refused to join in and whenever I left her or the session produced anything vaguely threatening, she would walk out. She was of course an impossible girl to cope with in a conventional talking group. After several months, she was able to stay longer in the group and would return to the group for short periods when she did walk out. The breakthrough came when most of the group were away on a school trip and Hazel was one of three adolescents left. For the first time she participated in some individual role-play involving a possible career. Although only capable of maintaining it for several minutes, she showed a level of sophistication which we had not observed before anywhere on the Unit. Several weeks later she discovered the address of her mother and rang her, only to be rebuffed. This led to new acts of aggression around the Unit. In psychodrama she verbally attacked the social worker when he refused to take her to her mother so that she could 'cut her fucking throat'.

Fortuitously this session was one in a series in which Pam, who is described earlier, was working through the death of her mother. Hazel was not yet ready to play herself in a psychodrama of this emotional intensity, so Pam was asked to play Hazel meeting her mother after eleven years of separation. Pam, of course, put a greal deal of herself into this role. Hazel curled up beside me and watched. One of the female co-therapists played the mother. Pam at first said how much she had missed her mother, what she had been doing and what her future plans were. Then some of her pent-up anger for her mother's loss was expressed. This was the part which involved Hazel the most. A co-therapist took over the role of Hazel from Pam and asked the mother directly why she had left her. The mother replied that she had a new family now and it would be difficult to have Hazel living with her and that Hazel now had to grow up and have her own family. The selfish and rather sick elements of the mother's position were not emphasized at this time because Hazel did not have the resources to take them. The group ended with a discussion about Pam's mixed feelings of sorrow and anger about her mother's death and the inadvisability of Hazel seeking her mother out in reality. We knew from the social worker that the mother did not want to have anything to do with Hazel and that a confrontation would only lead to greater sorrow. Hazel had managed to stay the whole session for the first time and had shown an ability to face up to some very painful feelings. After this session, she no longer tried to contact her mother and in the following weeks became much less aggressive towards the female staff. In following sessions she was far less disruptive and took a great interest in sessions involving sexual roles. She had always dressed in male-type clothing, talked of growing a penis and marrying another girl. This did not indicate a real homosexual inclination but her marked sex role confusion. In recent weeks she has shown far greater independence from me in the group and an ability to allow others to be dependent upon her. In various sociodramas we have worked towards showing her a status as a 'normal' woman in the outside world. In the early days, after years of institutionalization and the way she was treated because of her violence, she had accepted the role of a 'mad' person who would spend the rest of her life in mental hospitals. Recently she has been able to play rejecting mothers in other group members' psychodrama. She has grown to understand that her mother is the one to be pitied and that her own 'sickness' led to her rejection of Hazel — not because Hazel was sick and bad. Hazel has still some way to go before she can fend for herself outside but I feel that we have all managed to patch up a very damaged girl reasonably well and have great hope for her future.

Perhaps the preceding description of my psychodrama sessions with its emphasis on the therapeutic benefits, has tended to neglect the enjoyment and aesthetic aspects of this form of group. I believe it is fundamentally a creative activity calling upon the resources of both the therapists and the adolescents. The therapist must be able to 'read' the needs of the group and help construct a scenario without the benefit of a script. Likewise, the adolescents must be able to improvise upon these often vague directions.

After three years experience I now feel much more relaxed in the group and can accept the occasional dismal failures which can occur in any group. There were many times in the early days when I pined for the relative peace and ease of a conventional sit-down group. Failures will occur, not only because of poor direction by the therapist, but often because of the anxieties related to problems within the whole community e.g. the impending departure of a popular member of staff. It is difficult for the inexperienced therapist not to take a mass departure by agitated adolescents in any way but a personal vote of no confidence. However it is very pleasing when the following week the numbers attending are larger than usual.

Because of the arduous nature of psychodrama, I limit the number of groups of this type and take regular breaks to rest and reassess.

Pleasing spin-offs can occur from groups of this sort e.g. after a sociodrama on the running of an adolescent unit, the group decided that they would like to put on a play for Christmas. I suggested that they improvise something similar in sociodrama. A rough script was constructed and rehearsed with new improvisations at least twenty times before the performance. All the directing, set construction etc. was done by the adolescents themselves. The end result was quite magnificent and better than any school drama I had ever seen by 'normal' adolescents.

It is important that staff attending groups should have ample opportunities for discussing what has gone on in a particular group and also for mutual support and criticism. After each session the staff have a feedback period in which we attempt to analyse what we have learned about each individual. This will then be fed back to others in the Unit team later. This information can then be used in later psychodrama sessions from a therapeutic viewpoint. It also allows one to monitor progress more systematically.

I have described the use of psychodrama very much from the point of view of adolescents with severe enough emotional difficulties to have been admitted to a psychiatric unit. I am lucky to have the support of a variety of professions, well trained in the management of these difficulties. There will probably be many reading this chapter who hopefully can see the value of all or some of these techniques in their own work but who do not have this same support. Often one of the biggest difficulties is the initial starting of the group. It is necessary to have the support of the other members of staff. In my own situation I got to know the most powerful adolescent in the Unit, aroused her interest and let her recruit the other members.

It should be stressed that any directly therapeutic psychodrama should not be attempted until the leader has not only been well trained in the techniques of psychodrama, but has also had some training in group therapy. Courses are now available in the UK particularly in the London area which will train a variety of caring/professions in psychodrama, sociodrama and role play. [Full details of available training courses appear in Appendix 2. Ed.]

However, some of the techniques of psychodrama can be used sensibly without more intensive knowledge of group dynamics. Forms of role play and sociodrama can be used effectively as part of a drama group where the emphasis is not directly on 'therapy'. Sue Jennings' useful book

Remedial Drama describes the experiential approach using many of these techniques.

I have often heard anxiety expressed about the 'awful damage' that can be caused both by psychodrama and other remedial uses of drama. I am not convinced that this is such a real danger as is made out. I have stressed the need for 'sensible' use of psychodrama, of being aware of the dynamics of the group before instigating action, and especially letting a group member attend for some time before ever touching on the personal problem areas. Furthermore as far as my own group is concerned, attendance is voluntary and the adolescents have the freedom of choice to participate or not. I keep interpretations to a minimum and emphasize the fun and play element as much as the therapeutic element.

Summary

In this chapter I have described the unique role that I feel psychodrama can play in the treatment of disturbed adolescents. Since the adolescent often has weak ego strength, the emphasis in treatment should not be on the externalization of unconscious conflicts but on the providing of 'healthy' models on which the client can test his own present behaviour and also test the various fantasy roles he may have. The providing of models for learning are central to my use of psychodrama.

In describing some of my own experiences I hope I have encouraged others to attempt this type of work, but as I have emphasized, they must take advantage of the available training. Furthermore, it is essential to have the support of a therapeutic team and to start the work gradually, since, despite its enjoyment, it can also be extremely demanding, both physically and emotionally.

Finally I wish to stress that an adolescent psychodrama group should be a pleasureable, creative learning experience with an emphasis on the drama as well as the psycho.

References

1. A. Bandura, *Principles of Behaviour Modification*, Holt, Reinhart & Winston 1971, New York & London.

2. A. Bandura, 'Modelling Approaches to Modification to Phobic Disorders', in Ciba Foundation, *The Role of Learning in Psychotherapy,* 1968.

3. W. R. Bion, *Experience in Groups,* Tavistock Publications 1968, London.

4. K. G. Boires, 'Role playing as a behaviour change techniques: Review of the empirical literature', *Psychotherapy: theory, research and practice* 9, 185, 1972.

5. J. C. J. Bonarius, 'Fixed Role Therapy: a double paradox', *Brit. J. Med. Psychol.* 43, 213, 1970.

6. R. O. Boring & H. L. Deabler, 'A Simplified Psychodramatic Approach in group therapy', *J. Clin. Psychol.* 7, 371, 1951.

7. L. M. Caplan, 'Identification: a complicating factor in the in-patient treatment of adolescent girls', *Amer. J. Orthopsychiat.* XXXIV, 720, 1966.

8. H. Drabkova, 'Experience resulting from clinical use of psychodrama with children', *Group Psychother.* XIX, 32, 1966.

9. E. H. Erikson, *Childhood and Society,* Penguin 1969, London.

10. J. Evans, Lecture at Institute of Group Analysis, London, 1972.

11. R. B. Hass & J. L. Moreno, 'Psychodrama: as a projective technique in H. H. Anderson & G. I. Anderson (eds.)' *Introduction to Projective Techniques,* Prentice-Hall 1951, New York & London.

12. M. Hersko, 'Group psychotherapy with delinquent adolescent girls', *Amer. J. Orthopsychiat.* XXXII, 169, 1962.

13. S. Jennings, *Remedial Drama,* Pitman 1973, London.

14. H. Kreitler & S. Kreitler, 'Validation of psychodramatic behaviour against behaviour in life', *Brit. J. Med. Psychol.* 41, 185, 1968.

15. S. Lebovici, 'Psychodrama as applied to adolescents,' *J. Child. Psycho/ Psychiat.* 1, 298, 1960.

16. B. W. MacLennan & N. Felsenfeld, *Group Counselling and Psychotherapy with Adolescents,* Columbia U.P. 1970, New York.

17. J. Mann 'Experimental evaluations of role playing', *Psychol. Bull.* LIII, 227, 1956.

18. R. E. Shuttleworth 'Psychodrama in the rehabilitation of chronic patients', *Self & Society* 1, 7, 1973.

—— 'Psychodrama in the clinical applications', paper read at National Conference on Psychodrama, London, available from author, 1973.

19. L. A. Sullivan, 'Psychodrama in a child guidance clinic', *Sociometry* 8, 296, 1945.

20. T. D. Zadik, 'Effects of feedback on self identity in group therapy', unpublished dissertation for B.P.S. Diploma in Clinical Psychology, 1973.

9

Creative social work?
ANNE BATE

In this chapter I wish to discuss the relationship between
creativity and social work and consider whether 'creative
social work' is a realizable concept. I shall begin by looking
at the traditional role of the social worker in relation to the
problems he has to face in contemporary society. Comment
is also necessary on the changes already beginning to happen
within social work, the rise of radicalism and self-help groups.
The bulk of the material is based on my eight years experience
working with 'problem families' in London and it is both
specific and subjective. I feel that it may be of value if I
share some of the doubts, feelings and questionings which
I experienced in relation to my work and personal philosophy
rather than attempt to write about an ideal model of the
role of the social worker. I shall emphasize the influence of
creativity in my development. I do not mean that I just
discovered that I was able to draw but by experimenting
with my 'creative self' through different means (drama,
dance, mime and art) I was able to get in touch with my
own creative areas and also the fears associated with them.
These experiments in expression increased my self-awareness
and self-confidence and the alternative means of communication encouraged personal and professional growth. I found
that I was sometimes able to use creative skills in the course
of my work but more often I was able to use the social
work skills that I had in a more creative way.
   The traditional stereotype of the social worker has been

that of a psychoanalytically oriented counsellor whose job
is to care for clients who have been referred as 'suitable
cases for treatment'. The model is of helper and helped.

The ideal aim of social work is a dynamic, creative interaction taking place between social worker and client. As
in many political and religious belief systems, the hope is that
man may have life, and that he may have it more abundantly.
The forces militating against this are formidable, including
the ambivalent and relatively powerless role of social work,
the conflicting values of society, lack of knowledge and
personal confusions of both social worker and client.

Where the social worker perceives deficiencies of mal-
functioning in the clients' attitudes or behaviour, he endeavours
to change this. Where he perceives deficiencies in the environment he endeavours to change these by manipulating resources
and opportunities in what he judges to be his clients' best
interests. The social worker goes about 'doing good' for the
chosen few which constitute his caseload. Although it may
seem straightforward, the actual process of becoming a
client is mysterious and rather arbitrary.

When visiting those defined as problem families, I soon
began to meet their friends and neighbours, and I found that
they often seemed as beset with serious problems as were
my own clients. I recall seeing a group of mums, among
them my 'problem mum', coming through the austere arch
of their council flats, early on a winter's evening, on their
way to work as night cleaners. Dusk and the yellow street
lighting made their faces look insubstantial, grinning jauntily,
yet incredibly weary, they were determined to 'get a bit
extra for the kids'. They looked as poignant as coal miners
preparing to descend into the darkness for their livelihood.

As well as the arbitrariness of the clients' role, the work
of the social worker and his 'load' is not as easily evaluated as,
for example, the manufacture of objects, or the curing of a
disease. It is possible for social workers to perceive of their
clients as dispossessed. Somehow through personal and
environmental losses, they are not fully experiencing the richness, bounty and beauty of the world. In a situation of
environmental rather than individual poverty, an individual
may be adjusted to an impoverished life; but when for various

reasons he becomes no longer 'able to cope', he is administered to or helped by, the welfare services. Due to lack of finance and other resources, these services are not as good as those that a wealthier person could purchase, when he finds himself 'unable to cope'.

People in general do not welcome dependence on 'the welfare', do not value the system and thus have little compunction about abusing it.

The street chant of the children 'we all live on the welfare' is both a recognition of their condition and a defiant stance in relation to it.

The social worker no longer has a clearly defined role in relation to poverty. Gone are the days described by Virginia Woolf quoted by Noel Timms when pioneer social workers, Canon and Mrs Barnett could validate their work with their own perceptions 'their tale is made to unfold into full blown success, like some profuse peony!' (N. Timms: *Language of Social Casework*, Routledge 1968, London.)

The recognition of poverty as a structural problem rather than a direct result of an individual's pathology has led to one of the present conflicts in social work. We have the clinic as opposed to the community, the professional case worker versus the community action worker. The 'professionals' press for the development and sophistication of casework skills; the 'radical trade unionists' perceive social work as the opiate of the masses and seek to develop a revolutionary consciousness both in themselves and their clients.

Pressure groups have arisen to make a claim for certain needs to be met regardless of the pathology of individuals. The groups have been formed both on behalf of certain disadvantaged people like the Child Poverty Action Group, or by the individuals themselves as in the Claimants Union. In the struggle for better conditions in work and domestic life, people are increasingly making their own demands without the use of a filter. They have discovered that power lies with the group. The social worker's focus on the individual can be his greatest strength and also his greatest weakness.

It is possible to perceive the clients of social workers as dispossessed. Somehow, through personal and environmental losses, they are not at the centre point of their existence fully

experiencing the richness, bounty and beauty of all the
promises of the natural world and of the people that inhabit
the Earth.

The social workers, too, can be perceived as having suffered
a dislocation. Increasingly, the alienation of social workers is
being expressed. Many are not at ease with prevailing norms
and values. They distrust the high value given to power, status
and wealth and the apparent necessity of obtaining these
in order to 'be someone' or to 'get anywhere'. Increasingly
there is a demand for the needs of the client to be placed at
the centre of the stage even if this leads to conflict with
the social workers' employing agency. Despite their distrust
of bureaucratic power and prevailing values, social workers
are a mainly middle-class semi-professional group. From a
position of relative powerlessness and ambivalence can they
really offer anything to the poor and dispossessed? The social
workers seeking radical change in the attitudes of society or
the redistribution of the bounty of its economy find themselves in a double bind. Without the moral purity of a St.
Francis can they criticise society, identify the economic
needs of the poor or identify with them in their poverty?

As a backcloth to the life and work of the social worker
there is the frightening possibility that human society is
destroying itself. Food and space are limited and exhaustible.
Crime and violence against property and the person increase
in what are termed the most advanced countries of the
world. It seems the ultimate in horror when old people,
women and children are abused, attacked and killed in
zones of both peace and war. Already we accept that men
are expected to play the brave soldier — in fact their
torture or death should be no less horrific. The activities
of society which can be most deadly to the body or spirit
— smoking, drugs, TV, drink or cars — seem to have come
to dominate the lives of the despairing citizens. It is grotesque
to think that as specialization has increased we now have
individuals and groups who are paid to care about the feelings
of other people. By placing the task of caring on to 'the
welfare' society can refuse to take responsibility for the
suffering of individuals and groups within it. Is it a solution,
as each new problem area is revealed, for the cry to go up

for more social workers to be trained to work from bigger, more complex and more powerful administrative centres? A friend of mine, now an ex-social worker, had a day-dream of social workers demonstrating their plight by walking to Trafalgar Square carrying crosses to represent the problems of society and on arrival making a massive bonfire of them.

Social workers seem to have become trapped by the concept of blame, either holding the poor responsible for their poverty or blaming the organization of society for all human suffering. They seek one cause of the problem, one reason and one solution. It does not seem to me to be helpful to seek to blame or to polarize one's perception in this way. There is a need for social reformers, revolutionaries and therapists. There are dangers in both under- and over- stressing the significance of a social worker's intervention in a family's situation. It is easy to smile at the image of the social worker immersed in thought of deeply meaningful interchanges with their client while the client is pre-occupied with the absence of money, rain pouring through the roof and rats gnawing at the floor-boards. It is also an illusion to think that the social worker can make 'good' all of life's tragedies. Death, disaster, and mental or physical illness do not avoid certain income groups or classes. In certain situations some form of personalized help seems to be needed before people can find themselves. Therapeutic intervention does not preclude the possibility of the client becoming a revolutionary. At times it seems that to enable someone to speak from the heart of himself is a revolutionary act. In the confusion of fantasy, politics, blind spots, double binds, prejudices and predilections, it is easy for the social worker to get lost. A colleague of mine would talk of the loneliness of the long distance caseworker. There are implicit ground rules for conduct in the client/social worker situation but in the reality of the work situation, who defines the dynamic?

My training seemed to suggest that I should define the rules of the game by a process of remoteness, detachment and containment. This was certainly not how I felt, and a lurking sense of failure accompanied me on my chosen work. In my first contacts with clients I found that once having intervened in a situation I was irretrievably involved and inescapably committed. I remember taking some photos of a problem family to a case conference as I felt this would contribute to my communication about this family and make the discussion more valid. I felt very daunted when my act was seen as 'a sign of touching but excessive involvement with a family'; and I was asked if I 'always carried photos around of my clients'!

Human need is at the same time simple and immensely complex. The definition of the needs which it would be appropriate for me to meet and finding effective means of meeting them proved a far harder task than I initially imagined during my basic training. Working as a social worker I became less sure of having the answers to problems and more aware of questions that needed to be asked about my basic assumptions.

I want to now look at the reality of 'problem families' and my largely intuitive way of dealing with myself and them in a work situation.

These families are often in a state of deep apathy, depression and despair with scanty furniture, broken windows and the power supply more often 'off' than 'on'. They seem to need an on-going affirmation of their being by the continuing attention of a representative of society. In relation to many of them, there is the feeling that whatever one did it would never be enough. Words are not enough. Gifts of time and money seem to disappear into a void. Attempts at giving (in different forms), are made again and again by the social worker, but somehow they are never completely received. In what way would it be possible to enable these families to have warmth and colour and light both within and around them?

When I was helping with an under fives' playgroup for deprived children I used to give the children raisins to eat in the beakers of a baby's building toy. One boy asked for more, saying 'give me plenty, plenty'. He was not a boy who was deprived of actual food by family circumstances but rather than, as I usually did, emphasize the need to share equally, I poured a cascade of raisins into the beaker until it was on the verge of brimming over. 'Cor!!' he said as we gazed at each other in amazement over this change in the normal order of things. The giving and receiving of plenty was a satisfying moment for both of us.

Another situation where a gift seemed to be received and to be followed by growth, occurred while I was working with a small group of delinquent boys. We used to end the sessions with a cup of tea and somehow there never seemed to be enough tea in the pot. Someone always got landed with a rotten, weak cup. One day I saw a gigantic, brown, enamel tea-pot in a shop and despite the cost — 70p — decided to buy it as a joke for the group. It was a great success as it provided a seemingly inexhaustible supply of good tea. The boys christened it 'The Tit-pot'. In planning the group, I thought that they would want to make trips out of the house and be quite active but in fact they seemed content to stay indoors. We made two trips out, one to the West End and one to Alexandra Palace, but they insisted on returning 'home' for tea. I felt like Wendy in *Peter Pan* with my little group of lost boys crammed into the warm, tiny kitchen grouped around the giant, brown tea-pot. We talked about jobs, ambitions, hopes, violence, love, money, drugs and sex. In spite of my 'little mother' role the boys were more concerned about their lack of strong, effective caring dads.

The Unit worked with deprived, poor families and the tradition had developed that its representatives were often givers of practical and financial aid. The giving or withholding of money, food or second-hand goods was a fundamental concern. Could the giving or withholding of a bowl of soup initiate or destroy the relationship between worker and client? At times the Unit seemed to be pre-occupied with food. The shared Unit lunch symbolized the cohesion and strength of the group. Endless discussions took place about what we should eat, should we eat at all if some of the families didn't have enough money to buy food? But then, what about the families who hardly seemed to be able to stop eating and drinking? Who should be invited to share our food? If some families were welcome at the meal table why not all? If we invited the families to share our food with us, what should we do if they invited us to share their food with them? Should we ever share food with them at all? The soup and bread assumed far greater significance than their inherent qualities and became a symbolic sacrament, a fantasy of the parable of the loaves and the fishes.

In working with deprived families we used words as symbols and also symbolic actions. At the time of the initial referral we were uninvited guests in their homes. We tried to move towards the families, to share their lives and experiences. They in turn moved towards us but, of course, we kept our front doors firmly closed.

It seems to me that the symbolic words and actions could be enlarged and built on with the use of drama techniques. One summer the borough had a festival which was opened by a procession of floats. I was a member of a local art group and we together made a dragon with a magnificent head, long undulating body and a slightly obscene tail trailing in the rear. A group of us gave this monster life by walking along inside it. I formed about the third hump on the dragon's back with my face framed in a hood. I felt tremendously liberated by being part of a dragon, dancing, singing and shouting through the streets. A complete contrast to my usual sober progress in my work role, feeling under-valued and unsure.

The watching crowds were appreciative, laughing and clap-ping at our disorganized progress, bobbing their heads to the dragon, laughing and talking to him. The smaller children were mystified — was the dragon real or an illusion? We passed one of my most disturbing families which consisted of an overweight, inactive mum, a manic, violent dad and four wildly confused children. Mum stood solidly by the road with the children clamped to her like barnacles as the dragon's head bowed towards them. I had never seen the chil-dren unanimously subdued by anything before. Mum let our a cheer, lumbered into the road and endeavoured to fling her arms round me. We were holding wire hoops below the billow-ing tent of the dragon's body so a beautiful muddle of hoop and dragon, social worker and client ensued. The head of the dragon strained to go forward as the body concertinaed to a halt and the tail bobbed more wildly and suggestively in the rear. This mum always reminded me of a large animal lower-ing and rumbling with discontent prior to a charge but never able to find a moment or relevant target for the attack. I do not understand why, but the embrace she gave me in the guise of a carnival dragon seemed of deep significance. Maybe such moments cannot be repeated or increased but my admittedly overactive imagination cannot forget the idea of social workers metamorphosing into actors. Do social workers need to formalize their role as actors? The role of social worker requires quite astonishing acting ability and performances. At times social workers seem to deny their own selves, even to themselves. Does the social worker always have to play the same role of strength and security, leaving the client with the somewhat feeble supporting role of weakness and vulnerability?

My support system in my work at the Unit included three clients, one of whom suffered from a crippling depression and was usually hunched morosely over some sort of electric fire which we both knew was running up an enormous bill when I called. Cups were always being broken in this house, spoons and tea-leaves trapped down the sink or lavatory, causing dramatic overflows. I don't think there was always a tea-pot but she made the best cups of tea I have ever tasted. The tea seemed to have some sort of restorative quality to it. Often we would spend the time in silence while she made the tea and we drank it but afterwards we could begin to look at the gigantic problems of a divorced woman suffering with depression bringing up six children and dependent on supplementary benefit. It was difficult to trace where the depression had first arisen. Was it a reaction to her present circumstances or a legacy from the past? Her childhood had been bleak, with a caring dad but a mentally ill mum who used to tell her to get out of the home because she was afraid that she might kill her with a hammer. She married at sixteen, suffered a miscarriage — twins — and then lost her parents in a fire at their home. After this trauma she became increasingly burdened with babies, a disintegrating marriage and a husband who became mentally disturbed, violent towards both her and himself.

Another lady who had lost a leg in a playground accident as a child and had a violent, bitter childhood also was able to give support and strength to others with the warmth of a blazing fire, sparkling clean home and quick snacks. Despite this quality she could never be satisfied with herself, never feel that there was enough. She was always engaged in com-

plicated financial transactions, many of a very suspect nature which were to improve the family income but most of which ended in disaster. I seemed to make little headway in solving the riddle of the charm that held her trapped.

The third lady weighed over twenty stone and seemed to have eaten so much to provide a self-protective insulation from the world. She was seen by many as lazy, dirty and even downright wicked. I felt this at times myself but also drew strength from the quality she possessed of transmitting a warm calmness and the feeling that the world could be a good place. Was she the archetypal mad witch or the archetypal mother goddess? Her 'bad' aspects caused her to be rejected by most people and cut her and her family off from even the caring agencies in society. It took four years of patient work for her to change a little and become more acceptable and for schools, doctors etc. to change a little and become more accepting. We had some good laughs during the process and many tears. Fortunately the idea of clients having strengths is now becoming accepted and formalized in their employment by social work agencies.

Let us return to the dragon and the idea of social workers as actors. The children involved in the dragon encounter, whenever taken to the theatre or circus, spent most of the time trying to get on to the stage or into the ring. In everyday life they seemed to be bursting with good and bad humours and were quite capable of literally laying a trail of banana skins to trip up their trusting social worker. The youngest boy reminded me of Harpo Marx and could be amusing as long as it wasn't your chair seat that was spread with treacle! I felt like murdering the eldest boy one hot day when I had been stuck with all four of them in and around my mini-van waiting for mum to emerge from the social security office. Dad had temporarily deserted the family and mum was seeking financial assistance. This transaction took much longer than expected and I had collected the children from school. I was rapidly losing patience and the final straw came when the boy somehow climbed through the window of the van and zig-zagged out into the heavy traffic of the Euston Road. I pursued him, picked him up and flung him into the back of the van screaming that they were pigs and I hated all of

them. As his head whizzed past the metal of the van a ghastly
newspaper headline flashed into my mind — 'Social worker
kills child in Euston Road!'

These children were fascinated by witches and monsters
and liked acting out little plays which they made up. The
plays usually showed the terrifying power of a witch or monster but its ultimate subjugation by the forces of good. The
under-five play group was fascinated by a similar theme —
fear and the need to attack and destroy potentially evil monsters. All of the children could easily perceive the monster as
real and not just as someone with a cardboard box stuck
over their head. This dramatic expression of violent and powerful emotion did not lead to the situation getting out of
control or becoming destructive as one might fear. It allowed
for a necessary but controlled expression of alarming emotion
— behind a mask or within the role of monster the interaction
became intense and creative.

Perhaps a travelling social-workers' circus or mummers
group could be arranged to revive a form of drama and enliven
a semi-profession. It would give adults and children, social
workers and clients the chance to tangle with animals, throw
themselves around physically, dance, sing, wear fantastic
clothes and throw custard pies at each other. Why not let
the dreams become a reality — a *Midsummer Night's Dream*,
a play of a play within a dream. I suppose a lot of social
workers wouldn't really like the idea. I remember my own
disappointment at how frightened I became in drama sessions
at what lay behind my own persona. How frustrated I was
by my meagre creativity in trying to form dramatic situations
for children. How bitterly disappointed I was by not being
able to sing in tune, dance and act *in a less* restricted way.

The opening of the Remedial Drama Centre in Islington
in 1970 gave form to my fantasies. The centre seemed to me
to have a magical quality, to hold the key to some of the
charms, the solutions to some riddles. The drama sessions
it provided for children were an obvious and immediate
success enabling them to express their feelings with ease. The
group of children which I took on my first visit acted out
an improvised play involving a king, some loyal, and some
wickedly disloyal, citizens. At one point, the 'baddies' were

brought before the king for judgment and punishment. The eight-year-old king slumped regally in the massive wooden chair which was his throne: 'The sentence is to go to a children's home for nine years'. I thought at first that he said 'to go to some sort of hole' for nine years, I had not realized before how he felt about children's homes. He had already experienced 'being in care' and it seemed harsh of fate to consign him a few months later to a children's home yet again.

This reception into care followed a court case in which his parents were charged with wilful neglect, having left their six children in the charge of a fourteen-year-old boy. One of the children had gone out and been given drink by people sitting outside the local pub. He had become drunk, which attracted the attention of a passer-by who alerted the police. The police visited the home which was dark, disorganized and in the care of a fourteen-year-old. The children were removed to a place of safety and subsequently brought before the Juvenile Court as being in need of care and protection. The parents received a conditional discharge and a care order was made in respect of the children. The family were living in sub-standard council housing at the time which was in poor condition and due for demolition. Some of the evidence brought against the family focussed on the state of the house, a gaping hole in the floor of one bedroom where the ceiling below had collapsed; an overflowing outside toilet. I and the family had been trying to get repairs done by the council for weeks beforehand. It was obvious that the family were in urgent need of re-housing and the children were placed in homes and foster care for months until the housing department was able to allocate them a house in a clearance area due for demolition. Symbolic of its state was the fact that it was lit by gas and all the fittings were broken. We could not get this lighting system to function and eventually the Unit installed electric lighting. Stalwart male workers from the Unit also cleared mountains of rubbish and filth from the house.

The marriage was breaking up in this family, the home was poor and disorganized and there were a few skeletons in the cupboard but it was difficult to begin work at 'family dynamics' when the housing and financial conditions were so appalling.

The family were finally allocated a permanent tenancy. It was another old house, but it was newly decorated and renovated. For the first time in their twelve years as a family they had an inside toilet, a hot water system and a bathroom. Such vulnerable families are in particular need of a secure base with quick, efficient and genuinely caring supportive services around them. Some sort of crisis was perhaps inevitable for this family but did the children have to be separated by considerable distance and considerable time both from each other and from their parents, waiting with increasing distress for the reconciliation in a new home?

During this time I tried to keep the children's contact with the Drama Centre as constant as possible and at the same time began to explore my own creative ideas in drama and dance. Participating as a helper led me to realize that many of my social work responses had become stereotyped and static. Encapsulated in my car, I was using my ears, brain and behind as the tools of my trade. I became both more, and less, at ease with myself and my clients as I became aware of the lack of creativity in my life and work. Although taking part in the drama and dance and using them for my own discovery, I felt less able at first to use this approach in my work. However, in time, I found myself spontaneously integrating role play or other skills when the situation needed it. I began to value the significance of art and decided to develop my own skills in drawing. I realized that social work had stood in opposition to the development of personal creativity, because of its physical, emotional and intellectual demands.

After joining a local art group, I decided to work only four days a week and to spend more time developing my art. It was with great satisfaction that I was later able to stage a small exhibition and do some illustrating work.

I consider myself lucky to have been able to find myself in this way. I often felt that 'deprived families' in their bleak environments were living in a kind of frozen hell with little opportunity for escape.

A family on my caseload which had been charged with neglect of their children, who were far below average in weight and height, asked if the wife could be given elementary cooking lessons. As the handling, giving and sharing of food

seemed such a basic and major problem in this family it was
agreed that I should perform this task. The family were living
in sub-standard property and, following the court case when
the bad state of the home had been revealed, extensive
repairs were underway. The boards in the hall were pulled
up and the cupboard under the stairs full of water. Having
passed this hazard I entered the kitchen which was freezing
cold as the roof of the lavatory which led from it had caved
in and the builders were slow to repair it. Due to the bitter
cold both the mother and I kept our coats on and as there
were no chairs we stood around awkwardly while the food
cooked. Mum talked a lot about poison during our endeavours
and this, combined with the fact that she could cook quite
well, led me to think that the coffee she gave me might
possibly contain poison and that it was all part of some
bizarre plot to lure me to the house. I quite often used to
experience feelings of ill-defined fear and being trapped
when visiting families. In some instances it could be based
on the slight but real fear of physical or sexual violence,
but usually it was a feeling of being trapped and a danger
of being consumed. To make an obvious analogy it was
like a fly trapped in a web and paralysed by the spider.

I can feel my self-protective defences revving up for action
now and saying, 'don't tell them this, they will think you are
a fool lacking in casework skills and knowledge, and probably
inadequately supervised by your agency'. However, I think
that it is important to talk about personal and professional
weaknesses and inadequacies as these play a vital part in
the effectiveness and creativity of social work. The dynamic
between social worker and client is the traditional basis of
the helping process. How can this be most creative and productive for both concerned? A lot seems to be said about the
client's role in the social work situation, what is thought to
happen to him during the casework process, but what about
the social worker's feelings? Much of social work involves
crisis intervention when the whole being of the social worker
is called to pay attention. The social worker has an ideal of
professional control and restraint and tries to present a calm
professional persona at all times. Whatever happens in reality
there is an ideal model of the social worker able to handle

any situation, cope with anything, understand everything. What in fact happens to the social workers' feelings about the immediate situation they may find themselves in? What happens to their anger, their depression or despair, momentary fantasies which barely can be translated into words but seem of vital and intense significance? In the course of a day the social worker may pass through a myriad of whirlwinds. The harsh environment of poverty enters the soul of the social worker as well as the client. Where is the beginning and where the end? If each encounter is to be a creative act the strength of the social worker needs to be considerable. The social worker is often expected to cope with family and community dynamics single-handed. It seems to be a David and Goliath, Augean Stable situation. Society is asking its representatives to keep their clients in order, to make them good mothers and fathers and well-behaved happy children. The clients are asking the representatives of society to give them a home, health, money, love.

The trend at the moment is for one worker to be assigned to work with a problem family so that visiting is not unnecessarily duplicated. The reduction in the number of callers from 'the welfare' and the appointment of one worker to be responsible for the family seems a good idea, but I feel that it leaves the worker with a near impossible task. Also the worker and client in this one-to-one situation have a vested interest in avoiding the open expression of conflict and drama inherent in the situation. The active involvement of another worker either from the same or a different agency facilitates creative interaction. Different workers represent different facets of life, policeman and local authority workers represent the limits of acceptable behaviour while Family Service Unit workers are more indulgent and permissive figures. The intervention of an authority figure before a crisis rather than after it could be a great help in preventive work. I found it most helpful to have the support of a male social worker from the social service department in working with an aggressive, demanding family. The family flourished while he and I argued and quarrelled on behalf of the couple — he taking the part of the wife and me identifying with the husband. A shared, active involvement with the family even if only manifest in wrangles on the telephone seems to lead to a more dynamic situation where the possibilities for action and inter-action are much greater. The involvement of more than one worker from the same agency, particularly a male and female worker, seems to lighten and enliven the situation and bring more resources to it. I felt able to be the caring, supportive mum sorting our quarrels but did not feel that I was much good at setting limits, exercising control or the imaginative use of the provision of material aid. A solution seemed to be to work with someone who could provide at least some of the qualities which I lacked.

The presentation of case material often seems to lack life and to be removed from the actual experience of both client and social worker. Perhaps a solution could be the acting out of the situation of the family with their attendant chorus of social workers, housing department officials, doctor, teachers, neighbours, health visitor, psychiatrist, police or probation officer. This enactment could enable some of the myths and stereotypes in the network of interaction to be explored. It is surprising, for example, that social workers will defend their particular clients from all criticism yet bitterly attack other workers' clients or representatives of other agencies. The swopping of roles and the use of masks could lessen the barriers between the protagonists, clear up some misunderstandings, clarify and illuminate perception. Police-men, teachers, doctors and psychiatrists are the rather awe-inspiring guardians of authority, law, knowledge and wisdom. What would the social workers' role be in this scenario; minor god, magician, con-man scapegoat, angel or clown?

Civilized man with his improved health, housing, systems of transport and food seems to have lost the beauty of feeling within himself, the movement of the dance, rhythm, music or adornment with mud, paint and feathers. Maybe this lost world is an illusion of vitality but it always seems to have a deep power when viewed by the twentieth century voyeur. Drama can be seen as a rather self-indulgent form of exhibi-tionism, not what social work is *really* all about. Is it unnatural to want to disrupt an apparently meaningless process of existence, to attract attention, to give voice to the silent scream which gnaws at so many of our throats?

The role and training of the creative therapist: some reflections

JILL SAVAGE

Introduction

A training programme needs to be clear about what it is training its trainees to do. Trainees need to make statements about their aims and purposes. Too often, particularly in creative therapy or in the aesthetic subjects in education, too much training has been given in the practical aspects of the subjects, leaving the trainee with an impoverished ability to conceptualize about the work he is involved in. At the same time too much didactic training supplies information to passive trainees who never need to learn how to initiate thought and develop ideas. In this chapter I am not aiming at offering a didactic lecture on creative therapy training programmes. (The reader who wants facts can refer to the editor's appendix.) Instead, I am inviting the reader to form an alliance with me while we engage in a creative process of exploring the role of the creative therapist, using words and photographs as the media for communication. From an understanding of the role, we can imagine the training needs and the learning opportunities relevant to these needs.

Trainees need to be offered an educational growth process in personal relationships with their teachers and therapists. In this, they may experience creative therapy as an integrated approach to the human condition, involving intellectual learning, emotional and bodily experience coming together at a creative centre. This learning experience is the model for their future work, where they attempt to offer involve-

ment in the same creative exploration to others whether in
clinic, community centre or school.

To understand the continuing training needs of a particular
creative therapist, we need to understand the work that therapist will be required to do. We need to know what resources
and skills the person brings with him, and in which future
contexts his work will take place. The creative therapist
needs to learn how to develop his personal, creative resources
for the growth of the client and the collaborative endeavour
of the therapeutic team.

Creative therapy is an umbrella term. It implies the integration of experience of the creative processes in a range of arts
and human relations specialties. It includes such different
therapeutic endeavours as individual psychotherapy, music
therapy, art therapy and community drama therapy. A
professional trained in any of these areas may begin to think
of his work in the wider context of creative therapy. This
happens when his concern is not with the narrow basic approach
for which he has already been trained, but with his contribution to its development. Towards this aim, the therapist de-
rives inspiration from the enlightenment after the shared
creative confusion he experiences with each client. Equally
his creative approach to his own work is enhanced by a sharing of such experiences with creative therapists from other
backgrounds. This is not to say that an art therapist needs to
become skilled in dramatherapy to qualify for the title
'creative therapist'. Multi-disciplinary collaboration among
the disciplines gives the opportunity for wider sharing of
the creative processes of therapeutic work. As boundaries
clarify, shift or dissipate between the disciplines (analogous
to the blurring of familiar internal boundaries when the
creative person explores his unconscious), new relationships
and insights can be established.

The sociological perspective

Creative therapy is primarily concerned with the growth and
development of human beings. Unfortunately the term therapy
has had a medical connotation and there is an assumption
that therapy is treatment which is designed to remove symp-

toms of distress. Therapy goes beyond an attempt to make an impact on a symptom. And similarly, creative therapy goes beyond attending to those distressed people who are the symptoms of our distressed society. It is concerned with wider issues of relationships, conflicts, communication problems, and the dynamics of groups in communities.

In our society, which has valued independence, control and self-sufficiency during its technological phase, it has been relatively unusual to find people who are interested in exploring with others their relationships and experiences because of a fear of exposing personal areas which will be judged to be weak. Only in extreme distress would an individual open himself to the understanding of another. That is why the knowledge that we have about a person's inner world has been derived from work with patients who have been driven by their distress to reveal their experiences and their inner relationships in order to get help for their problems in relating to people or for their neurotic symptoms which are a signal of their distress.

During the technologically preoccupied phase of the industrial society there was no way in for creative therapy in this wider context. Now, however, there are signs that this is changing. The encounter movement in America reveals that people are becoming more preoccupied with the emotional, spontaneous parts of themselves and others, and of course the changing pattern of migration within and between countries has confronted people with the problems of engaging in relationships and separating from them. This encounter movement is spreading now in Britain, too, and its flourishing is not only a comment on the changes in society and its attitude to the personal aspects of living but also a reflection upon the failures of the educational system. People now are looking for ways of developing their potential as human beings that were not afforded during their striving for academic success at school.

Who becomes a creative therapist?

It is very rare for young people to mention any of the creative therapies as a primary career choice. Indeed even if they do

there is no training course which would train them from
start to finish. Perhaps the career choice closest to creative
therapy is that of occupational therapy where a young person
can enter college straight away and study for three years to
work as an occupational therapist. There are some similarities
in the role of occupational therapist and that of the creative
therapist, in that the occupational therapist learns to use a
variety of media for communication with and education of
patients. There is a heavy emphasis, however, on aspects of
rehabilitation of the physically ill, necessitating the understanding of physiological processes and anatomical structure.
Such knowledge is redundant to the needs of the creative
therapist in most of his work situations. Once qualified,
however, the occupational therapist may elect to work in
psychiatric wards of a clinic or mental hospital and by
apprenticeship learn about psychodynamics and the phenomena of group process. He becomes involved in understanding problems with relationships and in learning how to respond
to difficult behaviour. As that occupational therapist moves
away from the traditional old-fashioned occupational therapy,
keeping the patients physically active and occupied by making
baskets or soft toys, or something equally belittling, he finds
himself working in ways which really know no difference
from those of the creative therapist. He will, for instance, use
creative stimuli like Rorschach blots on to which patients
project their own perceptions and phantasies. The sharing of
these phantasies can then be discussed in the group situation.
He will find that the theme that emerges in the discussion
relates to themes discussed in other situations in the ward
where the patients belong during their stay in hospital. He
will learn to use examples from the occupational therapy
session as indications or even evidence for interpretations
which are made during verbal group therapy in the ward.

Other mental health professionals, hearing such feed-back
during the ward group, become interested in the value of
creativity in therapy. Those who may have had an individual
interest in an individual art are keen to integrate this aspect
of their personality with their professional skills. For instance,
a professional social worker whose painting competence has
been recognized by the Royal Scottish Academy was asked

to teach art to an evening class of prisoners. She soon found that her social work training enabled her to discuss the personal problems that arose in the prisoners' paintings and during their conversations with her as they came to know her. A psychiatric nurse who had enjoyed movement classes at school was interested in offering patients the kind of experience which had left her with a personal grace which was clearly an expression of but also an influence upon her personality. Her fluidity enabled her to tolerate the difficulties of long-term day patients and to represent for them a model of flexibility and harmony.

My own position is that I was trained as a community psychiatrist, working with individuals, families and groups of patients, and also with groups and communities. And I had a lively interest in the arts that was split off from my professional life. When I was at school good movement teaching allowed me to experience at a very early age the relatedness of mind and body and helped me to know how movements reflected inner feelings. At a later stage in my schooling a very sensitive English teacher taught Shakespeare by having the class enact scenes from the plays. The ensuing discussion had to do with the motivation of the characters involved and how this related to their personality structure and their background. In extra-mural drama lessons I became interested in exploring relationships by enacting the roles that the theatre used to represent these characters. Although I did not realize it at the time, I can see now how this had to do with the enactment of adolescent conflict, facilitating a working-through of aggressive and loving wishes without these having to be acted out in reality. Thus my motivation for an interest in creative therapy has to do with bringing together the parts of myself now located in the trained psychiatrist and the dramatist in me so as to provide situations for staff and patients where they can bring together in drama the different parts of themselves. It was from this base that I became interested in the potential of other art forms as well.

This divergence from a particular art form is commonly found among arts specialists too. A drama teacher, for instance, who uses music to create a mood for a particular play soon

discovers that there is value in the playing of the music
itself and that people can respond to it and improvise in
response to the feelings and images which it has stimulated
in them in the class. Similarly, an art teacher may find it
interesting to notice how painting style may be influenced
by different music playing in the background. Some potential therapists, trained primarily in a single art form, may
not have in mind to widen the range of media that they can
use; they may be interested only in translating their work
from the teaching situation into a therapeutic situation.
The motivation for this can arise from an experience of
tutoring some difficult children or working in an approved
school (community home) where emotional problems
intrude upon the teaching situation and require alternative
techniques than the standard classroom teaching methods.
They find they want to learn more about human relationships than has been afforded during the training college
period.

The creative therapist may come from any of the backgrounds
that have been described. He widens his role to that of the
creative therapist by gaining experience in the other areas.
For instance, the drama teacher may work as a volunteer in
a mental hospital; the art teacher may collaborate in a project with the drama teacher at the same school. There is
definitely an impression, however, that those who are wanting
to widen their horizons and extend their capabilities have
had to scratch around to find ways of doing so. Only in the
last few years have training courses in one or two of the
creative therapies and skill sharing creative therapy workshop
centres been established.

Where does the creative therapist work?

Creative therapy has a wide remit. The creative therapist
deals with individuals, groups, families, and communities.
The training has to prepare the creative therapist for this
wide range of context.

Some creative therapists will be involved with people
who come to them because of stress symptoms. Here I am
thinking not only of those who come at a time of breakdown

in their mental health, but also those who come as a result
of social breakdown. Within these two groups is encompassed
a rich and varied spectrum of human problems with special
needs of therapy, and knowledge specific to these different
areas has to be imparted during the training.

The creative therapist working in a psychiatric clinic needs
to know more about psychopathology and how to use his
own personality in a therapeutic relationship with patients
who have personality and mood problems. This knowledge
is gained only minimally from lectures or books. It grows
with experience and time spent in seminar discussion about
the problems encountered on the job.

The task is approached variously through verbal intervention and discussion techniques and arts media for communication. The arts media may be used in a number of ways.

Example 1. The therapist may elect to paint alongside a
person who has difficulty in communicating. As the
therapist carries out the same painting activity as the
person, a message of willingness to be part of that person's
experience is communicated non-verbally. As the shared
activity allows personal trust to develop, the client may
become able to talk to the therapist in personal terms
about his loneliness and difficulty feeling in touch with
people. Here the art of painting has had an initiating role
in the establishment of the relationship. In a different way
the patient or client might use the situation to express
some unspoken feeling in his paint-work, by painting a man
in a grey box, with shadowy coloured blobs around it.
Then the creative therapist has to read the unspoken
message in the symbols, colours and style of the painting.
He might respond with no more than a comment about
the greyness that was cut off from the colour to show
that he had appreciated what was in the painting. This
would give the client enough confidence in the therapist's
ability to be in touch, so that he might then respond with
more material in the paintings or with more verbal material.

At a different stage in the relationship, the therapist
could offer an interpretation of the art in the light of his
knowledge of the patient and his own feeling-response to

that person and his artistic work. For instance, he might
want to say that he felt that the man had been so envious
of the colour and spontaneity in his parents who had each
other that he had to shut himself away in a box to prevent
him from attacking them. By investing them with all the
enviable qualities he divested himself of interest and felt
grey and empty, a feeling which led him into the grey of
sadness and depression about the loss of the good,
colourful parents of his infancy who felt out of reach and
pushed away by his envious attack and withdrawal. One
cannot read such interpretations into any material, although
books have been based on such speculation, but one needs
to link the visual representations with the personal knowledge of the client.

Example 2. One may learn from the patient how the
present problem feels to him in an experience of its current
state, shared in discussion or role play. Then the patient
can associate the 'here and now' problem, perhaps feelings
of rivalry towards a younger patient of the same sex, to
an earlier trauma of wanting to outshine the wonderful,
attractive new baby sister and replace her in the parents'
affection. This can be re-enacted and worked through
and different alternative behaviours tried out.

The therapist has to learn by the examination and tolerance
of his own areas of conflict to be available to experience and
to respond to the patient's conflict. This flexibility of the
self is learned during supervised work with patients, in training groups for staff, and in personal therapy. The stresses of
work with patients tend to make personal therapy more of
a need for creative therapists in this field than for those
working with the less disturbed, although all creative therapists need to work towards their own growth if they are to
allow growth in their clients.

The therapist working in hospital has to understand something of the sociological dynamics of the hospital institution
from books on asylums, therapeutic communities and organizations. He has to be helped to clarify and define his role and
to understand its relation to other roles in the institution.
He needs to understand enough about patient care to be

able to communicate with the other professionals who are part of the ward team and he needs to know how to be a member of a team rather than an autocratic, independent therapist. During the training period, meeting with a variety of professionals in group situations offers the opportunity to understand attitudes and to find common ground. The understanding of the roles and attitudes of other professionals is fundamental to understanding the dynamics of the institution and the obstacles to change, which is also fundamental preparation for multi-disciplinary team work.

The creative therapist may work in a social centre where people during social breakdown may be helped by attending groups. The socially isolated adult can find something to share and can learn to communicate by going back to primitive beginnings, sharing in ritual and sounds or painting signs and symbols, until he feels safe enough to communicate in the verbal sense. Work with arts media is very effective with groups of immigrant and indigent children since it gives them the opportunity of building an understanding of each other unhampered by language difficulties at an age before prejudice interferes. The creative therapist will not necessarily set up a group deliberately, but may rather join a group that has arisen spontaneously as a community support group. These community support groups are emerging as antidotes to the feelings of isolation created by the previously described patterns of our changing society. Professionals need to give these groups every encouragement because of their value in maintaining community mental health.

The worker in the community has to know something of the life of that community. He also has to understand the phenomena of social breakdown and to bear in mind the wider issues of poverty and ignorance while dealing with the superficial symptomatic problems such as violent youths, or unemployed men, in his group. Thus, knowledge of sociology and techniques of social intervention and political action should be included in the training period. Some experience of this community work allows the creative therapist, who is mainly concerned with individuals, to see his work in perspective. Creative therapy in the community includes such

projects as theatre and arts in education programmes, planning
for parenthood groups, retirement and leisure preparation
groups.

   Example 3. As a community psychiatrist I had the
   opportunity to work as a consultant to a community
   group. This group was organized to promote creative
   opportunities for people living in their community which
   was culturally and socially rather deprived. They began
   by arranging violin lessons and had no thought of the
   creative therapeutic potential of this move. While
   mothers were getting together to arrange such violin
   lessons they began to feel they would like something for
   themselves too and arranged to have some drama lessons.
   Out of this grew a wish to put on a community drama.
   While they were developing the necessary dramatic skills
   their general communication was improving and a group
   spirit was growing, as was a social awareness of the needs
   that they shared and which were being frustrated
   by their life in this deprived community. At the same
   time their experiences in putting on the community
   drama gave them administrative expertise and management
   ability which means that they were in a very good position
   to make effective protest about the conditions of which
   they were now aware. So the coming together of the group
   which arose out of creative activity led to social and
   political activity. The community has named this cultural
   action.

   In schools now, there is a more creative approach to education with less tendency to think of creativity only as what
happens over in the art room. For fuller participation in the
creative process, teachers need a greater awareness of the
unconscious forces operating in the individual, in the classroom and in the whole school. With greater acceptance
and understanding of these, there can be less suppression
and censorship of unconscious impulse and thought so that
its creativity is available for learning and development.
Examination pressure is a ready constraint against this kind
of involvement. Education at its best, however, is concerned
not just with the intellect but with the growth of the whole

person. This approach can be learnt in the college of education and maintained by in-service seminars for teachers and counsellors given by educators and mental health personnel.

Attitudes concerning creative therapy

Not everyone thinks of creative therapy in an interpretive dynamic mode. There are those who view creative therapy in the light of the previously known recreational therapies. Their views are based on the idea that 'getting away from it all helps' or 'a bit of exercise is good for everyone', or 'everyone should have a hobby'. While one may recognize that diversion and amusement are important in everyday life, one is soon aware that it is only a short step across the boundary from where useful momentary diversion allows concentration and work to be resumed to the point where diversion is obviously an escape from painful reality of present situations. This is the point where 'distraction is a distraction from distraction'. I may say that this quote refers not only to the clients but also to the staff who have the task of facing the painful situation with the client. The creative therapist may find himself expected to work in this limited way. His training has to support him to understand the resistant attitudes to his involvement in a creative therapeutic process. People are afraid of the potential of creativity for shocking, healing, disturbing, and changing.

Another response which is less obviously defensive is to imagine that the creative therapist offers a situation where all the boundaries are let go. The philosophy is assumed to be based on the idea that 'if you can get it out of your system it is good for you', as if human emotions stemmed from some kind of abscess which once incised would no longer be present. People with this view appear to be supporters of an exploratory and radical creative therapy. In fact their ill-informed enthusiasm fans the fears of the other group. The ambivalence about any therapy which is going to offer change and will make the demands that change makes is embodied in these two opposite reactions, with attitudes focused on issues of control, of holding on or letting go.

This crude polarization of attitudes in others reminds us, however, of a dilemma in the creative therapist himself. As in other therapies, structure is important if the clients are to feel safe enough within the familiar to explore the unknown. Here we are talking not of the type of control that inhibits expression but of the kind of control that allows expression because it provides limits. Once he is able to show that he can maintain the boundary for a group or a client, the creative therapist can then work towards extending the boundary so as to increase the range of experiences of which that person or group is capable. He can also work towards getting the group to the stage where it has had enough experience of his ability to hold the boundary within which they can work freely, so that they are then able to hold the boundaries themselves in ways which are constructive rather than inhibiting, ways which are conducive rather than repressive to the further exploration of inner feeling and interpersonal relationships.

This leads us to another problem which occurs when therapists from different backgrounds meet to learn from each other to develop their creative therapy work. Is creative therapy non-directive like psychotherapy, with paint, or movement, or music being used as well as words by the therapist in response to the feeling-situation of the client group? Or are the media to be used as creative stimuli which will elicit responses which can then be examined verbally or explored further in related media? There is a tendency to polarize here, too, with some therapists working very much like teachers of the aesthetic subjects with the addition perhaps of a discussion at the end while others work in a more passive way, waiting during periods of inactivity until a need emerges which can then be responded to in an appropriate way, with an artistic medium that has been chosen as being the most helpful one. Each type may accuse the other of not really being a 'creative therapist'. It seems to me that what is required is a mixture of these approaches and yet it is so difficult to find the right balance. Starting a session with a warm up, for instance, can be looked on as a helpful, initiating exercise with which the therapist aims to warm up the group to its task. On the other hand, it can be looked upon as an intrusion of the therapist's wishes into the unrecognized feeling-state of the group. When the therapist prefers to sit around with the group, waiting until he knows where the group is at, we may view this as a helpful preliminary to let the group tune in to the feelings. Unfortunately the therapist's inactivity may tend to offer a passive model to the group who are then reluctant ever to be involved in a creative active exploration, preferring to sit around discussing things. This is a problem particularly in staff training groups who are used to group therapy and staff discussions (and this will be referred to later).

The experienced therapist can, hopefully, respond intuitively to the needs of the group, choosing initial activities which will bring out the hidden tensions or which will relieve the anxiety about them so that the tensions may emerge. This requires great skill and sensitivity. The therapist does have to face the problem of finding the balance between directiveness and non-directiveness since this creative therapy method will tend to come in conflict with the method learnt in the previous background training. A way of dealing with this is to think of one's approach as directive only at the technical, action-promoting level but non-directive at the unconscious, expression level. Then technical instructions and suggestions for action remain of subordinate importance and are used as a means to the end of expression of fantasy, and working through of conflict and reality testing. With this emphasis in mind, the therapist will not be confused into behaving in a directive fashion that would feel over-controlling and inhibiting at moments of revelation or personal feeling. Similarly, the therapist will not feel afraid of being directive at some points when this is required to facilitate the work. Really this is not different from verbal psychotherapy when therapists' responses to understand the spontaneously associated thoughts of the patient are in themselves stimuli which can direct the patient's further experience of his thought and feeling.

This problem of allowing parts of the self to come together in creative expression underlies the more superficial problem of professions' difficulties in coming together in a creative process. At a meeting of therapists and teachers brought

together through their mutual interest in creative therapy,
there was considerable difficulty in sharing skills. An art
teacher said: 'What would a therapist know about art?' She
thought it was wrong that a therapist had begun to use paint
since the therapist did not have the Diploma of Art, as if only
one with a Diploma of art could be allowed to use paint.
Some therapists felt that an artistic training was not required
and that it militated against a therapeutic use of the arts
media. One therapist blamed the artist for being so concerned
with the pure art form that he emphasized the achievement
of the end product at the expense of using the artistic process
to understand the being of the person involved. This is a
stereotyped view of the work of the artist who is in art
therapy. Preoccupation with goals to the detriment of
understanding method is not a prerogative of the artist alone.

I certainly feel that the intensity of the personal experience
of art in an art school training gives a person an understanding
of the media that no-one else can have. Similarly, I feel that
someone who has trained at a drama school understands that
medium from the personal commitment made to it in a way
that no-one else can. Similarly, a therapist who has undergone
personal analysis understands the relationship between
patient and therapist from the personal commitment as a
patient to that relationship in a way that no-one else can.
Acknowledgement of these separate valuable skills is not
intended to diminish the status of the others, and yet these
special skills are often used defensively.

Similarly, a therapist was heard to say: 'What would a
teacher know about people?' Teachers that I consulted to during that workshop seemed to me to be unwilling to accept the
phenomena of the unconscious; they were inclined to take
things at face value and to resist hidden meanings. Yet they
do know a lot about the behaviour of large groups and
individuals at different ages. A drama teacher who consulted
to a group of mental health professionals, of which I was
a member during the workshop, found us very resistant to
joining in or being spontaneous, preferring to delay by
constantly focussing on what was not being done and what
was not being said. We all have a lot to learn *about* learning
from each other before we are *able* to learn from each other.

Acceptance of this is required to interrupt the cycle of
resistance to growth.

Establishing skill sharing as training.

One important step taken to alter the cycle has been the
creation of multi-disciplinary skill sharing workshops. A
primary task of these workshops has to be to work at this
resistance to skill sharing and the fears people have of
their specialist territory being invaded. This in itself is
valuable training in understanding the fears of groups in
the community and the fears of a patient reluctant to enter
therapy with a therapist who, it is feared, will be invasive
and thieving. The one profession envies the other, imagining
its skill to be greater than it is so that the other profession
seems much better, more competent and more omnipotent
than they themselves feel. This kind of envy leads to an
inner feeling of emptiness, in comparison to the inflated other
profession, and it is hard to tolerate the despairing feeling
of impotence. In reality, however, all the professions are
confronted with their helplessness in the face of extremely
difficult problems. If that helplessness can be shared, constructive improvements in methods of approach can be devised
without recourse to omnipotent behaviour or slick fads chosen
as a way out of the present therapeutic impasse.

In sharing skills, the different professionals come together as
people prepared to explore the common ground, willing to
experiment and develop new shared ideas. They not only do
this by talking together about each other's work but by sharing in a practical workshop setting. Each has a personal
experience of the other's methods of work. Then these
personal experiences discussed in the post-action group are
of value in building cohesion in the group and in offering
the group a personal basis for the development of new methods.
It seems to me vital that anyone who intends to use creative
therapy should have had a personal experience of this in such
workshop situations. I do not, however, wish to imply that
anyone can go off for a weekend's workshop and return competent as a creative therapist. All that can be hoped for at
the present time is that one who is already skilled as a thera-

pist may be more flexible and creative in his approach while
one who is skilled as a teacher may be more aware of the
nature of the creative relationship involved between the
pupil and himself.

It takes a long time for new experience to be fully integrated
in the professional. If this time for integration is not allowed,
hasty incorporation of something foreign occurs and reappears
in the therapy like a misplaced foreign object which has a
disturbing effect on the group and also on the professional
who has to deal with it. When I worked in Edinburgh I ran
a staff training group for trained mental health nurses and
occupational therapists who wanted to develop a more
creative approach to their work, using body communication,
paint, music and drama as well as words. The seminar was
run on a workshop basis once weekly and it was over a year
before any of the people felt free to use the new skills in the
ward setting. During that year, too, of course, the other
professionals in their wards who were not interested in
attending the seminar were hearing of the experiences of the
seminar and gradually became used to the idea that this
might be helpful for the patients. _____

At the beginning of that course of seminars we appreciated
the resistance among staff to the use of new ideas and we
were careful to spend a considerable time discussing the
project with them until we felt that they were in agreement
with our experimenting in this workshop. We felt it was
important to establish their support prior to beginning since
this established the principle that it would be all right to use
these methods with the patients for whom consultants were
legally responsible. One consultant was against the idea,
saying that action methods were a flight from the slow,
painstaking and difficult process of psychotherapy. We reassured him that the new techniques (if we became competent enough to use them) would be an adjunct to the
present psychotherapy and would in no way diminish our
continuing concern to learn, evaluate and improve our verbal
psychotherapeutic approaches. A year later two of the
senior nurses from his ward were developing a weekly action
group for the community of day patients. In this situation
they were surprised at the responses of patients that they

had previously found to be very passive and withdrawn. The consultant was particularly interested in the action group as a diagnostic indicator but he was no longer denying its therapeutic implications.

Examples from staff training creative therapy groups

The trainee's experience

I have been careful to emphasize the point of a personal experience of the creative therapy method and so the first example described here comes from my own experience as a participant in a group run as part of a summer course on drama and creativity in remedial work organized by the Remedial Drama Centre in July 1970.

> *Example 4.* At the beginning of the group we were standing awkwardly on the studio floor wondering what would be expected of us. People were anxious, smoking, or looking at their course timetables. The director arrived and the music began. I felt a surge of anxiety. What would be expected of us? Sensibly the director expected very little. 'Just move one finger in time to the music.' My own relief was shared by the rest of the group who were just able to move that one finger since this did not seem too incriminating or exposing. Gently the director asked us to move a hand or an arm until we were all sufficiently involved in the warming up process to relax and move about.

Here I was learning how important the beginning is for the professional who has been unaccustomed to creative therapy. I learnt from that small beginning that it is important for the creative therapist to try not to do too much in the first session, just as it is for the group therapist starting a verbal therapeutic group. Towards the middle of the session people were more open to receive an experience of some impact.

> *Example 5.* We were asked to choose one word, such as 'spit', that could be said repetitively to express an angry

feeling in a nasty way. A rising intensity or anger developed
as the group repeated the words. I began to feel that this
was getting out of hand and to feel disturbed by the amount
of rage emitted. At this point, others of the group who had
been asked to be silent began to speak words with a calm
tone such as 'peace' or 'quiet'. It was reassuring for me
to find that my own intense rage gradually dissipated
with such gentle confrontation.

Here I was learning about the use of opposites to maintain
balance. I felt that the intensity of the rage was arising because
of the lack of relationship context in which it could hurt a
person who might also retaliate. Thus there was no limit to
the rage. It was useful to feel this unlimited rage and equally
useful to have it confronted. There were other controls used
during the group; for example, the word command 'freeze',
the noise of cymbols the introduction of periods of relaxation, the more subtle use of varying levels of pitch or volume,
such as the rise and fall of a drum beat roll. While these
various controls were certainly operating, it occurred to me
that basic to them all was the presence of a creative therapist
in whose ability to maintain the boundaries of the task we
could all have trust. I learnt, too, that it was important not
to imagine that the free-flowing expression of impulse and
feeling was in itself therapeutic, since I knew how frightening
my own rage was. On the other hand, I did feel that the
experience of the primitive feeling outwith the context of
the relationship was in itself an interesting experience of
rather primal phenomena. (The need for this kind of structure
was referred to in the part of this chapter about the attitudes
and expectations of other professionals to the creative
therapy session.)

Example 6. Half of us imagined ourselves to be inert
and alone. In this lonely shut-off state I found myself
approached by a helper. Gradually she held my hand.
Then slowly eased one arm into movement. Then the
other. Then rocked me by the shoulders. This unexpected personal contact was at first threatening and exciting,
but as trust developed it became reassuring. When she
moved away from me to change her point of contact

and let go my hand and moved around to hold my shoulder instead, I felt frightened in case she would go away altogether and leave me alone and shut off again. But always she did come back and it felt all right again. And gradually being alone felt all right too, because I knew she would be back.

This was a vivid personal experience of the usefulness of action techniques to promote insight about satisfaction and frustration. I realized at an emotional level the previously intellectually accepted theory of Erikson which refers to the resolution of the basic trust and mistrust conflict as an acceptance of the rhythm of satisfaction and frustration.

Example 7. We were asked to paint. Just as I was enjoying this, Indian music was introduced and we were asked to let our painting respond to its influence. I felt obstinately unwilling to put up with this interference in the process of my 'work of art', and sat aside listening to the music instead (and secretly sulking).

Another insight: my active mode and orderliness made passive acceptance of direction too difficult because of a feeling that it would spoil my production and make me make a mess if I was not in control. Here I was reliving an anxiety about letting go.

The trainer's experience

For two years the group of staff trained in mental health work met with me to learn about action methods. I had to devise action methods for overcoming their resistance to the task which they apparently wanted to be involved in.

Example 8. It was a struggle for them to move freely, so I suggested that they were to play the part of people struggling and battling against the wind, trying to move without panic even though the air pressure was steadily increasing and tending to restrict their movements.

When this external resistance was equal and opposite to their internal resistance the effect of the inner resistance was negated so that free movement was possible. I had experienced this myself in a training session and felt it could be extremely useful for staff who are more inhibited than are patients in responding to the newer action techniques.

Another problem was that of inhibition due to differences in status between members. This was reduced by mask work.

Example 9. Each member made a mask out of newspaper and clear adhesive tape, not a stereotyped face, but an undifferentiated, protective covering. In five minutes a wide variety of beaked, hooded, boxed, ragged creatures emerged and the staff members thus disguised were able to relate to each other. To circumvent the staff tendency of using clever words instead of expressing emotion I suggested that these creatures should emit sounds only. The members moved around the room emitting the noises they had chosen, developing particular movement patterns appropriate to the style of the creature. Different pairs of creatures confronted each other and communicated through gesture and noise.

During these contacts the most notable expression was that of aggression. Without the masks this degree of absorption in the task was not possible and self-consciousness showed itself in giggling, staring, and sitting down. But frequent repetition of masked followed by unmasked work led to a considerable improvement towards self-confidence and personal freedom.

We used living newspaper techniques to suggest situations on which we built improvisations, because at first the staff were reluctant to bring their problems of interacting with patients or ward-staff, for exploration by the group. From these first 'safe' situations we moved to a dramatic exploration of a real work situation.

Example 10. We considered what it felt like to be a patient admitted to a strange ward by recreating the scene at the admission area, with the receptionist trying to contact the charge nurse while answering the telephone. Then we moved to the scene in the duty room when the busy charge nurse is surprised by the new arrival, and followed this with a confrontation between the charge nurse and the psychiatrist who forgot to inform the ward that a bed would be needed. Those not taking part in the scene were encouraged to substitute for any of the players in the replays so as to demonstrate suggestions for improved behaviour. They were also able to double behind the back of the protagonists to reveal to them what their unspoken feelings were at each moment in the interaction. The experience was deeply moving for the one who played the patient. She said she had been so disturbed by the admission procedure that she would make a determined effort to be much more sensitive to the fears and needs of new patients in future.

Example 11. Later in the course we imagined a family consisting of an angry, dominant father, a quiet depressed wife, a daughter who could do no wrong and a son who could not live up to his father's ambitions for him as a sportsman. We began with the scene at dinner, focusing on the conflict between father and son, when father discovers that the boy has never worn the athletic club tie he gave him.

Working away at this, different staff members had the opportunity of knowing how it felt to be that boy, having demands made on him by the father. Role-reversal techniques showed how the father-son interaction could be modified. Then we imagined the son had turned to drugs as a way out, so our next setting was a psychiatrist's office where the boy and his father and mother were being interviewed by the psychiatrist and a social worker (played by two nurses). The bonds and tensions in the family were quite altered by this intervention. We, on the receiving end of the therapy, were able to experience this therapeutic effect subjectively. Those who were the family members reported on whether they felt supported or attacked and persecuted by the therapists' remarks. And apart from this verbal feedback about their performance the therapists were able to experience their own therapeutic efforts by reversing roles with the family members.

A group such as this is not only introducing the members to some of the techniques of creative therapy but is itself therapeutic in the sense of promoting spontaneity and crea-

tivity in the members. It helps the staff to dispense with
professional masks and to get in touch with the person behind
that, the person who is simple, honest and in touch with
his feelings. As well as experiencing the techniques which
they will themselves use, the staff members are having a
shared experience which will support them as a group in the
future so that then when the person leading the group has to
leave they will be able to use the resources within the group
to support them in future activities. This in itself is a model
for enabling therapists to transmit their authority to the
patients and to allow the patient an experience which he
can carry with him inside him as his own for his continuing
growth in the future.

The reports of these groups show that my main concern
was with drama-based action methods. At that time my
repertoire was rather limited and I felt uncomfortable about
using clay or paint. The experience of taking the group, however, put me in contact with a number of the occupational
therapists who were familiar with the use of clay. Although
they were versed in many media, they had been limited in ·
the use of the materials as media for communication. Two
of us decided to collaborate on running an event for a
conference of art therapists, who wanted to have a workshop
to explore action method and creative therapy. In the following description you will see that the range of media used in
the communication has widened since the earlier training
group. This is evidence of the growth-promoting effect of
skill sharing. It demonstrates my feeling that I as the leader
of that earlier group had been learning as much from the
members of the group as they were learning from me.

Example 12. We began with some introductory remarks.
I explained that the emphasis in this workshop would
be on teaching, not on therapeutic intervention. We did
not intend to produce a mass media emotional abreaction
at all, but were hoping to involve people in a learning
experience through the use of media, rather than offering
them the passive experience of a formal lecture. We would
emphasize the group situations and the group dynamics
throughout.

We began with a purely verbal response situation to the creative stimulus of music. The group was invited to listen to a five-minute section of music and to attend closely to the feelings, associations and fantasies that were evoked by it. Individuals sat quietly listening and then joined a small group to describe their experience.

Thereafter the practical dimension was introduced by the use of clay. The groups were asked to express the feelings or images evoked by the music in the clay. We reassured them that the emphasis would be on the expression rather than on the technical form of the sculptures. When completed all the sculptures were put in the centre of the groups. In each group, members were invited to share their feelings on seeing the sculptures of the other people in the group and to identify a group mood. That is not to say all the sculptures were expected to be the same. What one did find, however, was that although the sculptures were of different images the sharing of the task of discussing them introduced a shared feeling and a shared mood which could then be identified.

The sculptures were placed in the middle of each group and the members of each small group then moved away from their sculptures to form another small group around another set of sculptures. They passed the sculptures around the group, looking and thinking about them, touching them and trying to feel what it was the sculpture was expressing. Each member chose one sculpture that interested him and focused particularly on it. We then suggested that the person might use his body to echo the line of the sculpture in order to achieve some insight into the feeling expressed by the sculpture and thereby into the feeling state of the person who had made the sculpture. In the room at this time there were five small groups of individuals whose postures were moulded into the shape suggested by the sculpture they had been attending to.

The members of the small group were asked to look at the different shapes in the group and to find a way of putting these shapes together that represented a melange of feeling, and then to find ways of moving this group sculpture so that it could move towards another group and inter-relate with it. At this point in the room there were five sculptured groups with individual members articulating one with the other, and moving in a rhythm that echoed the feelings produced by the music. One group was unable to move and experienced a feeling of being stuck. Another group was quite invasive and tried to break up the stuck group and encompass it. This split within the large group echoed the form of the music which had a very quiet and withdrawn beginning that induced images of deserted seashores and black seagulls which gave way to a very vibrant and disturbing second part of the music.

Finally we all sat down in the large group and discussed our experiences during that part of the day. We tried to relate the particular feelings evoked by that music to the anlage of feeling that was present in the room on that particular day of that particular conference.

The last example from the training of the creative therapist is taken from a Scottish Association for Creativity and Communication workshop arranged for workers using creative methods in a variety of work situations from special schools, colleges of education, psychotherapy, psychiatric nursing, community work, and approved school education. Here I introduced some fantasy projective techniques.

Example 13. Sitting in circles of ten members we projected our own fantasies: first by finishing off the sentence starting 'When I was a child I used to pretend that . . .' and then by sharing some of our present pretences, hopes and wishes.

The excusable fantasies that could be indulged in childhood were a safer start than the area of adult fantasy. While the group shared the childhood fantasies the members were gaining enough confidence in each other to be able to move on to the area of present pretences, hopes and wishes. Many groups had common themes of wishing for more real confidence, of noting the difference between pretence to deceive oneself and pretence to deceive others. Again, the problem of the professional mask hiding the real person was brought out.

Example 14. Working alone then we each thought of just one of our personal characteristics that we felt strongly about, either hoping to develop this quality or feeling ashamed of it and wishing to diminish it. Putting aside our consideration of the whole personality for the moment we imagined ourselves each to be taken over by only that one aspect. How did it feel to us? Then we embodied this raw feeling in the form of a fantasy creature with a characteristic means of locomotion. A host of creeping, crawling, laughing, petrified, and quietly curled creatures emerged, confronting each other and exploring. Indeed, we moved on then from fantasy creatures to explore human embodiments of the aspects of the personality represented. We explored the conflict arising when these human beings found themselves in difficult situations.

I noticed that the fantasy creatures were impelled to change after meeting other creatures. This follows our life experience of having to give up selfish expression of individual fantasy when adapting to two- and three-person relationships. When we enacted scenes where the human beings were relating to each other in roles suggested by the limited attributes of the fantasy creatures, we noticed that the reaction to the individual behaving in that way provoked responses which tended to exaggerate the behaviour. The people playing the roles knew what it was like to feel taken over by that part of the self and to have this reinforced by the behaviour of others. The application of this phenomenon can lead to awareness of the self in situations so that there is no collusion with this expectation.

Conclusion

Intra-psychic, inter-personal, group and inter-group dynamics are a necessary training requirement for all creative therapists. Some of this knowledge can be got from reading psychology and sociology. Mainly it is learnt by the apprenticeship

Fantasy creatures begin to move.

Role Play.

Family Role Play.

method, namely by sitting in therapeutic groups or observing them through a one-way screen. Attendance at group dynamics conferences is an excellent, although expensive, way of appreciating the unconscious phenomena in group processes. Personal experience in a sensitivity group or indeed in an individual or a group therapeutic situation would be necessary for the person who has trained mainly in an arts subject.

Those, however, who are trained mainly in the human relations skills would need to spend more time in exploring other types of creative intervention, such as arts workshops, encounter groups or creative therapy workshops. When creative therapy becomes more established it may be sufficient for a prospective creative therapist to undergo a period of involvement in a creative therapy group. This would not currently be sufficient to fit a person to work in a fully professional way as a creative therapist.

At present, however, the situation is that the training for creative therapy is really a post-diploma training. The training should not however be seen as a short, sharp, post-graduate course, but instead as a preparation for work which will require continuing personal and professional development. This sort of development can be allowed for by continued practice in the artistic aspects of the chosen media by continuing one's individual art alone or by attendance at evening classes, by membership of study groups to understand the social processes of groups, by involvement in personal therapy, by attendance at lectures and seminars in the related disciplines.

The greatest hope, however, for maintaining professional competence is the provision of situations which will foster regular contact between workers using creative methods. They need to be able to meet and talk and also to work together in practical workshop settings. This continuing support for each other is important in such a new and experimental profession. A continuing sharing and communication of their professional experience in creative therapy maintains the flexibility of the self to participate in further creative process with clients, teachers and trainees.

Creative therapy will not emerge as a discipline unless the professional groups which it encompasses are able to get together for skill sharing in a multi-disciplinary setting. Out of that setting can grow the inter-disciplinary people of creative therapy who will have enough knowledge and experience to plan training programmes for creative therapists. As teachers of creative therapy they will then have to draw on the resources of sub-specialists particularly skilled in particular areas such as in group therapy, or in psychotherapy with young people, or in art, or sculpture, or drama, or music, or movement.

No chapter on role and training is complete without some mention of the career prospects which can be expected as a result of the special skills and competence developed by that training. At this stage, however, one cannot even predict about career prospects when at the moment there are so few posts for creative therapists. Indeed I know of none. Those workers whom I would call creative therapists are very often working under some other label such as diversional therapist, assistant nurse, assistant youth worker, or psychia-

trist. These manipulations of the present situation are valuable
in allowing the creative therapy work to be developed but
the titles under which the therapists have to work compro-
mise the identity of the profession. Creative therapists face
the urgent task of devising a combined creative approach to
the establishment of creative therapy in the health, educational, and social services.

Summary

The role of the creative therapist and the context in which
he works have been described. It has been seen that the
'creative therapist' is an umbrella term covering the creative
work of the human relations professions, the arts speciali-
ties and education. Training has to ensure continuing development of artistic skills and psychodynamic understanding
and sociological awareness of the creative therapist's impact
on the institutions of society. It is fundamental that the
training should be participant and practical and that the
creative therapeutic skills should arise out of this personal
experience of the shared creative process. Examples of
training sessions from my own experience as a participant
and as a leader have been given. The training of the creative
therapist has itself to be an educational growth process,
thus offering a model of therapy as a creative shared growth
process.

Notes on Contributors

Anne Bate, B.A. (Hons.). Social worker and artist; eight years experience as social worker with deprived families in London; currently working for higher degree at Oxford; experience in personal analysis and group therapy; has illustrated one book and exhibited her pictures.

Julienne Brown, B.Mus., LGSMT. Pioneer of Music Therapy at Goldie Lea subnormality hospital and tutor for three years on Music Therapy course at Guildhall School; extensive experience in all fields of mental illness and handicap; personal analysis and group therapy; married with one son, now living in Scotland and acting as music therapy consultant and lecturer.

Larry Butler. Actor, artist, dancer and poet. Founder and director of the Playspace Trust and co-director of the Drama Therapy Centre; special experience with probation service and work with young offenders and the handicapped; author *Dictionary of Games* (in press).

Elinor Goldschmeid. Formerly Froebel teacher, now trained PSW specializing in work with infants and babies; worked for thirteen years in Italy in a pioneer community for mothers and illegitimate children; experience in child guidance, child care; currently adviser in social work for ILEA; has collaborated in making seven documentary films about very young children.

Rosemary Gordon, Ph.D. Jungian analyst and professional member of Society of Analytic Psychology; divides her time between private practice and writing and lecturing on the psychology of fine art, University of London (Institute of Education); married to Peter Montagnon, Head of BBC Open University Productions.

Sue Jennings, LRAM, LGSM, Dip. Soc. Anthrop. Anthropologist, Drama Therapist and author; founder and consultant Drama Therapy Centre; extensive experience in drama with all types of mental and physical handicap; individual analysis and group therapy experience; currently engaged in doctoral research on body movement; publications: *Remedial Drama* (Pitman), *Anthropology and Dance* (in press).

Roy Shuttleworth, B.Sc., Dip.Ed., Dip.Clin.Psych., A.B.Ps.S. Clinical Psychologist Longrove Hospital Adolescent Unit; extensive experience in psychodrama with adolescents and chronic schizophrenics; trained group therapist;

presented papers at the first National Conference in Drama Therapy 1973 and the British Psychological Society Conference 1974.

Dr Jill Savege, MBCHB, MRC, Psych. DPM, FTLC, LGSM. Senior Registrar in adolescent psychiatry, Tavistock Clinic London, and Hill End Hospital St Albans; consultant, Laban Art of Movement Studio and Goldsmiths' College; Co-founder, Scottish Association for Creativity and Communication.

Veronica Sherbourne. Part-time lecturer in movement for teachers of ESN(S) Redlands College, Bristol; movement teacher in Dept of Drama and visiting lecturer Dept. Social Administration and Social Work, University of Bristol; chairman of Committee on Physical Education for Handicapped Children. Has made two films: *In Touch* (with handicapped children) and *Explorations*; lectures extensively in England and abroad.

Anne Ancelin Schutzenberger, Ph.D. Lecturer in Social Psychology, Nice University; European pioneer of T-groups and control of triadic group psycho-drama; organizer, First International Congress of Psychodrama, Paris, 1964; author of *Précis de Psychodrame* (Paris, 1966; translated in many languages); many publications in psychology, sociology, psychiatry and psychotherapy; lectures and holds courses world-wide.

Training Courses Available

Many local authorities, universities and teacher training colleges run courses in art, music, movement and drama which provide basic skills. Equally there are many part-time courses in group therapy, group dynamics, encounter and sensitivity training which are appropriate. It is not possible to include such information here, but individual schools and colleges, local authority subject advisors, and reputable therapeutic organizations can advise and recommend.

The following information is concerning specialized courses on the arts in remedial and therapeutic work. Since there is great variety in duration of courses, syllabus content and entrance qualifications, intending students should write for complete information.

Several centres run courses in psychodrama and sociodrama allied with other skills. For British psychodrama training limited to psychologists and psychiatrists, contact Edward Hazelton, (secretary) 3 Spring Terrace, Richmond, Surrey. For French psychodrama training contact Dr Anne Ancelin Shuzenberger, 14 av. P. Appell, 74014 Paris.

Organizations specializing in the arts in remedial and therapeutic work

British Assoc. Music Therapists (Juliette Alvin), 48 Lanchester Road, N6.
Drama Therapy Centre (Sue Jennings, Larry Butler, Dr Carlos Chan,
    Roy Shuttleworth), 30 Baker Street, London W1M 2DS.
Music Therapy Charity Ltd, 6 Queensdale Walk, London W11 4QQ.
Remedial Art Department, St Albans School of Art, 7 Hatfield Road, St Albans,
    Herts.
Sesame, 8 Ayres Street, London SE1 1ES.
Untie (Carole McIntyre and Brian Osman), 30 Priory Street, Colchester, Essex.

N.B. These organizations will recommend or send tutors for external courses.

Other organizations which include these subjects in training

A.R.I.P, (T-group training). 6 bis rue Bachaumont, Paris.
Backworth Drama Centre, Backworth, Newcastle-upon-Tyne.
Community, 15 Highbury Grange, London N5.
Franklin School of Contemporary Studies, 43 Adelaide Road, London NW3.

Laban Art of Movement Centre, Woburn Hill, Addlestone, Surrey KT15 2QD.
London Boroughs Training Committee, 3 Buckingham Gate, London SW1.
Mind (NAMH), Education Department, 22 Harley Street, London W1N 2ED.
National Soc. Mentally Handicapped Children and *National Gateway Federation,* Pembridge Hall, 17 Pembridge Square, London W2 4EP.
National Theatre for the Deaf, RNID, 105 Gower Street, London WC13 6AH.
New College of Speech and Drama, Golders Green, London NW11.
Playspace Trust, 22 Frognal, London NW3.
Quaesitor, 187 Walm Lane, London NW11.
Redlands College, Bristol 6.
Spastics Society, Castle Priory College, Wallingford, Berks.

Individuals who run courses in these areas

Dr Joel Badaines (psychodrama), 38 St Charles Square, London W10.
Peter Hawkins (creative remedial drama), 38 St Charles Square, London W10.
Dorothy Heathcote (drama) Institute of Education, Newcastle-upon-Tyne.
Pat Keysell (mime for the deaf), National Deaf Childrens Society, 31 Gloucester Place, London W1.
Gina Levete (dance and mime) & Ian Robertson (art), 8 Winthorp Road, London SW15.
Max Pagés (T-Groups, encounter groups), Laboratoire de changement social, Universitede, Paris—IX—Dauphiné, Paris.
Anna Scher (drama), 25b Elsworthy Road, London NW3.
Veronica Sherborne (movement), 26 Hanbury Road, Bristol BS8 2EP.

Other useful organizations

Association for Humanistic Psychology, 16 Crestview, Dartmouth Dark Hill, London NW5.
British Association of Art Therapists, 90 Liverpool Road, London N1
British Theatre Association, 9 Fitzroy Square, London W1.
Creative Drama Conference, Rea Street Drama Centre, Birmingham.
National Drama Conference, 26 Bedford Square, London W1.
Scottish Association for Communication and Creativity, 23 Belmont Street, Glasgow W2
Physical Education Association of Great Britain and N. Ireland, 10 Nottingham Place, W1.

Note.

The information was based on answers to questions. The Editor regrets any omissions and would like to hear from other practitioners in the field.

Suggested Reading

Some writers have given their own specialized bibliography. The following list, although not exhaustive, is designed to give the reader a wide span of approaches. Drama, movement and dance, music, art, creativity, psychodrama, encounter and other therapeutic approaches have been included. Some titles specialize in, and others have a section on the remedial and therapeutic application of the arts. These books are marked with an asterisk.

Art

Edith Kramer, *Art as Therapy with Children**, Elek 1973, London.
E. Neumann, *Art and the Creative Unconscious**, Tavistock 1959, London.
L. A. Reid, *Meaning in the Arts**, Allen & Unwin 1969, London.
Daniel Schneider, *The Psychoanalyst and the Artist**, Mentor 1949, London.

Creativity

Jean Duvignaud, *The Sociology of Art*, Paladin 1972, London.
Anton Ehrenzweig, *The Hidden Order of Art*, Paladin 1964, London.
Arthur Koestler, *The Act of Creation*, Hutchinson 1964, London.
Harold Rugg, *Imagination*, Harper & Row 1963, New York and London.
D. W. Winnicott, *Playing and Reality*, Tavistock 1971, London.

Drama

Rose Bruford, *Teaching Mime*, Methuen 1958, London.
Janet Goodridge, *Drama in the Primary School*, Heinemann Educational 1970, London.
N. Dodd & W. Hickson, Eds., *Drama & Theatre in Education*, Heinemann Educational 1971, London.
John Hodgson, Ed., *The Uses of Drama**, Methuen 1972, London.
John Hodgson & Ernest Richards, *Improvisation*, Methuen 1966, London
John Hodgson & Martin Banham, Eds., *Drama in Education* (the Annual Survey – nos I, II*, & III), Pitman 1972+, London.
Sue Jennings, *Remedial Drama**, Pitman 1973, London.
David Male, *Approaches to Drama*, Allen & Unwin 1974, London

William Mart & Gordon Vallins, *Exploration Drama*, Evans 1968, London.
R. N. Pemberton Billing & J. D. Clegg, *Teaching Drama*, University of London Press 1965, London.
Peter Slade, *Child Drama*, University of London Press 1954, London
Peter Slade, *Introduction to Child Drama*, University of London Press 1958, London.
Peter Slade, *Drama Therapy as an Aid to becoming a Person**, Guild of Pastoral Psychology 1959, London.
Viola Spolin, *Experience of Spontaneity*, Longmans 1968, London.
Viola Spolin, *Improvisation for the Theatre*, Pitman 1973, London.
Brenda Walker, *Teaching Creative Drama*, Batsford 1970, London.
Brian Way, *Development Through Drama*, Longmans 1967, London.

Encounter and sensitivity training

William B. Schulz, *Joy*, Penguin 1973, London.
Carl Rogers, *Encounter Groups*, Penguin 1973, London

Movement and dance

Vera Bruce, *Dance & Dance Drama in Education**, Pergamon Press 1965, Oxford.
Vera Gray & Rachel Percival, *Music, Movement and Mime for Children*, O.U.P. 1962, Oxford.
Marion North, *An Introduction to Movement Study and Teaching*, Macdonald & Evans 1971, London.
Marion North, *Movement Education**, Temple Smith 1973, London.
Marion North, *Personality Assessment Through Movement **, Temple Smith 1972, London.
Ferris & Janet Robbins, *Educational Rhythmics**, R. A. Verlag, Switzerland.
Audrey Wethered, *Movement and Drama in Therapy**, Macdonald & Evans 1973, London.
John Wiles & Alan Garrard, *Leap to Life*, Chatto and Windus 1957, London.

Music

Juliette Alvin, *Music Therapy**, Baker 1966, London.
Juliette Alvin, *Music for the Handicapped Child**, O.U.P. 1965, Oxford.
Jack Dobbs, *The Slow Learner and Music**, O.U.P. 1966, Oxford.
Paul Nordoff & Clive Robbins, *Music Therapy and Special Education**, John Day 1971.

Psychodrama

Didier Anzieu, *Le psychodrame analytique chez l'enfant*, Paris 1970.
Howard Blatner, Ed., *Practical Aspects of Psychodrama*, New York 1968.
Howard Blatner, *Acting In*, New York, 1973.
Raymond Corsini, *Role-playing in Psychotherapy*, Chicago 1966.
Robert Haas, *Psychodrama and Sociodrama in American Education*, Beacon House 1949, New York.
Ira Greenberg, *Psychodrama and Attitude Change*, Thyrsus 1968, California.
Paul & Jenie Lamoine, *Le psychodrame*, Paris 1972.
J-L Moreno, *Psychodrama I*, Beacon House 1946, revised 1964, New York.
J-L Moreno, *Psychodrama II,* Beacon House 1959, New York.

234 *Creative Therapy*

J-L Moreno, *Psychodrama III*, Beacon House 1969, New York.
J-L Moreno, *Psychotherapie de groupe et psychodrame*, Paris 1965.
J-L Moreno, *Who Shall Survive*, Beacon House 1953, New York.
J-L & Z Moreno, Eds., *The Sociometry Reader*, The Free Press 1960, Glencoe.
Zerka Moreno, *Le psychodrame d'enfants*, Paris 1973.
A. A. Schutzenberger, *L'observation*, Paris 1972.
A. A. Schutzenberger, *Vocabulaire des techniques de group*, Paris 1971.
A. A. Schutzenberger, *Précis de psychodrame*, Paris 1966.
Daniel Widlocher, *Le psychodrame chez l'enfant*, Paris 1962.

Other relevant individual and group therapeutic approaches

Virginia Axline, *Play Therapy*, Riverside Press 1947, New York.
Virginia Axline, *Dibs: In Search of Self*, Penguin 1973, London.
Raymond Corsini, *Methods of Group Psychotherapy*, McGraw Hill 1957, New York & London.
Patrick de Mare, *Perspectives in Group Psychotherapy*, George Allen & Unwin 1972, London.
S. H. Foulkes & E. J. Anthony, *Group Psychotherapy*, Penguin 1957, London.
Erving Goffman, *Presentation of Self in Everyday Life*, Penguin 1971, London.
Erving Goffman, *Interaction Ritual*, Penguin 1971, London.
R. D. Laing, *The Politics of Experience and The Bird of Paradise*, Penguin 1967, London.
R. D. Laing & A. Esterson, *Sanity, Madness and the Family*, Penguin 1970, London.
Carl Rogers, *Client Centred Therapy*, Constable 1965, London.